THE POWER OF REINFORCEMENT

SUNY series, Alternatives in Psychology
Michael A. Wallach, editor

The
Power
of
Reinforcement

Stephen Ray Flora

STATE UNIVERSITY OF NEW YORK PRESS

Published by
State University of New York Press, Albany

© 2004 State University of New York

For information, address State University of New York Press,
90 State Street, Suite 700, Albany, NY 12207

Production by Diane Ganeles
Marketing by Jennifer Giovani

Library of Congress Cataloging in Publication Data
Flora, Stephen Ray, 1963–
    The Power of reinforcement / Stephen Ray Flora.
        p. cm. — (SUNY series, alternatives in psychology)
    Includes bibliographical references and index.
    ISBN 0-7914-5915-2 (alk. paper) — ISBN 0-7914-5916-0 (pbk : alk. paper)
    1. Reinforcement (Psychology) I. Title. II. Series.

BF319.5.R4F58 2004
153.8'5—dc21
                                                    2002045264

10 9 8 7 6 5 4 3 2 1

CONTENTS

ACKNOWLEDGMENTS

This book would not have been possible without the support and help of my parents, Glenda Christine Flora and Joseph Martin Flora. Although that may sound like a cliche, as the introduction reveals, in this case the cliche holds true. Additionally, my mother served as the reader and editor of the first draft and other early drafts. After each convenient breaking point I mailed the work to her in North Carolina. Ever the outstanding English composition teacher, soon she returned the work marked with writing and grammatical corrections and other suggestions for improvement. Often she or my father included useful articles and references about the material that contributed to the richness of the work. My father offered several kind suggestions to make the work less polemic yet still remain convincing. My parents' steady support and encouragement was invaluable.

I have been fortunate to have numerous outstanding teachers (too numerous to give them all proper credit) that have been instrumental in shaping my academic accomplishments, including this book. Specifically, my major professor at the University of Georgia, William B. Pavlik, not only gave me stimulating experimental problems to work on (e.g., "rule governed behavior and reinforcement") and opened his laboratory to me, but he also opened his office and home to me. Taking turns at the keyboard, I learned to write concisely in Dr. Pavlik's basement. His guidance, early collaboration, and warmth set me down the path that led to this work.

The first seed of this book may have been sown as an undergraduate in Dr. David Eckerman's advanced learning course at the University of North Carolina. For my term paper in Dr. Eckerman's class I attempted to explain the material of my social psychology class in terms of basic learning and reinforcement processes. Dr. Eckerman has remained a touchstone for me over the years and has been highly supportive of my work.

Philosopher Bruce Waller was kind enough to be one of the first readers of a completed part 1. Although I had requested a harsh critical reading and marking, his feedback consisted almost exclusively of reinforcing comments. Although I did not realize it until I got it, his reinforcing support was exactly what I needed to press on and his tips lightened the load.

Likewise, Molly Burdette was a supportive early reader of many parts of the book. In fact, James "Bubskiluv" and Molly Burdette kindly let their family (Brendan, Katie, Colin, Brigid) become my surrogate family during the largely solitary endeavor of writing this book. They let me in the back door, fed me, and like a stray dog I never left.

Attendance at the yearly meetings of the Winter Conference on Animal Learning (first suggested by Dr. Pavlik) and the Association for Behavior Analysis have become invaluable as sources of inspiration and information. Already familiar with his work, at an early meeting of the Winter Conference I was fortunate to meet Professor Robert Eisenberger. Since that meeting he and his work have remained an inspiration. In fact Eisenberger's work forms the basis for much of this book. Robert Eisenberger has kept me involved in the area, provided me with any information or material I needed and is an untiring source of support and kindness.

Other constant supporters during the sometimes dark and stormy seas of my life during the writing of this book who deserve acknowledgment include Robert Morgan, Coreena Casey, Jane Kestner, Paul Weisbecker, and again my parents.

Although I have had great editorial, grammatical, and spelling support, given my atrocious spelling and grammar skills, no one could be expected to catch all my errors. I am solely responsible for all errors that remain. I understand that the final tasks of an author before a book ends up in a reader's hands is the proofreading of the page proofs and the compilation of the indexes. These tasks would have been brutally tedious, solitary, and frustrating for me, but Sarah Holowach's assistance made the work humorous and fun. Thank you all.

INTRODUCTION

Why do some children skip school to get drunk, "high," or "wasted" on drugs, while other children get to school on time, work hard on their homework, and participate in extracurricular activities such as bands, debate clubs, interscholastic athletics, or plays? It is for the same reason that one child with severe developmental disabilities bangs his head on the floor and repeatedly hits himself in the head until the cumulation of blows results in detached retinas and blindness while another child with equally severe developmental disabilities dresses and eats independently and uses sign language to communicate his wants and needs instead of relying on self-abuse. It is for the same reason that one elderly person takes numerous prescription drugs for pain, constantly complains of her ailments, and frequently visits the doctor while another elderly person in the same physical condition takes no prescriptions, hardly ever complains, or visits the doctor but instead attends continuing education classes at the local college, helps her grandchildren with their homework, and participates in book and dance clubs. The reason why all these people do what they do—the reason why *everyone* does what they do—is that *people do what they are reinforced for doing.*

Reinforcement is a basic process in nature. Understanding the reinforcement process is one way to understand behavior—why people do what they do. Other frameworks can be used to understand behavior. One can use a physiological or biological framework or one can use a poetic or artistic approach to understand behavior. While other approaches to explain behavior may have their place, explaining behavior from a reinforcement perspective has the advantages of being straightforward, directly observable, testable, and parsimonious (as simple as possible without "excess explanatory baggage"), and most important, when the reinforce-

ix

ment process is understood, a very effective *behavior change technology* emerges that is readily available to parents, teachers, counselors, managers, behavior analysts, and anyone who is involved with behavior—which is everyone!

For examples: When any academic behavior, from reading and math to sentence construction, is purposefully and systematically reinforced, academic achievement rapidly improves. Interest in, and enjoyment of, academics also increase following systematic reinforcement of academic achievement (chapters 1, 4, 5, 7, 9, & 10). When correct responding is reinforced on IQ tests or on other standardized tests, the scores of children from *all* socioeconomic backgrounds and prior achievement levels significantly increase (chapters 5, 9, &10). When following safety procedures was systematically reinforced for men working in dangerous open-pit mines, there were thousands less days lost due to injuries, lives were saved, and the company saved millions of dollars from the reduced cost of accidents and injuries (chapter 2). Compared to children given reinforcement for indicating common uses for common objects (e.g., using an eraser to erase), children given reinforcement for indicating creative uses for common objects (e.g., using an eraser as a fishing bobber or as a sponge) later draw more creative pictures and write more creative stories (chapter 7). When completing treatment goals, practicing social skills, and submitting negative urine samples is systematically reinforced, drug addicts have greatly increased rates of abstinence and successful employment (chapter 11). Emotionally disturbed children with conduct problems who participate in reinforcement based Teaching-Family model programs improve grades and decrease court contacts and criminal offenses (chapter 12).

Quite simply, a *reinforcer* is a consequence that increases the frequency of the behavior that preceded the consequence. *Reinforcement* is the *process* of increasing the rate of behaviors with reinforcing consequences. *Punishment* is the process of *decreasing* the rate of behavior with punishing consequences. Reinforcement can be positive or negative. Both *positive reinforcement* and *negative reinforcement increase* behavior.

Positive reinforcement occurs when an event or stimulus is presented (positive) as a consequence of behavior and the behavior increases (reinforcement). If reading a novel reveals a story and brings pleasure, and if the rate of reading novels increases to reveal more stories and brings more pleasure, then reading novels has been positively reinforced by the stories and by the pleasure produced by reading.

Negative reinforcement occurs when the rate of a behavior *increases* (reinforcement) because an aversive event or stimulus is removed (negative) or prevented from occurring. The behavior of saying "Not tonight, Honey. I have a headache" is negatively reinforced if it prevents or termi-

nates unwanted sexual advances. Reading novels may also be negatively reinforced if reading provides escape from the humdrum of everyday life, or allows one to forget, to escape from, one's problems.

Behaviors that are increased or maintained with reinforcement are *operant behaviors*, or *operants* because they "operate" on the environment to produce reinforcing consequences. For example, the verbal behavior of saying "Please pass the cake," is operant behavior because it operates on the social environment to produce the reinforcing consequence of receiving cake, just as operating a vending machine is operant behavior because it produces a reinforcing snack.

Both positive and negative reinforcement increase behavior or operants. A behavior, for example, reading novels, may be a function of positive reinforcement at one time and negative reinforcement at another time. "Channel surfing" with the TV remote control is positively reinforced if there are several interesting programs on at the same time and if the viewer wants to watch them all. But most of the time channel surfing is more a function of negative reinforcement because "nothing good is on," so the surfer changes channels to escape bad programs or to avoid commercials. Similarly, drug abuse may occur for positively reinforcing consequences— "to get high"—or for negatively reinforcing consequences—"to escape reality." As we will learn in the chapter on drug abuse, the abuser who engages in drug-taking behavior as a function of negative reinforcement—"to escape"—is much more likely to become addicted than the abuser who takes drugs as a function of positive reinforcement—"to get high." Unfortunately, much drug abuse occurs for both its negative and positive reinforcing characteristics, and therefore, drug abuse quickly becomes a complex behavior.

But using the concept of reinforcement to understand drug abuse, suggests that if drug abuse occurs because it is reinforcing, then drug abuse can be reduced or eliminated by teaching individuals new behaviors—such as communication skills and vocational skills—that may produce greater reinforcement than drug use produces. This is just one example of how using a reinforcement perspective to understand behavior suggests practical ways to replace maladaptive behaviors with adaptive behaviors.

Although positive reinforcement can be used to the great benefit of humanity, myths and misrepresentations of reinforcement have precluded the widespread implementation of systematic reinforcement. Even so, millions of people, including myself have greatly benefited from systematic reinforcement. For example, my parents were shocked when my first-grade teacher said I would never learn to read or write in the public schools. So during the summer between the first and second grades, I was taken to a reading laboratory at the University of North Carolina where they tried to teach me the basic skills I would need to learn to read and write. Each small success I had was reinforced with praise, affection, and encouragement.

My reading behavior was being *shaped*. *Successive approximations* of prerequisite reading skills (consistently looking at a word from left to right, writing words from left to right, etc.) were reinforced with praise. Appropriate discriminations were also differentially reinforced with praise and errors were gently corrected. For example, I learned that *d*, *p*, *q*, and *b*, did not all mean the same thing. "Tew" did not spell "wet," as I wrote on a school spelling test. "Deb" and "bed" were not the same and so on. Through this reinforcement program I was able to acquire some of the basic behaviors needed for success for reading and writing. For example, I learned to start at the beginning, the left, of words when reading or writing. I learned to associate sounds for letters with the shapes of the letters (*B* makes a "baa" sound; *P* does not, etc.).

My father, an English professor, feared I would never learn to spell or write at a minimally acceptable level. So out of desperation he took matters into his own hands. Dad guided me through a systematic positive reinforcement program that centered on reinforced "overlearning" (repetitions past perfection to improve performance). The program started on Sunday evening with a test of the next week's spelling words. Every word that I got wrong, which was usually every word, I had to write ten times. Then Dad gave me another test, and again I wrote every word I got wrong ten times. Afterward my efforts were reinforced with a Ping-Pong match against Dad in the basement. No matter how much I cried or yelled, I still had to do my spelling. I did not get to play Ping-Pong with Dad (or do anything else for that matter) until I had done my spelling.

We did this again on Monday, Tuesday, Wednesday, and Thursday evenings. By the time I took the test on Friday, I was spelling almost every word correctly, and Dad would reinforce my efforts with a new comic book. At first I just looked at the pictures in the comics, but my reading improved as my spelling improved and soon I was able to read some of the words. Eventually, as my reading slowly but surely improved, I could follow the adventures of *The Incredible Hulk* and *Sergeant Rock*. Some of the natural reinforcers that reading produces began to occur for me. Spelling, reading, and writing continued to be, and remain, a challenge for me (e.g., when writing this I just typed "continueb" instead of "continued"!). I still frequently misread words, read slowly, and spell worse than most people. But the reinforcement of my spelling efforts in childhood taught me not to give up. This reinforced persistence helped me to earn undergraduate, master's, and doctoral degrees.

During my senior year of college, and during the summers while working toward my master's degree I worked at Annie Sullivan Inc. Named after Helen Keller's teacher, Annie Sullivan Inc. was centered on one-on-one instruction and behavior management programs based on positive reinforcement. Clients had severe hyperactivity, aggression, autism, mental retardation, and/or life-threatening self-injurious behavior (SIB). In other words Annie Sullivan took only the "worst of the worst" when it came to dangerous behaviors and developmental disabilities. I worked with and observed several such clients.

To protect himself from SIB, which had already permanently disfigured his face, one autistic teenager came to Annie Sullivan wearing a lacrosse goalie's helmet and padded arm restraints that would not bend at the elbows. "Carl" cried and screamed almost constantly. Out of his restraints, he would attempt to severely injure himself. In his restraints and helmet, Carl was little more than a human vegetable. Our first goal was to get Carl out of his restraints without SIB for increasing amounts of time. Once out of his restraints without self-abuse, Carl could be taught basic life skills (i.e., basic personal hygiene behaviors). This program eventually resulted in a greatly improved quality of life for Carl. But there were storms before calm.

We never deprived Carl of food, but we started by requiring Carl to eat without his helmet (initially he could wear a hat as a replacement), without his restraints, and without attempting SIB (we blocked the blows to his face). If Carl attempted SIB his helmet was put back on and the meal was taken off the table. Carl was allowed three chances to eat each meal without SIB. If he attempted SIB a fourth time the meal would be taken away. Carl's reinforcement, the meal, was contingent on proper eating behaviors without SIB. Carl's eating requirement was not really unusual. He was required to "behave" at the table or he was "asked" to leave. This is just like millions of families where children are required to behave properly, eat without hitting oneself or others, or be sent from the table without finishing the meal.

Carl's appropriate behaviors were systematically, contingently, reinforced. After a few intense days Carl was eating happily without his arm restraints, without his helmet, and most importantly without self-injury. The next few summers when I returned to Annie Sullivan I observed further improvements in Carl's behaviors. His restraints were gone. He was attentive and worked on various vocational skills. While still very limited, his vocabulary improved. Best of all, Carl seldom screamed, cried, yelled, or attempted to injure himself. Instead he appeared calm and at ease. He now frequently smiled and often laughed.

I also observed that the very infrequent times when Carl did attempt SIB or other inappropriate behaviors, it was because this behavior was reinforced. Carl usually attempted SIB only when Ann was working. Ann was a hypnotically beautiful staff worker whom I unsuccessfully attempted to date. Carl had a crush on her as well. Following an SIB episode, Ann would get a millimeter away from Carl's face and plead with him in her voice that melted all males within hearing distance: "What's wrong Carl? Oh, Carl you shouldn't do that. I want to help you." Tears were in my eyes as well as Carl's. I told the other male staff "I'll injure myself too if Ann will get in my face and talk to me like that. Maybe she'll help me out too." Now that's social reinforcement of inappropriate behavior! Be that as it may, without exception at Annie Sullivan, I saw the *planned* reinforcement programs make significant positive impacts on the lives of all of the clients served.

My experiences during graduate school working as a psychology aide and as a behavior specialist for the Georgia Retardation Center were similar to those I experienced at Annie Sullivan in that every time a systematic reinforcement program was implemented for a client, the client's well-being improved. Once a reinforcement program was put into place, the involved clients screamed and cried less and smiled and laughed more.

The aggressive behaviors of one fourteen-year-old female, "Jane," were so severe that many staff members avoided her, ran from her, or outright refused to work in any area where she was. Observations revealed that Jane usually became aggressive when there was basically nothing else for her to do. Because she enjoyed being active, I designed a program that simply gave her more to do, for instance, doing more puzzles and taking out the trash, and reinforced her, usually with verbal praise, for task engagement. Jane also enjoyed being tickled and piggyback rides, and while many staff members were afraid to turn their backs on her, I gave Jane many piggyback rides without incident. Reinforcing Jane's task engagement greatly decreased her aggression. This may not seem like much. But before systematic reinforcement procedures began to be used with institutionalized individuals, most state institutions were nothing more than human warehouses for medically sedated, psychotic, retarded, and autistic individuals. Systematic reinforcement programs have allowed many previously warehoused individuals to be returned to their respective communities where their quality of life is usually greatly improved.

However, as reinforcement's power becomes increasingly clear and profound, some people—including many psychology professors—dismiss the study of reinforcement as "insufficient," "irrelevant" to psychology, or "overly simplistic." Some people consider reinforcing children for "appropriate" or academic behaviors as "bribing children to behave." I never felt I was being bribed when learning to read and spell was reinforced.

There is an entire literature—a movement—that argues that if reinforcement, or "reward," is not downright *evil*, then at the very least it should never be used in education or purposefully in any human affairs at all because the effects of reinforcement are invariably detrimental to humans! It is argued that using reinforcement is the same as "turning play into work" (Lepper, Green, & Nisbett, 1973). It is claimed that reinforcement "undermines intrinsic motivation," prevents "self-determination," deprives children of a "sense of competence," and is aversely "controlling" (see Cameron & Pierce, 1994, 1996; Dickinson, 1989; Eisenberger & Cameron, 1996; Flora, 1990 for reviews of these claims).

If it is true that reinforcement is evil, then did the hundreds of situations I have been involved in that systematically used reinforcement to better the lives of people (including my own) not really happen? Were the thousands of studies and experiments investigating reinforcement all fraudulent? Were the thousands of applications of reinforcement I had read about, observed, helped implement, and even designed all *unethical?* Should we really keep self-injurious and/or violent individuals in restraints or isolation and medically sedated 24 hours a day, 365 days a year? Or could we use reinforcement systematically to better human lives? I believe we should use positive reinforcement to improve the human condition. But this may be a minority position.

Although *false*, the argument that "extrinsic rewards" (e.g., reinforcement) "undermine intrinsic interest" is impressive to roll out at academic cocktail parties. But as with so many psychological "factoids" when you scratch beneath the surface, the argument is without merit. Basically, the myth is that if one is given an "extrinsic reward" (this usually means a "reinforcer") for an activity in which one has an "intrinsic interest" (i.e., the activity is engaged in without contrived reinforcers), then the "intrinsic interest" will be "undermined" by the "extrinsic reward." At first glance the myth of "undermining intrinsic interest with external reward" seems counterintuitive: "If someone is rewarded for something they like doing already, doesn't that mean they should like it even more? Isn't it icing on the cake?" Yes, they will like it more. It is only a myth that interest will be undermined. But the explanations for the myth sound logical enough, and once it is given, the intelligentsia, feeling smug at their elite "insight into human nature," are likely to reply, "Of course, I should have seen that all along."

The basic explanation, the "overjustification hypothesis," goes as follows: If I like doing something, supposedly I am "internally justified" for the behavior. Then if you reward me for it, it becomes "overjustified" (internal justification *plus* external reward): Later if you no longer reward me, supposedly because I came to believe that I was engaging in the behavior only because it was being extrinsically rewarded, I will engage in it less and less. The behavior is now "un-," or "less," "justified." (e.g., Lepper et al., 1973). "Ah-ha," claims the intelligentsia, "we wouldn't want to overjustify a behavior now would we?"

According to the myth, if you liked to teach, and taught as a volunteer, but then I started and then stopped paying you for teaching, you would never teach voluntarily again. "I'm a professional now; I only teach if I'm paid." Overjustification. Mysteriously, the original "intrinsic interest" in teaching has been lost.

But just as logical as "overjustification" may sound, the absurdity of it all is blatantly obvious in the world around us. If "extrinsic reinforcers" really did "undermine intrinsic interest," then no veterinarians would have pets; all former professional athletes (especially those with incentive contracts) would never play or want to be involved with their former sport; no carpenters, electricians, or painters would ever volunteer for "Habitat for Humanity," an organization that builds houses for the working poor; teachers would not want to teach; doctors would not want to practice medicine; in short, NO professional would enjoy his or her profession and no professional would want to be involved with the profession unless he or she were being paid to do so. *If the myth that extrinsic reinforcers undermine intrinsic interest were true, humanity would be a complete mess.* To assume that a teacher, formerly a volunteer, would remark, "The pay is nice and I need it, but the real reason I chose teaching for a profession is because I love teaching," is just as, or more, logical as the "overjustification hypothesis." The overjustification hypothesis, like the *myth* that extrinsic reinforcers undermine intrinsic interest, is wrong.

Despite copious evidence on the beneficial, lifechanging, lifesaving effects of reinforcement programs, Edward L. Deci and Richard M. Ryan's book, *Intrinsic Motivation and Self-determination in Human Behavior* (1985), and Stanford University's Mark R. Lepper's writings argue that reinforcement programs have too many unwanted effects and should be avoided or removed from human institutions, which were, and are, being cited in the educational and popular presses.

Chapters on learning or motivation in many introductory psychology textbooks conclude with a statement that reinforcement undermines intrinsic interest and therefore it is really harmful to use reinforcement procedures with humans. Parenting magazines publish articles warning parents against rewarding—even against praising—the appropriate behaviors of their children because of supposed detrimental effects of rewards on their children's development. Within the academic community and applied psychology professions there is widespread skepticism, and sometimes even outright hostility, toward the study and use of reinforcement. Behavior analysis (the discipline that studies and applies reinforcement) has been ghettoized (Leahey, 1991, p. 373) by psychologists who feel that their domination of the academic and applied study of human behavior is being threatened. Many psychologists have belittled and ignored advances in behavior analysis and reinforcement theory.

In 1993, the popular book *Punished by Reward (sic): The Trouble with Gold Stars, Incentive Plans, A's, Praise, and Other Bribes* was published by "social critic" Alfie Kohn. An easy read, Kohn takes virtually every myth, misrepresentation, caricature, and criticism ever made against the use of reinforcement to attack the use of reinforcement. If it were not for the fact that Kohn is a skillful self-promoter (an Oprah Winfrey guest) and that the book is so widely read and cited, primarily in education and business management textbooks, the book would be laughable. However, the book has brought to the public, in easily readable form, the argument that *reinforcement is evil.* Incredibly, Kohn argues, among other things, that "rewards" (by which he means "reinforcers") do not improve performance or behavior and are bad for relationships and creativity. Kohn further argues that incentives, reinforcers, should not be used in the workplace or in school, and that children's work should not be graded (evaluated). Indeed, according to Kohn, *children should NOT even be praised*!

Throughout my life I have been witness to, and often a part of, the systematic use of the power of positive reinforcement to improve the human condition. Yet others, like Kohn, continue to pound the misguided message that purposefully using reinforcement with humans somehow treats humans as less than human. Improvement of the human condition has been hampered because myths about reinforcement have precluded effective implementation of many reinforcement programs. A widely available response is needed to counter the myths about, and misrepresentations of, reinforcement. With such a response the purposeful use of reinforcement procedures may more likely be utilized, and, when gains are being made, those involved with reinforcement programs can be better informed to respond to criticism and defend against the attacks on the good they are doing. This book is meant to respond to the myths, misrepresentations, and criticisms of the purposeful use of reinforcement in human institutions and human relations and to accurately present the use and potential uses of reinforcement in society.

Part I

Myths and Misrepresentations of Reinforcement

1

REINFORCEMENT AS "RAT PSYCHOLOGY"

A new vaccine has been developed. Hailed as a miracle, the vaccine protects against ALL sexually transmitted diseases including AIDS and herpes, and prevents the flu, the common cold, and all childhood diseases such as chicken pox. The vaccine is available starting tomorrow. Would you take it? Would you want your child to have a shot?

Sorry, one piece of information concerning the hypothetical vaccine was left out. The vaccine has never been tested on animals and is not based on animal models of the diseases. The pharmaceutical company manufactured the drug by looking at people with the illnesses and put together something that seemed logical to them. Knowing this, would you take the vaccine? Probably not. In reality, before new drugs are even allowed to be tested in a very limited and controlled manner on humans, the drugs must undergo numerous tests on animal models of the disease.

While laws require pharmaceutical companies to test their new drugs on animals before they are allowed to be tested on humans, the opposite is true with many psychological and educational "treatments." The treatments are seldom, if ever, tested on animals and seldom based on animal models of abnormal or inappropriate behavior. Often the "treatments" are not based on any valid research of any sort (Singer & Lalich, 1996; Watters & Ofshe, 1999). Psychologists and educators simply develop the treatments by looking at people with the problem behavior(s) and develop something that somehow relates to what they have seen. This anything goes attitude in psychotherapy has produced, by the estimate of University of Pennsylvania researcher Alan E. Kazdin (1994), over 400 different approaches to psychotherapy! Ed Anderson, trustee of the Cambridge Center for Behavioral Studies lamented on this state of affairs: "Being a

3

chemist by profession, I often wondered why there is only one chemistry, one biology, one physics, and there are 10,000 psychologies" (from Daniels, 1994, p. xii). While not ethical for physical problems, this "invent a therapy" approach is standard practice when it comes to behavioral and educational problems. The result is that millions of dollars are wasted on such quackery as "past life regression," "facilitated communication," empirically invalidated psychoanalytic "therapy" (e.g., Singer & Lalich, 1996; Watters & Ofshe, 1999; Wolpe, 1981), "whole word" reading instruction, and "new math." Indeed, one child died in a "rebirthing" effort to get her to "bond" to her adopted mother.

The systematic, purposeful use of reinforcement is seen as too elementary, ineffective, irrelevant, or even as unethical for human problems. The science of behavior, called "behavior analysis" that is based on an experimental analysis of behavior (EAB) that often uses rat and pigeon behavior as a source of data to unveil the reinforcement process, is held in disdain by many in psychology, management, and education. Ironically, however, the *most effective* psychological and educational treatments and programs can all be ultimately traced back to animal models or data from animal behavior and behavior's systematic relation to reinforcement. Likewise, *performance management*, developed by Aubrey C. Daniels, directly applies behavior analysis, primarily the effective application of positive reinforcement, to business management. This direct systematic application of reinforcement to management has resulted in improved quality and productivity at such companies as 3M, Kodak, Rubbermaid, and Honeywell, as well as other companies in the United States, Canada, Mexico, Great Britain, France, Italy, and Brazil (Daniels, 1994).

RAT PSYCHOLOGY IN INNER-CITY EDUCATION

In 1975, in one of the poorest, most violent sections of the Houston, Texas, area, Thaddeus Lott took over as principal of Wesley Elementary, a school with a 99% minority population. Only 18% of the third graders were reading at grade level. However, by 1996, 100% of the third graders passed the Texas Assessment of Academic Skills. In 1998, Wesley first graders ranked in the top 13 of 182 Houston schools in reading, out-scoring many upper-class, predominantly white schools. Similar results have occurred with functionally similar programs in other run-down "ghetto" schools, such as Public School 114 in the Bronx (Lemann, 1998).

Despite his truly amazing success, rather than being applauded, Principal Lott is vilified by many in psychology and education. Lott's success is discounted and criticized because his school program is based on reinforcement that is contingent on progressive achievement by teachers and students and uses the method of "direct instruction." In direct instruction students are constantly drilled with correct answers reinforced and errors immediately corrected. In other words, the approach Lott uses to run his school is based on principles of learning derived from the study of animal behavior, or derogatorily, his approach is said to be based on "rat psychology." Indeed, according to critics such as Kenneth Goodman, professor of language, reading, and culture at the University of Arizona, not only is Lott's approach called "rat psychology," but it is directed at poor, minority children and is something "that middle-class parents wouldn't stand for" ("Despite Test Scores," 1988).

Despite such unsubstantiated attacks and inaccurate portrayals, progress continues. At Wesley Elementary, the behavior of both the students and the teachers is reinforced according to a strict, purposeful, programmatic, research-based behavior management program centered on reinforcement contingent on successive academic gains. Teaching cannot be said to have occurred if no learning has occurred. Therefore, teaching effectiveness is measured by students' academic progress. Promotions and raises for teachers are contingent upon their students having end-of-year test scores higher than their start-of-year scores. That is, effective teaching behavior is reinforced with raises and promotions. As a result effective teaching behaviors are selected, increasing in frequency, and ineffective teaching repertoires tend to die out or become extinct.

Direct instruction is largely based on the concepts of *shaping* (the method of reinforcing successive approximations) and *fluency*. Behavior that occurs with ease, accuracy, and at a high rate is fluent. Understanding the fundamental nature and the systematic use of both shaping and fluency was derived directly from studies using rat and pigeon subjects in basic experimental analyses of behavior.

Shaping involves the reinforcement of closer and closer responses to a final behavior and the extinction, or nonreinforcement, of previous approximations. To shape a rat to press a lever, first being near the lever is reinforced with a food pellet. Then, touching the lever is reinforced, but just being near the lever is not. Then, pressing the lever is reinforced, but simply touching the lever is not. The rat has been taught to press a lever by reinforcing successive approximations to lever pressing and by not reinforcing, or extinguishing, previous approximations.

A cheetah mother starts to bring meat to her cubs to supplement her milk. Later, she brings small wounded gazelle calves to her cubs so they can kill and eat them. Still later she brings largely uninjured and larger gazelle calves for her cubs. Finally the cheetah mother does not allow her offspring to share in her kills. The cheetah mother, by bringing successively more difficult prey, has shaped the hunting behavior of her offspring.

A child is taught to read the word *was* by first being socially reinforced for making the "waaa" sound in response to the printed stimulus *W*, and by making the "as" sound in response to the printed stimulus word *as*. Next the sound "waaa.......aaaasssa" in response to the stimulus "was" is reinforced. Then the sound "wa...as" is differentially reinforced and the sound "waaa.......aaaasssa" is not reinforced or is corrected. Finally, only the verbal behavior of saying "was" in response to the printed stimulus "was" is reinforced. Learning to read "was" was shaped by reinforcing successive behavioral approximations to the desired response. Learning to read by phonics depends in part upon shaping. While seeming simple, shaping can build complex behavioral repertoires and may require thousands of repetitions. Learning basic math (addition and subtraction) for example, may require over fifty thousand responses (L. K. Miller, 1997, p. 261).

If learning simple math requires thousands of repetitions, then it is easy to see that to learn basic elementary academic skills, hundreds of thousands, if not millions, of repetitions are required. Fluency building is dependent on rapid repetitions, with correct responses reinforced. To have a functional skill, fluency is required (Johnson & Layng, 1992).

Most college graduates and some high school graduates have had a few years study of a foreign language. However, the vast majority of these adults cannot speak, read, or understand the language they studied. They do not have a functional foreign language skill because they never became fluent in the language. Instead, they achieved a minimum level of acquisition necessary to pass the next exam. But the few who did become fluent in a language often enjoy speaking and listening to that language.

Similarly, fluency in math brings appreciation of the power, beauty, and utility of math. In addition to calling a solution "beautiful" mathematicians may call a proof or solution "eloquent." But those with poor, dysfluent math skills are said to have "math phobia." Those who cannot read well do not like to read. But fluent readers enjoy reading. A heart surgeon who has acquired only the basic skills to perform bypass surgery may perform the operation correctly but take many hours. In contrast, a surgeon who is *fluent* in the operation will perform the operation equally well but may take less than two hours. Even though both doctors perform the surgery correctly, the fluent doctor's patients are much more likely to survive. Fluent behavior is needed whether the operant behavior is auto mechanics or heart surgery.

When a behavioral skill is not fluent, it is effortful. According to the law of least effort, effort is aversive (Eisenberger, 1992), and will tend to be avoided. Therefore, teaching basic academic skills to a high degree of fluency increases the probability that more advanced academic skills will be acquired. Conversely, learning only to a minimum level of acquisition increases the probability of later academic failure.

In colleges across the United States, direct instruction is often belittled as a "drill and kill" teaching method (Cheney, 1999). A more accurate phrase may be "drill and thrill." When a behavior is highly reinforced and built to fluency, as behavior is in direct instruction, it builds "self-esteem" (Cheney, 1999), and the students enjoy learning.

A fluent behavior is one that has been strongly selected and is therefore very likely to occur under the appropriate environmental conditions. The method of fluency building in direction instruction is based on the ("rat") laboratory concept of "free operant responding." In free operant responding, as long as the organism is in the environment, the organism is "free" to perform the operant behavior as frequently or as infrequently as the organism's physiology allows. "Percent correct," the standard educational measurement, captures only part of what is necessary for a behavior to become fluent. Fluency requires a high *rate* of accurate performance.

Lever pressing by a rat may be reinforced when a light above the lever is on but not when it is off. Initially, lever pressing will be equally likely whether the light is on or off. If the training is stopped as soon as seven responses are made when the light is on and only three when the light is off, (70% accuracy, a typical goal required for promotion in education), correct responding is not overly probable for the next training session. Furthermore, training a new behavior that is based on the previous discrimination learning (press when the light is on; don't when the light is off), will be next to impossible because the initial learning, while demonstrated at 70% accuracy, never became fluent.

Conversely, if lever pressing at a high rate while the light was on, one hundred responses per minute, and a low or zero rate when the light was off, was required to end a session or before a new behavior based on the initial discrimination learning was taught, then correct responding during the next session and learning new responses based on the previous learning is highly likely. High-rate, reinforced, free operant responding builds fluency.

If attempts are made to teach a child new math skills based on simple addition and subtraction, *before* the child is fluent, but *after* the child can make 70% correct responses (perhaps the child still uses his fingers to count or it takes one minute per problem), then teaching a new skill such as multiplication, division, or word problems, will be very difficult if not impossible. However, if the child is required to become fluent in simple addition and subtraction, for example, ten correct flash cards for every incorrect flash card, *at the rate of one card per second*, before teaching a new skill, then learning multiplication, division, and word problems will be much easier.

According to educational researchers and reformers Kent R. Johnson and T.V. Joe Layng, requiring fluency in academic behavior is a direct product of "Skinner's (1938) discovery of the importance of response rate as a dependent variable" (Johnson & Layng, 1992, p. 1476). Skinner's classic text *The Behavior of Organisms* (1938), is based entirely on research with rats. Perhaps, the claim that "using reinforcement on humans is 'rat psychology,'" is not a myth after all. The general principles of reinforcement (e.g., how delay, magnitude, frequency of reinforcement, and other variables, e.g., the concurrent availability of alternate responses and sources of reinforcement effect the rate of behavior) have all been systematically established almost exclusively by studying rat and pigeon behavior under various reinforcement contingencies.

Every science-based discipline develops an understanding of general principles in controlled *simplified* laboratory conditions before the general principles are applied to human situations. General principles of a chemical reaction may be established in a test-tube with isolated variables before the principle is applied in a pharmaceutical medication. Electricity, transistors, resistors, and all other components of modern computers were first studied in controlled, simplified, laboratory situations before their systematic application was possible. However, when an experimental analysis of behavior develops general principles in controlled *simplified* laboratory conditions before the general principles are applied to human situations, the general principles are discounted in their applicability to humans. The procedures are discounted, and the promoters are often held in contempt. "People are not rats. Studying rat behavior can't help people."

However, such attacks are inciting but not insightful. To be valid, an attack must be accurate. If what is meant by "rat psychology" is the systematic application of general principles of reinforcement in applied behavior analysis programs, then, in fact, when children are having behavioral difficulties, middle-class parents are increasingly using "rat psychology" themselves, or run to programs based on "rat psychology" for help. Fortunately for these middle-class parents, the data make it clear that they have made the best choice. Furthermore these programs offer the best hope for impoverished minority children to succeed in school.

RAT PSYCHOLOGY IN THE HOME

Upper- and middle-class parents often rely on "timeout" rather than spankings to correct the behavior of their children. For good reason too. Murray A. Straus's research spanning over twenty years consistently shows a direct correlation between the number of spankings a child receives and increased social, psychological, and behavioral problems, both in childhood and adulthood (e.g., Straus, 1994). Over the course of a person's lifetime, spanking causes many more problems than it ever helps. Spankings frequently occur not because they help the child, but because spankings are often negatively reinforcing *for the parent.*

Parents who use timeout instead of spanking should know that the full term for "timeout" is *timeout from positive reinforcement,* and that, as noted by University of Florida researchers Cynthia J. Pietras and Timothy D. Hackenberg, the general principle of timeout was derived directly from the animal (rat and pigeon) laboratory.

> Timeout from positive reinforcement is one of the most commonly used procedures in educational and therapeutic settings. Like many behavioral procedures used in applied contexts, timeout from positive reinforcement has origins in basic laboratory research. . . . In applied settings, . . . their response-contingent application is typically used to suppress unwanted behavior. (Pietras & Hackenberg, 2000, p. 147)

Every time parents use timeout instead of a spanking to suppress unwanted behavior, they are using "rat psychology" on their children!

In the laboratory, for example, timeout from positive reinforcement may be programmed to teach sequenced lever pressing. During training, if the rat pressed a lever out of sequence the cage would immediately go dark and no lever pressing could produce reinforcement for a brief period of time, usually a few seconds. That is, by pressing a lever out of sequence, a "timeout from positive reinforcement" occurred during which time no responses are reinforced. A timeout from positive reinforcement for an unwanted lever press may be just as, or more, effective than electric shock in producing response suppression. (Is shock a rat's equivalent of a spanking?) Should a rat be shocked or have a timeout from positive reinforcement? Should a child be spanked or have a timeout for "misbehavior"? Timeout from positive reinforcement, "rat psychology," has reduced or eliminated severe, dangerous, and frequent behavioral excesses in children where other methods have failed.

In a classic example of timeout, researchers at the University of Vermont (Knight & McKenzie, 1974) trained parents in the use of timeout from positive reinforcement in a program to eliminate persistent thumb sucking in children six to eight years old who began this habit during infancy. First, each night parents read their child their favorite stories no matter what the child did. The children sucked their thumbs. But when the timeout procedure started the parents simply stopped reading whenever the child's thumb touched or went in their mouth. Reading started again as soon as thumb sucking ceased. That is, this habit produced a "timeout from positive reinforcement" (reading). Thumb sucking was eliminated in all children. Three cheers for rat psychology!

RAT PSYCHOLOGY IN PRIVATE SCHOOLS AND COLLEGE

The application of basic operant conditioning principles, or "rat psychology," has produced large rapid academic gains for academically disadvantaged beginning college students. In 1991, 40% of all the students in Malcolm X College in Chicago scored below the eighth-grade reading level; 30% scored below the sixth-grade level. A significant number of these students, virtually all of whom were either Hispanic or African-American, failed to make up this deficiency with remedial education, much less graduate. A summer term, pilot program in 1991 for Malcolm X students, based largely on fluency and general principles of Skinner's "rat psychology," increased reading vocabulary and comprehension 1.1 years in just 20 hours of instruction. Gains in mathematics computation, problem solving, and concepts ranged from 1.9 years to 6.0 years. No homework was required. On the strength of these results, Malcolm X College has established a Precollege Institute modeled after the pilot program (Johnson & Layng, 1992).

With students diagnosed as learning disabled and/or as having "attention deficit disorder," results that are as good or frequently superior to the Malcolm X program are *invariably* obtained at Morningside Academy in Seattle, Washington. In fact, the Malcolm X program is based on the Morningside model (which in turn is based on operant, or "rat" psychology). At Morningside, not only middle-class children, but homeless teenagers having criminal records have made outstanding academic gains. Morningside offers two money-back guarantees. Students will advance at least two grade levels in one year, and those *diagnosed* with attention deficit disorder will increase their average time-on-task behavior from 1 to 3 minutes to 20 minutes or more. *No* parent has asked for their money back (Daniels, 1994; Johnson & Layng, 1992).

Labeling an individual with attention deficit disorder (or with "obsessive compulsive disorder," or with any label for that matter) has as much meaning and does as little good as labeling a program *rat psychology*. The most valid approach for overcoming behavior deficiencies and excesses is to conduct an analysis of the individual's behavior-environment interactions and then to implement an intervention based on that analysis and on the systematic application of general principles of behavior including reinforcement of appropriate operant responses.

The systematic application of reinforcement principles in the education of disadvantaged children is the most effective, pleasant, and agreeable method of raising the educational achievement of lower-socioeconomic-class minorities to the level of the white middle-class majority. In a success story similar to that of Lott's success in Houston, when Harvest Preparatory Elementary School, a school that serves many children from poor families in Minneapolis, introduced direct instruction, the kindergartners' reading scores went from average to the 89th percentile (Cheney, 1999).

While many of the intellectual elite deny it and cling to romantic notions of human achievement, the elite's children's academic behaviors are richly and frequently reinforced. It is this rich, frequent reinforcement that selects academic, artistic, and intellectual behaviors. Systematic reinforcement programs such as direct instruction can supply the reinforcement needed to select academic, artistic, and intellectual behaviors of disadvantaged children whose environments are otherwise lacking in appropriate and sufficient reinforcers for academic behaviors. It is a human's history of reinforcement for particular operants, whether artistic or anarchist, and not some intrinsic, mystical, inner quality of the human that is responsible for what the individual achieves.

THE RAT PSYCHOLOGY OF READING

Earning by Learning is an example of a reinforcement program for academically at-risk children. Reading behavior is reinforced by paying a child two dollars for each book read. This reinforcement may also be contingent on reading part of the book to an adult volunteer, or writing a report on the book. Alfie Kohn, author of the polemic *Punished by Rewards*, claims that "It would be difficult to come up with a less effective way to help children value reading" (Kelly, 1995). Yet the research is clear, that is, paying academically at risk children to read does indeed teach children to value reading. Research conducted by West Georgia College professors found that the Earning by Learning reinforcement program increases positive attitudes toward both academic reading *and* recreational reading (McNinch et al., 1995). By increasing their reading skills, over ten thousand academically at risk children have benefited from this reinforcement program and learned to value reading.

Earning by Learning generally serves lower-socioeconomic-class children. Middle-class parents, whose children generally go on to college, are more likely simply to pay their children money themselves in order to increase a child's reading frequency (Flora & Flora, 1999; Flora & Popanak, 2001). Middle-class children are also likely to participate in Pizza Hut's Book It! reading program. During the 1995–1996 school year over twenty-two million children in the United States, Canada, and Australia participated in Book It! and the program is expanding. Book It! reinforces reading with certificates for a free personal pan pizza when reading goals set by the student's teacher are met. Book It! is a plain and simple reinforcement program (Flora & Flora, 1999). A report by the Institute of Human Science and Services of the University of Rhode Island on the "Book It!" program concluded "the basis behind the program was to offer *immediate positive* reinforcement to reward *individual accomplishments. . . .* it was this rewarding of effort and not ability that probably made Book It! so attractive to both parents and students" (Institute, 1986, p. 17, emphasis in original). Furthermore, teachers reported that Book It! increased positive attitudes toward learning (61%), reading level (69%), and enjoyment of reading (80%); the longer the children were in the program the more their reading level rose and their enjoyment of reading increased. Through the Book It! program, over twenty-two million children benefit from "rat psychology" each year.

When middle-class children are facing serious academic difficulties, parents typically will do whatever is necessary and use whatever resources are available to overcome their child's deficiency. Increasingly, to remedy a child's educational deficiencies, middle-class parents are paying out hundreds of millions of dollars, at the rate of $35 to $65 an hour, to private for-profit "learning centers" such as Sylvan Learning Centers. Sylvan operates in the United States and in a hundred seventy countries. Now Sylvan is going into public schools, taking federal Chapter One dollars for remedial education (Hancock, 1994). While Sylvan claims to use customized curricula for each child, the engine that drives the academic success of the children tutored at Sylvan is nothing more than a simple *token reinforcement* program or a *token economy*. Furthermore, at Sylvan, as in direct instruction, correct responses are frequently and immediately reinforced and errors immediately corrected. Like Morningside Academy, Sylvan also guarantees that each child will advance one letter grade in thirty-six hours of instruction or less. Most of what Sylvan does is nothing a parent couldn't do with a little investment of time and a minimal knowledge of reinforcement.

TOKEN ECONOMIES

The modern systematic application of token economies, used at Sylvan Leaning Centers and in other organizations across the globe, is a direct descendent of general principles of reinforcement established in the rat laboratory as explained by University of Exeter, United Kingdom, researcher S. E. G. Lea:

> "Operant psychology" does not just consist of those still carrying out fundamental research with rats and pigeons in Skinner boxes. Another important influence comes from those who seek to put operant principles into effect, for example in educational or clinical psychology—the behavior modifiers. . . . In an ambitious and original clinical research project, Teodoro Ayllon and Nathan Azrin (1968) sought to apply reinforcement principles to raise the level of behavior in an entire ward of severely regressed schizophrenic patients. . . . Ayllon and Azrin . . . introduced "tokens," which were given to the patients as rewards whenever they performed any desired response, and could be exchanged for any of the range of "backup reinforcers." Ayllon and Azrin's rationale for the token system lay in the well established principle of conditioned reinforcement, which had been studied in detail in animals, and shown to extend to the use of tokens at least in rats and apes. . . . Token economies had considerable success and soon spread widely. (Lea, 1987, p. 97)

In a token economy, *generalized reinforcers*, or tokens, are delivered contingent upon a specified behavior. The tokens have no worth in and of themselves. It is the backup reinforcers that tokens are exchanged for that make the tokens effective reinforcers. Backup reinforcers may be anything that has value for the individual. They could be food or computer time, depending on the individual whose behavior is being reinforced with tokens (see Martin & Pear, 1999, for a review of token economies). As noted by Lea, the systematic use of tokens is derived from the concept of conditioned reinforcement. When lever pressing is reinforced with a pellet of food and a tone immediately precedes the delivery of the pellet, then the tone will become a powerful conditioned reinforcer that a rat will work to produce. When a wife always plays Vivaldi before her husband's sexual advances are reinforced with sex, then Vivaldi will become a powerful conditioned reinforcer and the husband will engage in other behaviors to receive the conditioned reinforcer (buy CDs, request Vivaldi on the radio, etc.). Conditioned reinforcers associated with several backup reinforcers are generalized reinforcers of which tokens are one example. Based on the variety and value of the backup reinforcers, tokens can become very powerful motivators. "Token reinforcement programs have repeatedly proven of value in increasing academic productivity and decreasing inappropriate behavior, and they have proven very effective in large-scale comparative evaluations in inner-city schools" (O'Leary, 1991, p. 5). Regular classroom teachers have used token reinforcement systems to improve test perform-ance and study hall behaviors (e.g., Karraker, 1971) to name a few. Infor-mal surveys of teachers in my graduate learning classes find that over a third of them employ some kind of token reinforcement system in their classrooms. Furthermore, when teachers are explicitly taught about token economies they are more likely to employ them in their classroom and report good results (Kestner & Flora, 1998).

At Sylvan, appropriate academic behaviors are reinforced with tokens (nothing more than poker chips with "Sylvan Learning Centers" stamped on them). The tokens are then exchanged for CDs, movie tickets, balls, games, or other items of value to the children at the "Sylvan Store." It is the simple application of basic reinforcement principles (e.g. "rat psychol-ogy") that makes Sylvan so successful. And it is this success that brings the middle-class parent to Sylvan's door.

"I TRIED REINFORCEMENT. IT DOESN'T WORK IN MY CLASS"

As with other natural phenomenon, when the systematic application of reinforcement principles is attempted, a little knowledge may be a danger-ous thing. Occasionally, a teacher may try to increase academic behavior by "rewarding" it with gold stars, or smiley faces next to the student's name. Because the students' behavior doesn't change, or changes only temporar-ily, the teacher soon finds that they don't really care about the stars or faces. Because the behavior the teacher tried to increase did not increase, she concludes that "reinforcement doesn't work." The teacher is not alone, as we shall see; many psychologists and educators also believe that "reinforce-ment doesn't work." But that is just like saying that "natural selection does-n't occur."

In this example, the teacher has developed a system of delivering tokens, or conditioned reinforcers, but failed to associate the tokens (the stars), with any backup reinforcer of value. Therefore, the tokens have no reinforcing strength and cannot increase the rate of the behavior on which they are contingent. If the stars or faces were associated with, or had been exchangeable for, backup reinforcers, the teacher would have found that reinforcement does indeed work. It would have been more accurate for the teacher to conclude that "I rewarded academic behavior with gold stars that looked nice. But since I neglected to associate the stars with any backup reinforcers, ultimately the stars had no value for the students, and they were not effective in changing the children's academic behaviors. If I had made the star have value by associating them with backup reinforcers, like an extra five minutes of recess for each star, then academic behavior likely would have improved."

REINFORCEMENT VERSUS REWARD

Most people use the words *reward* and *reinforcer* interchangeably. In many cases rewards do function as reinforcers. However, the words *reinforcement* and *reinforcer* have functional meaning that is not explicit in the term *reward*. A reward is something given for special behavior. But, a reward is not necessarily a consequence of a behavior, is usually not given repeatedly, and most importantly does not have the explicit meaning of an increased rate of the behavior that the reward was given for. In contrast, a *reinforcer is a contingent*, explicit *consequence* of a behavior, usually occurring repeatedly, which *by definition increases the rate of the preceding behavior*. (Appendix 2 defines and explains several basic terms related to reinforcement.) If a behavior is "rewarded," but the rate of the behavior does not increase, then the behavior was not reinforced and reinforcement did not occur. Rewarding a behavior with a gold star will not necessarily reinforce (i.e., select or increase the rate of) the behavior that was rewarded.

Gold stars *could* become conditioned reinforcers if every time a child showed them to Mom, the child got a hug and kisses. Being kissed, hugged, and praised for bringing home good grades is one way grades become conditioned reinforcers for many people. If grades are not associated with praise and affection or other reinforcers, they are unlikely to become conditioned reinforcers for academic work. The child who is not given affection, praised, or reinforced in some way for academic accomplishment will not care what kinds of grades he brings home.

Reinforcement is a natural phenomenon just as natural selection or gravity are natural phenomena. Claiming that "reinforcement doesn't work" is as logical as claiming that "natural selection doesn't work" or that "gravity doesn't work." A jet flying across the Atlantic or a person's light weight on the moon doesn't mean that "gravity doesn't work." If we fail to understand why the jet flies or why the person is light on the moon, it means that we haven't considered all the other relevant variables operating on the phenomena (e.g., jet propulsion and the differential air pressure created by the wing's shape operate on the jet to allow it to fly) or that we don't understand, or are ignorant of, other relevant factors (perhaps we don't understand or are ignorant of the fact that because the moon has less mass, its gravitational force is less; therefore objects are lighter on the moon). Likewise, a teacher's "reinforcement program" may fail because the teacher is ignorant of the fact that for tokens, or conditioned reinforcers, to *reinforce*, the tokens *must* be exchangeable for backup reinforcers of value to the child. That is, tokens must be exchangeable for reinforcers that *reinforce* (perhaps each star could be exchangeable for ten minutes of free time, computer time, or an extra snack).

BEHAVIORAL ECONOMICS

All the world's economies are, in fact, token reinforcement programs, or token economies. Tokens, or money, have replaced the barter system. In reinforcement terms, *inflation* means that the same number of tokens are now exchangeable for less backup reinforcement or that more tokens are required for the same amount of backup reinforcement. In the 1980s 2 tokens ($2) were exchangeable for two beers. In the year 2000, one beer often required 4 tokens or more.

Deflation means that the same number of tokens are now exchangeable for more backup reinforcement, or that fewer tokens are required for the same amount of backup reinforcement. In the 1980s, 2,000 tokens ($2,000) or more were required for what now would be considered a shamefully weak, virtually useless, personal computer. At the start of the twenty-first century, 1,000 tokens are exchangeable for a personal computer a thousand times more powerful than the 1980s version.

Because the same amount of behavior produces the same number of tokens, but the same tokens are exchangeable for less, inflation decreases the reinforcing value of money. ("I won't work for $5 an hour anymore.") Because the same amount of behavior produces the same number of tokens, but the same tokens are exchangeable for more, deflation increases the reinforcing value of money. ("During the depression I worked twelve hours a day for $1 and I was glad to get it.") When a country's currency completely collapses, the currency is no longer exchangeable for backup reinforcers and it is worthless. People will no longer work for that country's tokens. The collapsed currency no longer functions as a generalized reinforcer. So too, if a teacher's gold stars are not exchangeable for backup reinforcers, students will no longer work for gold stars.

Of course it would be absurd to argue that the world's economies are nothing more than "rat psychology." However, economic behavior and operant behavior are often synonymous. In economics an employee works (behaves) in order to receive pay, commodities (reinforcers). In operant psychology an organism behaves (works) to receive reinforcers (commodities and money). As first noted by Skinner (1953), the contingency and resulting response pattern of animals responding on fixed ratio schedules of reinforcement is nearly identical to the contingency and resulting work pattern of employees paid on a piece-rate wage. For example, when a rat's lever pressing is reinforced on a fixed ratio schedule of reinforcement, the schedule produces systematically high steady rates of responding with a break in responding after each reinforcer is delivered. Likewise when an employee is paid on a piece-rate wage, for example $1 for every 25 socks sewed, typically the employee will sew at a fast rate pausing only after 25 socks have been sewed. The behavioral pattern is identical for the human factory worker and the laboratory rat because the reinforcement contingency is identical. The basic experimental model of behavioral economics builds on this observation by arranging various reinforcement schedules, contingencies, and constraints on responding and reinforcement to model economic phenomenon, hypotheses, and problems. The resulting behavior of animals working under such constraints then informs economic theory of the accuracy of economic assumptions and can provide possible solutions to economic problems.

"Laboratory experimentation based on behavioral analysis is the most powerful method for defining, testing, and refining economic theory," argue Steven R. Hursh and Richard A. Bauman from the Walter Reed Army Institute of Research in Washington, D.C. For example, "the most basic concept is the equilibrium of supply and demand. Supply is experimentally controlled by a schedule of reinforcement. Demand is determined by the level of consumption observed across a range of prices. Response rate is determined by the equilibrium point at each price" (Hursch & Bauman, 1987, pp. 154–155).

In response to possible criticism that the nonhuman animal results are not applicable to human economic problems, John H. Kagel, Raymond C. Battalio, and Leonard Green argue that "our results put the burden of proof on those who support a particular position for which our data are incompatible. It is they who must show how our results are not applicable, or are irrelevant, to the human condition" (Kagel et al., 1995, p. 5). Using this approach useful data has been obtained on such economic topics as income-compensated price changes, economic demand theory, the representative consumer hypothesis, labor-supply theory, budget constraints, labor supply curves, alternative jobs with different wage rates, income-compensated wage changes, risk preference, expected utility, cycle-of-poverty, inelastic and elastic demands and substitution, and price consumption curves (e.g., Green & Kagel, 1987; Kagel et al., 1995).

"Animals provide a way of testing *elementary* microeconomic principles" state Kagel, Battalio, and Green in their book *Economic Choice Theory*. They continue:

For some questions . . . animal models are the only practical means to investigate an issue. They allow us to conduct precise, controlled, and demanding experiments using rewards and punishments of real consequence to test individual choice theory. . . . In applying animal models to the study of economic behavior, we are following the same approach used in biomedicine, where animal models are accepted with few reservations. . . . We use our model to address complicated social issues—such as the "cycle-of-poverty" and the "welfare trap" hypothesis, [that] deal with the effects that wide differences in income and extremely low levels of income have on individual behavior; an experimental treatment cannot adequately approximate these conditions with human volunteer subjects. With rats and pigeons, however, one can impose large differences in income for extended periods of time to address directly the effects on behavior." (Kagel et al., 1995, pp. 3–4).

Economics—back to "rat psychology"!

The basic analysis of economic behavior in reinforcement paradigms using a variety of subjects including rats, chimpanzees, and humans has been instrumental in increasing our understanding of the general principles of drug abuse behavior and has been used to inform drug policy (e.g., Hursh, 1991; 1993). The scientific understanding of the behavioral economics of drug abuse behavior and the implications for an effective humane drug abuse public policy is a product of the basic scientific approach. As exemplified by Hursh's work at Walter Reed, the scientific approach begins with controlled laboratory experiments using the behavior of animal subjects and builds to practical knowledge that can be applied to improve the human condition:

The concepts of behavioral economics have proven useful for understanding the environmental control of overall levels of responding for a variety of commodities, including reinforcement by drug self-administration (Hurshm 1991, p. 377). . . . An overall strategy . . . would draw on the findings from laboratory research and naturalistic econometric investigations to design model intervention projects. Evaluation and improvement of these projects would then serve as small-scale test-beds for more general public policy initiatives. . . . If future work confirms the utility of this behavioral economic agenda, then we have made the first step toward the development of a more humane society." (p. 392)

BEHAVIORAL PHARMACOLOGY

Like behavioral economics, the foundation of behavioral pharmacology and the effective treatment of substance abuse is also a product of basic research centered on reinforcement using animal models of substance abuse. Indeed, the ubiquitousness and explanatory power of the reinforcement process has been so well established and proven so useful in the field of behavioral pharmacology that it is taken as a given that Newfoundland researcher William A. McKim noted in what may be the most popular introductory textbook on behavioral pharmacology, *Drugs and Behavior*: "The principles of operant conditioning are thought to apply to nearly all behavior of all animals" (McKim, 2000, p. 36). That includes human behavior. Mckim adds that "most human behavior, although very complex, is ultimately controlled by reinforcements, just as the behavior of the animal in a Skinner box is ... by carefully studying the effects of a drug on operant [reinforced] behavior, we can provide valuable information that will help us understand the effects of the drug on the behavior of humans" (p. 38). That reinforcement is ultimately in control of both rat and human behavior is not presented as an argument or as a hypothesis but as a scientifically established given. If this reality were more widely accepted, then the suffering of both humans and animals could be greatly ameliorated.

Indeed, West Virginia University researchers C. W. Lejuez, David Schaal and Jennifer O'Donnell argue that "the moral implications of drug use and abuse have long since given way to the quest to understand it as a biopsychological phenomenon" (Lejuez et al., 1998, p. 116). The basis of drug use and abuse as a biopsychological phenomenon is the reinforcement process. Understanding the reinforcement process is vital to understanding drug abuse:

> rats and monkeys ... self-administer most of the drugs commonly administered by humans, including opiates, stimulants, barbiturates and other anxiolytic drugs, phencyclidine, and alcohol [and] physical dependence on the drug is not necessary for drugs to serve as reinforcers. ... First, self-administration of drugs by animals causes one to question the notion that human drug abuse reflects weak morals or a lack of will; the morality of a rat has little place in understanding a rat's drug self-administration. Second, the conceptual contribution of "reinforcement" to an understanding of drug abuse can hardly be overestimated. Drugs of abuse exploit behavioral processes that have evolved in animals for other reasons; therefore, understanding those behavioral processes *in general* aids in our understanding of drug abuse.

Third, starting with relatively simple drug-reinforcement procedures, researchers have studied many factors involved in drug
abuse, including behavioral, pharmacological, and physiological
factors. Such research has often suggested straightforward
approaches to treating drug abuse in humans. (Lejuez et al.,
1998, pp. 117–118)

In short "the conception and study of drugs as reinforcers has been the
most significant contribution of behavioral pharmacology for understanding and treating substance abuse" (Lejuez et al., p. 121). (Reinforcement in
drug use, abuse, and treatment is covered in chapter 11 in this book.)

THE REALITY OF RAT PSYCHOLOGY

What direct instruction, fluency, shaping, time-out, the Malcolm X College Precollege Institute, Morningside Academy, Earning by Learning,
Book It!, Sylvan Learning centers, token economies, behavioral economics, and behavioral pharmacology all have in common is that they all are
directly derived from general principles of operant behavior and reinforcement or are programs based on the general principles of operant
behavior and reinforcement. Almost all of these general principles have
been established by studying the operant behavior of rats and pigeons in
simplified experimental environments. *This is a strength not a weakness.*
Almost all of our medical and pharmaceutical advances have come from
studying animal models of illness and injury. Establishing general principles in simplified situations and cautiously applying the previous findings
to increasingly more complex situations is the inductive approach that has
advanced all areas of human understanding. The approach to understanding human behavior and behavioral dysfunction should be no different.
The success of this approach is begrudgingly admitted by Jeanne Ellis
Ormrod in her *Educational Psychology* textbook: "Students in my own educational psychology classes sometimes resent the fact that . . . their behavior is being compared to the behavior of rats and pigeons. But the fact is
that behaviorist theories developed from the study of nonhuman animals
often *do* explain human behavior" (Ormrod, 1998, p. 376, emphasis in
original).
    Animal experimentation and animal models of human behavioral
problems, such as depression (see chapter 13 in this book), are the most
successful models for studying the factors involved and have produced the
most effective treatments for behavioral problems. Indeed, our ignorance
of causes and cures of many behavioral problems stem in no small part

from our reluctance to use animal models of human problems. Instead of clinging to the scientifically untenable romantic belief that humans are such unique creatures that knowledge about their behavior can only be learned by studying their behavior, we could gain more practical knowledge of the problems humans face if we put more effort into searching for general principles of behavior in laboratory models using whatever animal model was most pragmatic. Then the scientifically established principle could be more confidently tested with humans. Medicine has long relied on animal models to understand the medical problems humans face. Millions of humans would be dead if it were not for the general principles uncovered and applied to humans from "rat medicine." Millions of humans with behavioral problems will not be effectively helped without application of "rat psychology." But these people could be helped if we relied more on "rat psychology" to understand the general principles of behavior.

A PARTIAL REJOINDER AND CAUTION ON RAT PSYCHOLOGY

While far more has been learned about behavior and about reinforcement from studying the behavior of rats than has been learned by studying the behavior of humans, it would be overly simplistic to assume that any systematic behavior-environment relation established in the animal laboratory would automatically work identically for human behavior outside the laboratory and to cavalierly attempt application to humans. Again, basic laboratory research attempts to isolate and uncover basic principles and relations in controlled environments. But humans (and most other animals) face a "stimulus collage" in life (Baldwin & Baldwin, 2001), a complex environment with a multitude of constantly changing stimuli that occasion, and are discriminative for, a multitude of behavior-consequence relations. For example, a teenage male may usually work diligently on his homework for contingent tokens but not if his girlfriend is present (a competing source of reinforcement); he may work if his tutor is also present (a discriminative stimulus for studying) but not work if his tutor is talking on the phone; he may work if his tutor is on the phone talking to his mother; and so on. The inductive approach requires that laboratory findings are systematically replicated in increasingly complex situations. Each validation of the finding increases the generalizability of the finding, often to human behavior in certain contexts. Therefore, whether or not a finding from the animal laboratory applies to human behavior is not a matter of a priori belief, but an empirical question to be answered by systematic investigation. In most cases the exploitation of basic behavior-reinforcement relations to human behavior has proven successful. To claim that because a principle was derived from experiments using rats, the principle is therefore automatically inapplicable to humans is untenable and unethical.

2

INSULTS AND MISCHIEVOUS MISREPRESENTATIONS

M&Ms for the Retarded

It is a myth of reinforcement that while reinforcers such as M&M candy, or tokens exchangeable for candy, other goods, or activities, can produce compliance in developmentally disabled individuals, such reinforcers are ineffective in changing the behavior of nondisabled humans; "reinforcement may work on retarded children but not me; I'm too smart for that." The first part of this myth is certainly true; reinforcers such as candy can produce compliance in developmentally disabled individuals if the reinforcers are contingent on compliant behavior. However, as we have already seen, tokens are effective reinforcers across the human species, and candy is often an effective reinforcer for many humans. When dessert is contingent upon eating vegetables and vegetable eating occurs, then dessert has reinforced vegetable eating. When a child receives money for returning empty soda bottles, and recycling increases, then recycling has been reinforced. When an author receives payment for writing an article and article writing increases, then writing articles has been reinforced. When an office worker puts coins into a machine, presses buttons, and a bag of M&M candy falls out, then the operant behavior of operating the candy machine has been reinforced with M&Ms. If cod-liver oil had come out instead of M&Ms, then it is unlikely that operating the machine would occur again.

While it is true that reinforcement has been used in institutions and in the classroom to shape children to "be still, be quiet, be docile" (Winett & Winkler, 1972), it is a misconception that reinforcement is used *only* to make classrooms more manageable and behavior more compliant. Vocational skills for the developmentally disabled are routinely taught using reinforcement programs. If reinforcement is contingent upon vocational behaviors then vocational skills are selected. Behavior modification programs centered on contingent reinforcement are simply the most effective treatment for developing life skills of the developmentally disabled.

A lack of understanding of the inductive scientific approach may be responsible for the myth that simple reinforcers work only for simple behaviors of individuals with relatively simple (limited) behavior repertoires. With the inductive approach, general principles are first isolated and established in simple laboratory situations. For example, the principle of "differential reinforcement" is used to teach a rat to lever press when a light is on, but not when it is off: Lever presses when the light is on produce reinforcement. Lever presses when the light is off go unreinforced. Because lever pressing is "differentially reinforced" only in the presence of the light, eventually lever presses occur only when the light is on. As the basic finding is replicated in other controlled, slightly more complex environments, the generalizability of the principle is established and applications often become apparent.

For example, in a classic example of generalization of differential reinforcement, William Redd and Jay S. Birnbrauer (1969) used differential reinforcement to produce "stimulus control" of cooperative behavior of developmentally disabled children. One adult provided praise, ice cream, and soda to the children only when they were playing cooperatively. Another adult provided just as much praise, ice cream, and soda to the children regardless of whether they were being cooperative or not. Because the first adult made praise, ice cream, and soda contingent upon cooperative behavior, or differentially reinforced cooperative behavior, the children greatly increased the amount they were cooperative for the first adult, but remained uncooperative for the second adult.

Once a principle like differential reinforcement is established, it is applied to increasingly complex situations such as teaching a normally developing child to spell or to do mathematics (see Alberto & Troutman, 1999, pp. 334–338). Each successful replication further establishes the principle's generalizablity. Finally, the principle's operation in a vast range of situations becomes apparent (in this example the principle of differential reinforcement). For example, if an adult makes time for his elderly parent only when the parent is sick or complaining about aches, pains, and disability, then the adult has differentially reinforced the operant of "sick behaviors" relative to "well behaviors." The rate at which the parent complains will increase. (This example is in fact a very frequent occurrence; see chapter 13 in this book.) Likewise, within the operant of "computer software programming," incorrect placement of parentheses is differentially punished with a crashing program or a programming "flag"; however, the correct placement of parentheses is differentially reinforced by the correct execution of the software program. Through the process of differential reinforcement the behavior of correct placement of parentheses will be selected. Basic processes, such as differential reinforcement, may be initially observed in the animal laboratory, and early applications may be relatively simple, but this does not mean that they apply only in the animal laboratory or in simple situations. Reinforcement selects the behavior of not only the developmentally disabled, but the behavior of the "most able" as well.

WORKING MEN IN MINES

From developmentally disabled children in the classroom to working professionals in open-pit mines, whenever reinforcement programs are correctly applied they are likely to produce beneficial results for all parties involved. For example, when "a token economy that used trading stamps as tokens was instituted at two dangerous open-pit mines . . . [there were] large reductions [thousands per year] in the number of days lost from work because of injuries, the number of lost-time injuries, and the cost of accidents and injuries" (Fox et al., 1987, p. 215). That is, a program that reinforced safety with artificial, contrived, trading stamp reinforcers in extremely dangerous open-pit coal mines saved the company millions of dollars and benefited the health, safety, work-environment, and home-environment (with backup reinforcers that the employees exchanged their tokens for) of "foremen, shift supervisors, laboratory technicians, field engineers, surveyors, . . . mechanics, laborers, maintenance workers, . . . bulldozer, front-end loader, shovel, dragline, and truck operators . . . electricians, scraper operators, and fuel and lube workers" (p. 217) "The number of days lost from work due to injuries during the last ten years of the token programs was about one-fourth the national mining average at the Shirley Basin Mine and about one-twelfth the national mining average at the Navajo Mine. . . . In addition to suffering fewer injuries, disabilities and deaths, the workers earned the benefits of the backup prizes that they received in exchange for their trading stamps" (p. 221). The hard-working men who toil in open-pit mines are hardly developmentally disabled. But token reinforcement programs work well for them, proving to be injury-reducing and lifesaving additions.

In addition to increased worker productivity and safety, reinforcement programs produce emotional benefits as well. "The token economies added to the general morale of workers at both [open-pit mine] locations" (Fox et al., 1987, p. 222). In fact, contingent pay or "pay for performance," that is, contingent reinforcement is the strongest determinant of job satisfaction, and a determinant of job commitment and self-efficacy (Locke & Latham, 1990). This is hardly M&Ms for the retarded.

Just as failure to recognize the effects that exercising has on the cardiovascular health of an individual does not mean that the effects of exercising are not operating, failure to recognize reinforcement processes operating on an individual's behavior does not mean that reinforcement processes are not operating on behavior. Ignorance of scientifically established general principles does not mean that principles do not exist or are not operating. Reinforcement "works" for everybody, whether the human has developmental disabilities or is an engineer. "Human behavior, although very complex, is ultimately controlled by reinforcements" (McKim, 2000, p. 38).

3

CARROT-AND-STICK CONTROL, BRIBERY, AND VALUE

While ignorance about a general principle does not mean that principle does not exist, ignorance does lead to inaccurate criticisms. For example, establishing and increasing the rate of behavior with reinforcement has been criticized as a "carrot-and-stick" approach to behavior management and child care. Indeed, Alfie A. Kohn titled a chapter "The Trouble with Carrots," in his book *Pubished by Rewards* and disparagingly refers to reinforcement as a carrot-and-stick approach no less than ten times. "The carrot-and-stick approach in general is unsuccessful" (Kohn, 1993, p. 201). Relating to the criticism that reinforcement is "rat psychology," under a section titled "Treating People like Pets," Kohn remarks: "Before these words came to be used as generic representations of bribes and threats, what actually stood between the carrot and the stick was, of course, a jackass" (p. 24). The implication is that rewards (i.e., reinforcers) are bribes, and that purposefully using reinforcement with humans makes them something other than human (in Kohn's example, jackasses).

"The unconscious assumption behind the reward-punishment model is that one is dealing with jackasses, that people are jackasses to be manipulated and controlled." The relationship is "inevitably one of condescending contempt whose most blatant mask is paternalism" (Levinson, 1973, pp. 10–11). This absurd polemic assumes that my parents, millions of other parents, and the hundreds of thousands of teachers who participate in Book It! (just to name a small subset of people) or other reinforcement programs, have "condescending contempt" for their children and all "assume" that their children are jackasses!

The carrot-and-stick criticism generally reflects an ignorance of the reinforcement process and is a thinly disguised insult to professionals who use or advocate the use of reinforcement to ameliorate human problems. An image of a carrot-and-stick falsely implies that those who use reinforcement in a programmatic purposeful fashion are simple and largely ignorant of more sophisticated and more effective methods to enrich children. Yet, the editorial boards of journals that focus on the practical application of reinforcement such as the *Journal of Applied Behavior Analysis,* and *Behavior Modification,* are filled with professionals from many of the world's top research and academic institutions such as Vanderbilt, Johns Hopkins, the University of Pennsylvania School of Medicine, the Universidade Federal de Sao Carlos, the University of Oslo, the University of Wales, and the University of North Carolina (to name a few). It is highly unlikely that these people are simple and ignorant in their chosen profession (the study and application of reinforcement).

But the question remains, Is the purposeful use of reinforcement analogous to the carrot-and-stick approach? The *American Heritage Dictionary of the English Language* defines "carrot-and-stick" as "combining a *promised* reward with a *threatened* penalty" (*American Heritage,* 1992, p. 294). A promised but not received reward and the threat of penalty is a gross misrepresentation of the reinforcement process. At least in fables, a mule may be tricked into plowing a field by tying a carrot to a stick tied to the mule's head, in front of the mule's face. The mule walks toward, but never gets to the dangling carrot. The carrot is snatched from the mule just before he can eat it.

The carrot-and-stick approach dangles a prize just out of reach to trick someone to work, but the prize is never obtained; the carrot is snatched away at the last moment. But *with reinforcement,* if the behavior that reinforcement is contingent upon occurs, *the reinforcer is obtained.* You get to have your cake or carrot and eat it too! It is this *frequent, repeated, behavior-reinforcer relation* that selects operant behavior. There is no repeated behavior-consequence relation in the false carrot-and-stick analogy. Like the fable *boy who called wolf,* if individuals are repeatedly offered rewards for work, but the rewards never occur, and instead are snatched away just before they are obtained, then the people would quit working. That is, the work behavior would undergo extinction as would instruction following behaviors in general when rewards were offered in the instructions. The carrot analogy is simply dishonest and does not represent the reinforcement process.

The "threat of penalty" or "stick" side of the carrot-and-stick approach to motivation is an approach based on *negative* reinforcement. Negative reinforcement is a process in which the rate of behavior increases (reinforcement) because the behavior removes (negative), escapes, or avoids an aversive consequence (see appendix 2 in this book). In farming, instead of a carrot, a plow mule may be hit with a stick, whipped, or shocked in the buttocks. The mule moves forward to escape or avoid the aversive stimulus being applied to its rear and thus plows the field. In this manner plowing is selected as a function of negative reinforcement. Likewise, a horse is made to move forward by the digging of a rider's heels (which may have spurs to increase the aversiveness) into the side of the horse. When the horse reaches the speed desired by the rider, the aversive stimulus being applied to its sides is terminated. Therefore, as a function of negative reinforcement a horse moves forward to escape and maintains its forward movement to avoid being heeled in the sides. (Incidentally, in recent years the field of animal training and the zoo industry has been revolutionized by embracing a positive reinforcement approach and eliminating or reducing aversive control techniques previously relied upon.)

However, with humans the use of programmatic application of reinforcement has virtually *always* used positive reinforcement, not negative reinforcement or other aversive control techniques. None of the reinforcement programs covered so far (e.g., Book It! Earning by Learning, and Morningside) use negative reinforcement, or aversive consequences of any sort. Quite simply, there is no threat, there is no "stick." The reality of the carrot-and-stick analogy to the systematic use of positive reinforcement is that (1) *the stick half simply does not occur* and (2) a "carrot" occurs each time the behavior occurs. Therefore, a more accurate analogy of positive reinforcement than "carrot-and-stick" is "carrots, carrots, and more carrots, and while you are at it, throw in some candy, hugs, and kisses!"

BRIBERY

As exemplified by the *Woman's Day* article, "The Bribery Curriculum: Since When Did Corrupting Our Kids Become Part of Their Education?" (Hechtman, 2000), a particularly widespread myth of reinforcement programs is that they amount to nothing more than bribery. ("I shouldn't have to bribe Johnny to do his homework. He should do it on his own.") Alfie Kohn describes reinforcement as bribery no less than a dozen times and titled a chapter "Bribes for Behaving: Why Behaviorism Doesn't Help Children Become Good People." As a universal criticism of reinforcement, the myth that reinforcement is nothing more than bribery is untenable. However, depending on the bribe's relationship to unethical, corrupt, and/or illegal behavior, it is admitted that *bribes can function as reinforcers*. (But this does not mean the inverse, namely that reinforcers always function as bribes, is true.)

Just because bribes can reinforce corrupt behavior, it is absurd to claim that all contrived reinforcement situations *necessarily* involve bribery. Is an author bribed when being paid for an article increases the rate of article writing? Is it bribery if the receipt of productivity contingent bonuses by factory workers increases the rate of work productivity? Are Sylvan Learning Centers bribing children to study when they give children tokens contingent on studying? Is it bribery when professional athletes meet the performance standards in the incentive clauses of their contracts and are consequently paid more? Is it bribery when a child receives a certificate for a free pizza when the child meets her reading goal? Kohn thinks so: Pizza Hut started a program "to encourage children to read more. The strategy for reaching this goal: bribery" (Kohn, 1993, p. 11). Yet, while a bribe is typically a one-time occurrence, a child in Book It! may receive many reinforcers for reading. Book It!, Sylvan Learning Centers, and reinforcement programs generally provide *repeated, immediate positive reinforcement for individual* accomplishment, *reinforcing effort, and improvement.* This is hardly bribery. Furthermore, bribes typically involve threats and other aversive elements that are not part of systematic reinforcement programs.

Definitions of the word *bribe* usually include the word *corrupt* (as in "to corrupt judgment or behavior"). The *American Heritage Dictionary* defines "corrupt" as "1. Marked by immorality and perversion; depraved. 2. Venal; dishonest" (*American Heritage,* 1992, p. 423). It is hard to see how giving a child tokens or pizza for meeting reading goals is immoral or depraved. Of course, most children learn to read without pizzas, tokens, or money having to be contingent on reading. It does not follow, however, that making tokens, money, or other reinforcers contingent on reading is corrupt or somehow bribery. "First," argue Patrick J. Schloss, of Bloomsburg University, and Maureen A. Smith, of the State University of New York College at Buffalo,

> by definition, bribery involves paying someone in advance to do something wrong or illegal. Edibles and tokens are used after a desired behavior has been demonstrated to increase the likelihood that it will occur again. They are comparable to the paychecks we receive from our employers for doing our jobs. As [Marcia] Smith (1993) noted, "all employees work for pay ... but most would resent the implication that they are working for a bribe" (Schloss & Smith, 1998, p. 279).

"Second, . . ." Schloss and Smith continue, "teachers can use edibles and tokens to enhance learning . . . these techniques will be faded over time and replaced with events that occur naturally in the classroom. For example, edibles will be presented simultaneously with a smile. Eventually, the smile will be sufficient for a job well done" (p.11).

If a behavior occurs, it must occur for *some* reason. If reading and learning to read occur without obvious contrived reinforcers, such as pizza or money, learning to read still *must* have been reinforced, and reading *must* still be reinforced in some manner or else it wouldn't occur. For many children, perhaps for most children, the reinforcers for learning to read (among other skills) and for reading are usually copious, spontaneous, frequent, and natural. *The ultimate reinforcement for learning to read is being able to read!*— a great source of pleasure for many people and a very useful skill to have for getting along in the world (e.g., once someone can read, many other reinforcers become available).

In middle-class families it is likely that parents will read to their children; serve as models for reading; have many reading materials available; prompt (encourage) attempts at reading; and provide attention, praise, affection, and other reinforcers for reading. Once some reading behaviors are acquired they will begin to produce more typical and natural reinforcers for reading. For example, once a child who has been encouraged to, and reinforced for, reading billboards ("Do you know what that sign says, Honey? That's great, Dear"), begins to produce some accurate reading, then reading billboards will produce consequences that otherwise may not have occurred. Reading out loud "Dairy Queen 5 Miles" is more likely to be reinforced with an ice cream treat than the cry of "I'm bored! I wanna stop!" As a function of the consequences that reading billboards produce, the child's rate of billboard reading will increase. Has the child been bribed to read billboards?

Beginning in infancy, middle-class children are likely to have books with thick, firm pages that are easy to turn. Turning pages is likely to be reinforced with bright pictures, possibly "pop-ups," and socially by the parents: "Look at Sally! What are you reading Honey?" Eventually these books will contain letters and simple words that the child will be encouraged to say and sound out. Successive approximations of reading will be reinforced by the parents (even if they are not "aware" that they are using reinforcement). Once reading begins to occur, reading will increasingly be reinforced by the natural consequences that reading provides.

Once reading has been shaped, a middle-class parent may remark, "We never taught Johnny to read. He just picked it up naturally." However, this is a case of missing the trees for the forest. Reading is no more a "natural" behavior than doing calculus or shooting three-point baskets is natural behavior (although all of those behaviors seem natural when they become fluent).

ALL children learn to read through dynamic behavior-environment interactions. The physical and social environments of the typical middle-class home and school contain reading material, prompts for reading, and consequences for reading. In these homes and school environments, reading materials and prompts set the occasion for reading and the consequences of reading select reading behavior. In many of these cases, the parent may *not* have overtly taught the child to read. However, the child still *learned* to read by the differential reinforcement of successive approximations to reading behaviors. The parent may not have purposefully provided differential reinforcement for reading behavior. But the parent or teacher did provide an *environment* that differentially reinforced this behavior.

Although I came from a middle-class family and my father is an English professor, for some reason, the natural prompts and consequences for prereading behaviors and reading were not sufficient for me to learn how to read. Reading did not come "naturally." Therefore, my father and various tutors used contrived reinforcers (Ping-Pong, comic books, and money) for reading to reinforce reading. Now I read for many reasons, including pleasure. I hardly feel that I was "bribed" to read as a child. I was provided with special programs and consequences for reading because I needed special help. Unfortunately, many who need special help do not get it, and calling reinforcement "bribery" makes effective help less likely.

CONTRIVED AND NATURAL REINFORCEMENT

Systematic reinforcement of a desired behavior may appear to be a "payoff" for what the person "should have been doing anyway." In "The Bribery Curriculum" article, *Woman's Day* asks, "What happened to teaching kids to do something just for the sake of doing a good job?" (Hechtman, 2000). Kids learn they have done a "good job" only when the job is reinforced! The reinforcement may just be praise and affection, but if a job is not reinforced in some way, how can it be considered "good?" When a job goes unreinforced, unnoticed, or worse, punished, then obviously the job could not have been a good job in any sense of the word *good.* In fact the very phrase "good job!" itself becomes a conditioned reinforcer when repeatedly paired with other reinforcers such as hugs, kisses, and yes, even candy or pizza. Once the phrase "good job!" has become strongly associated with other reinforcers the phrase itself will function as a reinforcer and the candy and pizza may be faded. (Just as "good job!" becomes a conditioned reinforcer when parents and teachers associate the phrase with other reinforcers, "you're a *bad man!*" becomes a conditioned reinforcer for many children and teenagers when the phrase is said by a peer. *Bad* comes to mean *good*, because the word is associated with many social reinforcers such as companionship and sharing. The *functional* meaning of words is determined by their association with reinforcement.)

Still, a critic may ask, "Why should Johnny get payoffs and bribes for doing his chores and homework? People should do the proper thing just because it is the proper thing. " But what is "proper?" One functional definition is that *proper behavior is reinforced behavior.* Indeed, the only way that animals and humans with no verbal behaviors (expressive or receptive) such as severely retarded individuals, know what is proper is by which behaviors are reinforced, or not punished. The only way that these organisms know what is improper behavior is by punishment or lack of reinforcement. That is, proper behavior is differentially reinforced and improper behavior is not reinforced or differentially punished. Therefore for most middle-class children "proper behavior" is selected. For example, a middle-class child may be told, "I'll read you your bedtime story (reinforcer) *after* (contingency) you put on your jammies, wash your hands and face, and brush your teeth (*proper* behavior)." A middle-class teenager may hear, "you can call your boyfriend (reinforcer) *after* (contingency) you do your homework and practice your flute (*proper* behavior)." Is this bribery and payoffs? Proper behavior is reinforced behavior.

Unfortunately, not all humans are so lucky as to come from the stereotypical middle-class family. If doing what is normally considered "proper" is not reinforced then it is unrealistic to expect proper behavior to occur. A child in a lower-class home may hear, "Turn off that damn water and get your butt in bed before I have to come up there." Instead of reinforcing proper behavior, such a parental statement decreases the likelihood of doing bedtime chores. A teenager from a dysfunctional, broken home may be told, "Get this school mess off my table. Shut up that racket before I bust that flute on your head. Why don't you just go over to see that good-for-nothing Johnny and stop tying up my phone unless you want to pay the bill." Instead of reinforcing proper behavior—doing homework and practicing—with such parental statements, homework and music practice are less likely and sexual promiscuity has been prompted. (As covered in chapter 12 in this book, behavioral parent training that teaches parents to replace coercive parenting tactics with child-rearing practices based on positive reinforcement helps reduce delinquency and improve academic performance.)

When people are in, or come from living environments where behaviors that society considers "proper" were never reinforced, or even punished, then "proper" behaviors simply will not have been selected by the environment for those individuals. In such cases, the educational system, correctional system (here the word *correctional* may actually have meaning), or other social agency may purposively set up a contrived reinforcement system, usually using a token economy, which will reinforce "proper" behavior. Once these socially desired behaviors have been sufficiently reinforced they will be selected (at least in the environment where they are reinforced). Once these behaviors have been selected, as they are in the stereotypical middle-class family, proper behavior will be reinforced behavior.

"Still" the critic may insist, "it's just not the natural way humans learn, giving them treats, tokens, or check marks for what they should be doing anyway. Won't children expect a reward for everything they do?" Sure, they will, and they always have. Reinforcement *is why* people do what they do. If a behavior is occurring, it's occurring for some reason. The reinforcer responsible for the behavior may just not have been identified. Unfortunately, in some cases the natural or usually occurring reinforcers have not selected, may not be present, or do not maintain socially desired behaviors (e.g., cooperation, or personal hygiene behaviors). In these cases, it may be desirable or necessary to set up *contrived reinforcers* to shape and maintain these behaviors. It is when contrived reinforcement contingencies are being used that reinforcers are most likely to appear to be bribes, unnatural, or unethical. But if the behavior is not corrupt or illegal there is nothing unethical about using contrived reinforcement. In fact, in many cases, doing nothing (i.e., neglect) is unethical, and implementing a contrived reinforcement program necessary for life skills is the most ethical action possible.

Ideally, once a contrived reinforcement contingency has established a behavior, the behavior will be "trapped" by the natural contingencies. For example, reflecting on the deplorable conditions that so many of her clients lived in, a friend employed by a local county's children's services asked, "What's so hard about the concept of some water and a bar of soap?" For possibly many reasons (e.g., lack of resources, and caregivers who never taught hygiene), the contingencies of reinforcement for keeping clean were not having a functional effect on her clients' behaviors. If contrived reinforcement, such as vouchers for food and hygiene products, were offered for personal hygiene, then it is likely that personal hygiene would increase. Once hygiene is occurring, hygiene may be trapped by the natural reinforcers that hygienic behaviors produce such as decreased disease susceptibility, itching, infection, an increased probability of job offers, and an increased rate of affectionate and affirmative interpersonal interactions. In fact, contrived reinforcement, tokens, or what some would misleadingly call "bribery," for behaviors from taking a bath to doing the dishes to doing homework is standard practice in many church-run orphanages, group homes for predelinquent youths, and institutions across the United States (see Sarafino, 2001, pp. 341–346). Additionally, contrived reinforcement or tokens are regularly employed in classrooms and work sites to develop and maintain situationally desirable behavior.

CONTRIVED REINFORCEMENT: TOKEN ECONOMIES AND THE *TEACHING-FAMILY MODEL*

Contrived reinforcement, tokens, is the fundamental ingredient for the teaching-family model for delinquent and "predelinquent" juveniles. The teaching-family model is used in over two hundred programs, including Boy's Town and Methodist group homes. In the teaching-family model, juveniles earn tokens for behaviors that an uninformed critic might say "should be expected anyway—without bribes or threats" (reading, home-work, personal hygiene, turning out lights, etc.). Tokens are lost for antisocial or socially inappropriate behaviors such as fighting, lying, or using bad grammar. Tokens are exchanged for backup reinforcers such as snacks, TV time, allowance, or critically, "what they should have anyway." As appropriate behavior is trapped by the natural reinforcers for appropriate behavior (better grades, increased positive social interaction, etc.) the contrived reinforcement is faded out. Juveniles go from a daily point system to a weekly point system to a merit system where tokens (points) are not used. When good behavior remains consistent, the juveniles are returned home. While in the teaching-family environment, juveniles' grades and school attendance go up, criminal offenses, police, and court interactions go down (Kirigin et al., 1982; Wolf et al., 1987).

Are the Catholic Church, which runs Boy's Town, the Methodist Church, and numerous other charitable, religious organizations all corrupt, unethical, immoral—*evil*—because they "use carrots" and "bribe" juveniles to behave with contrived reinforcement? Critics of the practical use of reinforcement would lead one to believe so. Although the back cover of Kohn's book proclaims, "the more we use artificial inducements to motivate people, the more they lose interest in what we're bribing them to do" (Kohn, 1993) a reasoned, objective conclusion is that those who use contrived reinforcement are following the wise advice of Montaigne. "Where their profit is, let their pleasure be also. One should sweeten the food that is healthy for a child, and dip what is harmful in gall" (Montaigne, 1580/1958; reprinted 1992, p. 176). One should reinforce children's healthy and productive behaviors.

Critics of token economies *selectively* point to data indicating that for some individuals behavioral gains made while in the token economy may be lost after a period of time when they are no longer in the program (e.g., Kohn, 1993). But the larger picture is ignored along with other evaluations and research summaries of token economies (e.g., Kazdin, 1985) that find token economies to be effective with diverse populations and to produce gains that are maintained for years after the token economy. Yet, even if a juvenile returns to antisocial and criminal activities after leaving a teaching-family program, it does *not* mean the program is ineffective or much less *evil*. The juvenile's return to antisocial behaviors means socially appropriate behaviors were not trapped by naturally occurring reinforcers for the behaviors or that the juvenile's home environment provides more reinforcement for criminal and antisocial behaviors than it does for socially appropriate behaviors.

But in fact, following treatment that includes participation in a token economy, many juveniles do not return to antisocial behaviors. For example, Trent Hicks and Richard Munger of the South Carolina Department of Youth Services adapted the teaching-family model including a structured token economy to a school day treatment program and found that there were significant improvements in school grades, parent-reported behavior, and "consistent decreases in contacts with the juvenile court, self-reported criminal offenses, and residential placements" (Hicks & Munger, 1990, p. 63). Reinforcement is a natural process, by which the *environment selects (reinforces)* behavior. The extent that we can arrange the environment, including the use of contrived reinforcement, to select adaptive, socially appropriate behaviors, is the extent that we can improve the human condition and ameliorate human suffering.

THE MYTH THAT "REINFORCEMENT DEVALUES THE REINFORCED BEHAVIOR"

Although reinforcement is often used to select adaptive, socially appropriate behaviors, critics of applied contrived reinforcement—of "rewards"—claim that the use of reinforcement conveys the message that the reinforced behavior is not worth doing and its only value is in the reinforcer it produces. "'Do this and you'll get that' automatically devalues the 'this': that is," argues Kohn, "the task comes to be perceived as a tedious prerequisite for getting a goody" (Kohn, 1993, p. 140). In a *Better Homes and Gardens* article on rewards that is illustrated with a cartoon of parents dangling carrots in front of a child (thus, promoting the carrot-and-stick myth), Kohn tells the reader what *he thinks* the child is thinking. "When you say, 'Do X and I'll give you a gold star or an ice cream,' a child's immediate response is, 'Gee, X must be something I wouldn't want to do, otherwise they wouldn't be offering me a bribe.'" Kohn continues, "The more rewards you offer for something, the more a child's commitment to doing it for any other reason evaporates" (Holman, 1997, p. 114).

In reality, rather than devaluing the reinforced behavior, reinforcement *adds value* to the reinforced behavior. When a child is told, "Do X and I'll give you a gold star or ice cream," it is more likely that a child's immediate response will be, 'Gee, doing X must be something really important; otherwise they wouldn't be reinforcing me for it. I'll be sure to try my hardest." When a parent offers a child a reward for a behavior, it conveys to the child that the task is valuable and important to the parent and should be for the child as well. When a reinforcer occurs, it is associated with the behavior that produced the reinforcer. Behaviors that are reinforced take on "secondary reward value" as a result of the behavior's association with reinforcement (Eisenberger, 1992). Through this conditioning process, to the extent that reinforcers are valuable, whatever behavior, or dimension of behavior (e.g., high effort), which is reinforced becomes "valuable behavior."

Conditioning reinforcement value to behavior forms the basis of Robert Eisenberger's theory in *Learned Industriousness*. "Extensive research with animals and humans indicates that rewarded effort contributes to durable individual differences in industriousness," argues Eisenberger. "Reinforcement for increased physical or cognitive performance . . . conditions reward value to the sensation of high effort. . . . The conditioning of secondary reward value to the sensation of effort provides a dynamic mechanism by which reinforced high performance generalizes across behaviors" (Eisenberger, 1992, p. 248). Reinforcement of high effort produces industriousness because reinforcement of effort *adds value* to effortful, industrious behaviors. It does not devalue effort.

Because the reinforcement of effort adds value to effortful behaviors, in addition to increasing behavioral persistence, the reinforcement of high effort in humans produces increased self-control, moral development, and academic performance specifically as well as industriousness generally. "Differentially reinforced effort in a given dimension should result in greater performance in that same dimension . . . [and] increasing the variety of tasks in which high performance was reinforced would . . . increase the generalization of high performance across tasks" (Eisenberger, 1992, p. 250).

For example, moral behavior may be directly selected by the reinforcement process. If immoral behavior such as stealing or cheating is punished and moral behavior such as honest work and telling the truth is reinforced, then moral behavior will be differentially selected. Moral behavior becomes a "valuable" behavioral pattern because, relative to immoral behavior, moral behavior differentially produces reinforcement. The greater the variety of reinforced moral behaviors (sharing, honesty, helping, etc.), and the more situations (home, school, playground, etc.) that moral behaviors are reinforced in, the more strongly and more generally moral behaviors will be selected.

But because moral behaviors are often more effortful than immoral behaviors and immoral behavior produces immediate reinforcement with little effort, immoral behavior is tempting (studying for an exam is more effortful than looking at another student's exam, researching and writing a term paper is more effortful than downloading a term paper off the Internet, and making commission sales is more effortful than stealing from the cash register). Fortunately, the prior reinforcement of high effort makes immoral behavior less likely. For example, college students who were reinforced for completing difficult mathematical and perceptual problems (reinforcement of effort), cheated less on a subsequent anagram task than other students (Eisenberger & Masterson, 1983). "These results, replicated in a second study with a different cheating procedure (Eisenberger & Shank, 1985), suggest that an individual's honesty is affected not only by prior direct reinforcement of honesty, but also by the conditioned secondary reward value of effort" (Eisenberger, 1992, p. 257). The message is clear. If a parent, teacher, or employer wants to teach a child, student, or employee that a behavior is valuable then that behavior should be richly reinforced. Additionally, because honest behavior is often effortful relative to dishonest behavior, when honest work is desired, then in addition to reinforcing honesty directly, effort should also be reinforced. Reinforcement adds value to behavior.

4

THE MYTH THAT "EXTRINSIC REWARDS UNDERMINE INTRINSIC INTEREST"

In addition to making behavior that produces reinforcement "valuable behavior," conditioned, contrived reinforcement programs can and do have many powerful and beneficial effects; however, the use of conditioned reinforcement and contrived reinforcement contingencies to shape and maintain behavior has led to the most damaging and widespread myth regarding reinforcement: The myth that rewarding behavior undermines, or eliminates, any "intrinsic interest" in the behavior (interest in the activity "for its own sake"). The myth, (see the introduction in this book), holds that if I am given contrived reinforcers of any type (money, a game of Ping-Pong with Dad, or even simply praise) for reading, then I will no longer want to read for the sake of reading. I will view reading as only a means to an end, and reading will no longer be a reinforcing activity in and of itself.

This myth is most damaging to the effective use of planned reinforcement procedures because it argues that reinforcement will ultimately produce the opposite effect of its intended one. The myth holds that if I want Susan to read more, praising, hugging, or giving her a treat for reading may make her read then and there. But ultimately the reinforcement will make Susan read as little as possible, and she will have an expressed dislike of reading. Hugging her for reading will "undermine her intrinsic motivation" for reading. Likewise, according to the myth, if I pay Sam for bringing home good grades, he will learn to dislike school and will possibly drop out as soon as possible. Every believer in the myth that reward undermines interest is lost to any opportunity to help people through positive reinforcement. Tragically, this myth is part of the dogma of the United States' educational establishment. "The expectation of reward can

39

actually undermine intrinsic motivation and creativity," argues a primer by the National Education Association (NEA) under a heading titled "How to Kill Creativity." "A wide variety of rewards have now been tested" continues the primer, "and everything from good-player awards to marshmallows produces the expected decrements in intrinsic motivation" (Tegano et al., 1991, p. 119).

Although hundreds of studies have shown the powerful, beneficial, and lasting effects of reinforcement across a vast range of human situations and behaviors, the NEA and others came to believe the myth that reinforcement undermines intrinsic interest based on a few studies in the 1970s that claimed to demonstrate "detrimental effects of reward" (See Cameron et al., 2001, for the most recent objective review of these studies). Typically in these studies, children or college students were given a simple puzzle or other easy task to do; then they were given a sticker, praise, or trinket after doing the task; later the task was made available to them again. *Some* results have shown that *some* subjects engaged in the task less at the end than they did during their initial exposure, and *some* subjects report that they like the task less. Inferences from these results have snowballed from claiming that in some situations rewards may have "detrimental" effects on task enjoyment to claiming that rewards "turn play into work" to Alfie A. Kohn's (1993) polemic book *Punished by Rewards* that argues that all rewards (by which he means reinforcers) in all situations are inherently evil, ineffective, detrimental and should be avoided at almost all costs.

What is the truth? Are reinforcement programs the most effective tool for behavior analysts, educators, and psychologists, or are rewards really "punishers" as Kohn argues? (By definition *reinforcers* can't be punishers and punishers can't reinforce. But "rewards" that have nontechnical meaning, can be reinforcers or punishers.) Should rewards be used or avoided? In an attempt to answer these questions, several "meta-analyses" have been conducted on the effects of rewards on intrinsic interest. (Meta-analyses are statistical analyses of the statistical analyses of many studies pooled together.)

Not surprisingly, when opponents of the use of rewards have conducted the meta-analysis they have found that rewards have detrimental effects (e.g., Deci et al., 1999). But when proponents of the use of rewards have conducted the meta-analysis, they have found beneficial effects of rewards (e.g., Cameron et al., 2001; Cameron & Pierce, 1994; Eisenberger et al., 1999). (Meta-analyses of the same subject by different investigators may produce different results because the studies, manipulations, control conditions, and other characteristics of the previous studies on which the meta-analyses are based may be labeled, defined, and categorized differently by the different meta-analytic investigators. This is one of several reasons why validity of the entire enterprise of meta-analysis has been challenged.)

The most objective of these meta-analyses may be that of Judy Cameron and David Pierce (1994) published in the *Review of Educational Research*. At the time the analysis was conducted, Cameron was a doctoral student in education at the University of Alberta. The purpose of the analysis was not to support or promote a theory on which book sales and professional reputations were based, but to weigh the evidence for or against the use of reward programs in educational settings. (Cameron had promoted no theory that she needed to support.) The conclusion from her analysis of over twenty years of research was that "rewards can be used to maintain or enhance students' intrinsic interest in schoolwork. . . . When tangible rewards are offered contingent on level or performance . . . students remain motivated in the subject area" (Cameron & Pierce, 1996, p. 40). Because the data have shown that rewards are beneficial, Cameron has subsequently written from a theoretical orientation that supports reinforcement programs (e.g., Eisenberger & Cameron, 1996).

Due to the conflicting results of previous meta-analysis, Cameron, Banko, and Pierce (2001) conducted yet another meta-analysis that included *all* relevant studies. Cameron and Pierce's (1994) analysis included 96 studies. Deci and his colleagues' (1999) analysis included 128 experiments. Cameron and her colleagues' (2001) meta-analysis included a total of 145 experiments. The results of this most recent and comprehensive meta-analysis are essentially the same as Cameron and Pierce's initial meta-analysis:

> Our analysis shows that rewards can be used effectively to enhance interest without disrupting performance of an activity. . . . Rewards can be arranged to shape performance progressively (Schunk, 1983, 1984), to establish interest in activities that lack initial interest (Bandura, 1986), and to maintain or enhance effort and persistence at a task (Eisenberger, 1992). (Cameron et al., 2001, p. 27)

The findings that do support the view that rewards may have detrimental effects generally come from highly contrived, very artificial laboratory situations. In such studies, among other limitations, the task and reward are likely to be trivial or meaningless (paradoxically, the researchers manage to call the tasks "intrinsically interesting" anyway), the reward given only once, or never given but only promised, and the task engaged in for only a very brief period of time (see Eisenberger & Cameron, 1996; or Flora, 1990 for an in-depth discussion). To put it frankly, "fake" reward procedures are needed to produce a so-called undermining effect of reward. This is admitted by some promoters of the myth. Mark R. Lepper of Stanford University and his co-workers conceded that "many important experiments employed exotic procedures or deceptive methods without counterparts in real life outside the laboratory . . . unrealistic procedures . . . are widespread in this literature" (Lepper et al., 1999, p. 671). The unrealistic procedures researchers must use to "undermine intrinsic interest with reward" make any generalizations of these studies to practical applied reinforcement programs invalid. Indeed, in describing one such study, Lepper and his co-workers noted that it was "totally unrepresentative of the normal uses of rewards in everyday life to which researchers would like to generalize the results of this literature" (p. 671).

Compare this to actual reinforcement programs or studies. The behavior of interest is usually very important for the individuals in the study, typically involving life-skills, academic accomplishment (e.g., Hicks & Munger, 1990), or occupational productivity such as safety performance in open-pit coal mining (Fox et al., 1987). The "rewards" have been demonstrated to *reinforce* behavior (i.e., to increase the rate of behavior on which they are contingent), and the reinforcers are earned repeatedly contingent on behavior. In these situations, reinforcers almost invariably have beneficial, not detrimental, effects. The results of such studies as these have widespread generalization (e.g., Baldwin & Baldwin, 2001; Rawson, 1992; Rawson & Cassady, 1995).

Why then would highly educated, intelligent people with humanity's best interests at heart argue that the *purposeful* use of reinforcement is *bad*? Arguing that reinforcement per se is bad would be tantamount to arguing that natural selection is bad. Reinforcement of behavior throughout the animal kingdom is simply a fact, just as natural selection is a fact. Like natural selection, not good or bad, reinforcement just *is*. However, just as people argue whether *artificial* selection is good or bad (e.g., breeding greyhounds, or breeding disease resistant crops), people can, and do, argue whether *purposeful* reinforcement is good or bad (e.g., arranging the environment to provide contrived reinforcers contingent on socially desired behaviors). *Ironically, people argue against the use of reinforcement because they have been, and are, reinforced for so arguing!* This is not to say that these people are conniving, unethical, or have malicious intent, just as people who systematically use reinforcement are not in favor of bribery. What it says is that reinforcement is powerful. Some of the earliest studies on reinforcement have shown that through systematic reinforcement of specific behaviors or viewpoints, people's behaviors and viewpoints can be reinforced, changed, and maintained, that is, *selected*, without their awareness (e.g., Endler, 1965; Greenspoon, 1955; Verplanck, 1955).

Findings contrary to accepted theory (e.g., rewards having detrimental effects, e.g., Deci, 1971, Lepper et al., 1973) that suggest provocative hypotheses or theory (e.g., cognitive evaluation theory, see, e.g., Deci & Ryan, 1985), immediately produce reinforcers that are very valuable for the discovering scientist(s). For one, the study is likely to be published in an academic peer-reviewed journal. (Sometimes this may happen even if the results do not meet minimally accepted standards of statistical significance such as Deci's [1971] initial "result" that supposedly found rewards to be detrimental). Peer-reviewed publications are the scientists' lifeblood. Publications are associated with tenure (job security), promotions, raises, paid release time, invited conference presentations, professional recognition, and possibly lucrative speaking appearances. All very powerful reinforcers. If you develop a catchy-sounding theory with jargon currently popular in the field, such as "cognitive evaluation theory," and write a book on it (Deci & Ryan, 1985) the reinforcers for your position are likely to further increase in frequency and magnitude (just as I am hoping for various reinforcers for this book). In short, even *in spite of contradictory evidence*, the strength and frequency of your expressed belief is a function of *the reinforcement contingencies* that have operated on and selected your expressed belief. Consequently, you are likely to continue to defend your position even when almost all knowledgeable outside observers know your position is untenable.

For example, it has been experimentally established that a person's conformity or deviance, expressed beliefs for everything from attitudes toward the church (e.g., Goldstein & McGinnies, 1964) to attitudes toward federal aid to parochial schools (e.g., Sarbin & Allen, 1964) to agreeing that obviously incorrect geometric shapes are correct (e.g., Endler, 1965), can be controlled by social reinforcement. These repeated confirmations of the power of reinforcement led Endler to conclude that "reinforcement is a potent force in shaping . . . behavior, often more potent than the objective state of affairs" (p. 197). The defense of "creation science" is one example, and the belief that extrinsic reinforcement undermines intrinsic interest is another example showing that a history of reinforcement for expressing a particular belief is more powerful than the objective state of affairs.

Science methodology as presented in textbooks informs students that theories are modified to account for findings that do not fit the theory. If the findings against the theory are too strong or too many, the theory should be abandoned and replaced with a theory that can accommodate all the data. But, if a scientist has written, spoken on, and advocated a particular theory or viewpoint for a quarter of a century or longer and had those behaviors reinforced, contradictory findings, no matter how strong or numerous, are unlikely to make the scientist abandon his position. When espousing a particular view has been reinforced for most of an individual's life, contrary evidence is unlikely to erase the selective forces of such a history.

Many preachers, for example, Jimmy Swaggart and Jessie Jackson, and numerous politicians from former president Bill Clinton to former speaker of the house Newt Gingrich have preached the value and importance of "family values" and monogamy for years, but often these same people have repeatedly engaged in adultery. At one level, the adulterous acts are completely hypocritical. But when understood in terms of reinforced operant response classes, these actions are completely logical. The *verbal behavior* of preaching family values as an *operant response class* has a strong reinforcement history for these people. *Preaching* "family values," which is different from practicing family values, has been strongly selected with reinforcers such as increased donations, promotions, politically important invitations, and especially by winning elections. Apparently, however, the *practice* of sexual behaviors, congruent and incongruent with "family values," also has a strong reinforcement history for these individuals coupled with mild or no punishers for such behaviors. As a consequence of the reinforcement histories for these two different operant classes, both classes have been strongly selected. Since both operants, preaching family values and practicing sexual promiscuity, have been reinforced in different (usually mutually exclusive) environmental contexts, they are both likely to recur in their respective contexts, *independent* of the strength of the other operant. The behaviors are under differential stimulus control. Given a pulpit, Swaggart will preach, given a prostitute Swaggart will . . . you get the idea.

Instead of admitting wrong, which opens the door for punishment, politicians hem and haw and offer pseudo-explanations ("It depends on what the meaning of 'is' is": Clinton). Psychologists are no different. The opponents of applied reinforcement argue that reinforcement contingencies interfere with "innate psychological needs" and "evolved inner resources for personality development" (e.g., Ryan & Deci, 2000). But, there is absolutely *no* evidence of any "*evolved* inner resources for personality development." Where are these make-believe "inner resources" stored? In the brain? Endocrine (hormonal) system? The musculature? The best answer is "nowhere." There are *no* "evolved inner resources for personality development."

The *true resources* for personality development reside exactly where an objective, natural science based account of personality would put them: in the social, physical, and historical *environment* of the person. Personality is a product of the dynamic interdependent interrelationships between the physically developing person and the person's environment. There were no "inner-evolved resources" for the sexual or political aspects of Jackson's or of Clinton's or of Gingrich's personalities. The resources for this development were the selective forces of the various environments (social and physical) that the politicians were in and the reinforcing consequences of various behaviors. Personality is *shaped* by the behavior-environment interactions just as speaking Chinese or English is shaped by functional behavior-environment interactions. While there is no "inner-evolved resource" for personality, there are *physically* evolved organisms and selective forces in the environment—"*environmental* resources"—that shape "personality characteristics."

The "innate psychological needs" are just intellectual hocus-pocus. Ryan and Deci "postulate" that "competence, autonomy, and relatedness" are "innate psychological needs" (Ryan & Deci, 2000, p. 68) and that reinforcement contingencies reduce or otherwise interfere with competence, autonomy, and relatedness. But in reality, objectively and parsimoniously, "competency," "autonomy," and "relatedness" actually *boil down to a human need to have behavior positively reinforced*!

COMPETENCE

Competence suggests an adequate performance of one's job. Adequate performance produces reinforcement. Therefore, an objective functional definition of competence is "engaging in reinforced behavior." A pigeon can be trained to peck a series of key lights in a specific order. Competent pecking, pecking the correct sequence, will be reinforced. Incompetence, pecking the incorrect sequence, will produce a time-out from positive reinforcement. *Competent behavior is reinforced behavior.* Reading behaviors are reinforced for a child who is competent at reading. An incompetent reader is not naturally reinforced for attempts at reading (this is precisely where contrived reinforcement programs are most useful). By maximizing tax returns, keeping a balanced checkbook, and so forth; an adult who is competent at math has math behaviors reinforced. Adults who are incompetent at math do not have math behaviors reinforced. They may pay someone else to do their taxes and may be fined for overdrawn accounts. As suggested by Stanford University research-theorist Albert Bandura, reinforcement may increase intrinsic interest *precisely* because competent behavior is reinforced behavior; "rewarding quality of performance enhances perceived competence which, in turn predicts intrinsic interest" (Bandura, 1997, p. 221). That people are interested in activities they are competent in because their competence produces reinforcement is exactly what Robert Eisenberger and his co-workers at the University of Delaware found when they paid college students for meeting a performance standard on a perceptual task. "Reward increased perceived competence" (Eisenberger et al., 1999, p. 1030). Furthermore, "performance-contingent reward increases students' subsequent expression of task enjoyment. . . . These results suggest that . . . reward for high performance has incremental effects on intrinsic motivation . . . [and] reward indicates competence" (p. 1031). The reality of reinforcement is that reinforcement increases intrinsic interest, and competent behavior *is* reinforced behavior.

AUTONOMY

When we feel we have "autonomy" over our actions, it is because the actions are positively reinforced rather than under aversive control. Some (e.g., Kohn, 1993) argue that any contingencies, including contingencies of positive reinforcement are an imposed environmental constraint and therefore undermine autonomy; however this assumption is contradicted by research findings. Only contingencies based on coercion, punishment, and negative reinforcement decrease perceived autonomy. *Reinforcement increases perceived autonomy.* Norway researchers Geir Overskeid and Frode Svartdal found that "participants promised a high reward demonstrated a higher feeling of autonomy relative to those who received no, or only low, reward— regardless of whether the participants were instructed to engage in the task or allowed to choose" (Overskeid and Svartdal , 1996, p. 319). Similarly, when Robert Eisenberger and his co-workers paid college students for meeting a performance standard on a perceptual task, they found that:

> Performance-contingent reward increased students' perception that they were free to choose [autonomy] whether to carry out the assigned [experimental] task [in addition to increased expression of task enjoyment and increased free time performing the task just mentioned]. This finding is *inconsistent with the assumption* that performance-contingent reward is experienced as an aversive form of social control that reduces perceived autonomy. Instead, the results support the present view that performance-contingent reward increases perceived self-determination [autonomy] by conveying that the person, group, or organization giving reward has little control over the potential reward recipient; the potential recipient therefore feels free [autonomous] to decide whether to pursue the reward by attempting to attain the performance standard. (Eisenberger et al., 2000, p. 1031, emphasis added)

In other experiments Eisenberger and his co-workers surveyed hundreds of employees of a chain of large discount electronics and appliance stores in the northeastern United States. The organization gives bonuses and pay raises for superior performance. Results from the surveys revealed that

> Employees with strong performance-reward expectancies showed an increased perception of self-determination [autonomy] concerning how they carried out their usual job activities. . . . Reward for high performance appears to strengthen the perception of freedom. . . . The expectation of reward for high performance was positively related to employees' perception of autonomy. . . . [Furthermore] employees who experienced high autonomy, stemming from performance-reward expectancy, reported that they felt more active, enthusiastic, and energetic on a typical day at work. . . . These effects are the *opposite of* [the belief] that reward for meeting a performance criterion is an invasive form of social control that reduces perceived autonomy and intrinsic interest (Deci, 1995; Deci & Ryan, 1985, 1987). (Eisenberger et al., 1999, pp. 1033–1036, emphasis added)

In short, research findings of Eisenberger, Rhoades and Cameron, and the findings of Overskeid and Svartdal converge on the conclusion offered by the latter two researchers: "If a reward can reinforce behavior, it will also increase the feeling of autonomy" (Overskeid & Svartdal, 1996, p. 330). The objective reality of reinforcement is that reinforcement increases perceived autonomy and intrinsic interest.

RELATEDNESS

Relatedness is defined by Ryan and Deci as "the need to feel belongingness and connectedness with others" (Ryan & Deci, 2000, p. 73). One feels belongingness and connectedness with others when one receives social reinforcement from others. A schoolboy feels he belongs with, and is connected to, his teammates when his teammates reinforce his behavior. When yelling "Pass! I'm open!" is reinforced with a pass; when a joke is reinforced with laughter; when a score is reinforced with cheers, slaps on the back, and hugs; a teammate feels connected and that he belongs. When the yell "Pass! I'm open!" is ignored, when attempts at humor are punished with mocking, when a person does not receive social reinforcement from peers and family, the person does not feel connectedness or relatedness.

Indeed, Eisenberger, Rhoades, and Cameron found that employees felt relatedness and connectedness to their employing organization to the extent they were rewarded for high performance. "The expectation of reward for high performance was positively related to employees' perception of autonomy which, in turn, was positively related to employees' belief that the organization valued their contributions and cared about their well-being" (Eisenberger et al., 1999, p. 1033). The reality of reinforcement and relatedness is that the more a source reinforces an individual's behavior, the more that individual will feel related and connected to that source, be the source an employer, school, family, or friends.

RELATEDNESS: "THE PRAISE PROBLEM" VERSUS THE POWER OF PRAISE

Relying heavily on the work of Deci and Ryan, in his chapter "The Praise Problem," Kohn argues that "words of praise that take the form of verbal rewards generally do more harm than good, particularly when they are doled out as part of a deliberate strategy to reinforce certain ways of behaving" (Kohn, 1993, pp. 101–102). However, the reality is that reinforcement, especially verbal reinforcement, that is, praise, is the glue that holds social relationships together. Studying the relationships of over two thousand couples, marriage researcher John M. Gottman (e.g., Gottman, 1994) can predict with over 90 percent accuracy which relationships will last. Those relationships that contain a ratio of at least five positive interactions (e.g., high levels of praise) to every negative interaction will last; those relationships that do not contain a ratio of praise to criticism of at least a five to one will not last. How "in love" the couple say they are does not predict how long relationships will last but the amount of praise in a relationship does. Indeed, according to a review in the *Chronicle of Higher Education*, all successful relationships "require far more acts of positive reinforcement (a ratio of about five to one seems to fare best, [Gottman's] research suggests)" (Monaghan, 1999, p. A9).

In a study of children and parents conducted over two years, University of Kansas researchers Betty Hart and Todd R. Risley (1995), found that regardless of whether families were on welfare, in the working class, or in the professional class, the amount the children were talked to and specifically the amount of praise children were given were the strongest predictors of vocabulary and IQ gains. Children who received a ratio of at least six phrases of praise for every put-down had the highest vocabulary and IQ gains.

A homework assignment is given in both learning class for professional teachers and in an applied behavior analysis class where students, without trying to alter how they usually behave, must first record their ratio of approvals (verbal praise) to disapprovals for a few days during a standard period of social interaction (e.g., during dinner, homework time, or during a specific class during the school day for teachers, Flora, 2000). After this, the students attempt to reach a ratio of five approvals for every disapproval and then report on any effects of the task. Invariably, there are three common findings. The first, revealed by the students' baselines, is that most people did not give as much verbal reinforcement as they believed they did. Second, as the students begin to increase praise and reach a high level of praise, those who they are praising improve their behavior. Children act out less, complain less, and pester less. Both children and adults become more helpful and affectionate as they are praised more. Finally, the people who are doing the praising almost always report feeling much happier and less stressed than before they increased the amount of praise they dispensed. That is, people who give verbal reinforcement feel better, just as the people who receive verbal reinforcement feel better. Praise, verbal reinforcement, is the power behind "relatedness." The results from Hart and Risley, John Gottman, and Flora clearly suggest that if you want to have a successful marriage, bright children, and good friends, give copious, sincere praise. When praise produces such beneficial results, to argue against the use of praise is indefensible.

Yet, opponents of applied reinforcement hold that praise, and all other reinforcers for that matter, should be avoided because reinforcement is an invasive form of social control. According to this belief, such social control will undermine our "intrinsic interest." If it were true that for a behavior to be "intrinsically interesting" it needs to be "self-determined," then the question of why the "self" "determines" to do what it does, needs to be answered. The answer based on reality is that *reinforcement determines what the self does.* People freely admit that they perform behavior for praise and other reinforcers, and that it *feels good too*! (Eisenberger et al., 1999, p. 1034; Flora & Flora, 1999; Flora, 2000; Gottman, 1994). Behavior is *perceived* as autonomous when behavior is a function of positive reinforcement and competent behavior is reinforced behavior. Reinforcement increases both perceived self-determination and preceived competence.

WHAT DOES "INTRINSIC MOTIVATION" MEAN?

Definitions often vary even within the same article (e.g., Ryan & Deci, 2000).One of the definitions of both *extrinsic* and *intrinsic motivations* is that "*extrinsic motivation* refers to the performance of an activity in order to attain some separable outcome and, thus, contrasts with *intrinsic motivation*, which refers to doing an activity for the inherent satisfaction of the activity itself" (p. 71). "By definition, intrinsically motivated behaviors, the prototype of self-determined actions, stem from the self" (p. 74). But paradoxically "our theory of intrinsic motivation does not concern what causes intrinsic motivation (which we view as an evolved propensity, see Ryan et al., 1997); rather, it examines the conditions that elicit and sustain, versus subdue and diminish, this innate propensity" (p. 70).

Calling intrinsic interest an "evolved innate propensity" sounds plausible, but the actual cause of seemingly intrinsically motivated behavior is right under our noses—REINFORCEMENT! Claiming that intrinsically motivated behaviors *stem from the self* is a pseudo-explanation, a cop-out. How does behavior "stem from the self"? Why does behavior "stem from the self"? What does it mean to "stem from the self"? Other than claim an evolved propensity as a way to escape actual explanation, Deci and Ryan never address these seemingly basic questions about intrinsic motivation.

Incredibly, Ryan and Deci claim that "all expected tangible rewards made contingent on task performance do reliably undermine intrinsic motivation" (Ryan & Deci, 2000, p. 70), arguing that reinforcement "subdues and diminishes" interest rather than causes or, "elicits and sustains" interest. If this is true, then don't pay Tiger Woods when he wins a tournament or he'll really hate golf! People who believe this statement should never buy crafts from craftspeople lest they undermine the craftsperson's interest in his craft.

The preposterousness of the argument that reinforcement is detrimental to intrinsic motivation is clear when examined from a natural science, reinforcement perspective, or even with an honest look at everyday life. Replace the words *extrinsic* and *intrinsic* with *contrived* and *natural,* and the illogic is clear. For example, breathing fresh air and catching fish are natural reinforcers for fishing, part of what may make fishing "intrinsically interesting." Getting a dollar for each pound of fish is a contrived reinforcer, or an extrinsic motivator for fishing. Often the same behavior may be a function of both natural and contrived reinforcement contingencies. Is the woman who fishes with her father, enjoys the fresh air and her father's companionship, eats some of the fish she catches and sells the rest, extrinsically or intrinsically motivated to fish? Does it matter? The woman's fishing behavior is a function of several natural and contrived reinforcement contingencies; her behavior does not "stem from the self."

To argue that "intrinsically motivated activities are those that occur for the inherent satistisfactions that accompany them and which, therefore, are not dependent for their occurence on separable rewards or reinforcement" (Ryan et al., 1997, p. 710), and are "autonomous" and "self-determined" on one hand and that intrinsic motivation is an "innate," "evolved" propensity on the other hand reveals an extreme lack of understanding of natural selection. Natural selection, evolution, *is dependent on, a function of, environmental interactions!* Autonomous and self-determined actions by definition must be independent of environmental interaction, but environmental interaction is absolutely necessary for any phenomenon that has supposedly evolved.

Consider two individuals. Both "love to fish." They fish for "the inherent satisfaction that accompanies" fishing; baiting the hook, the breeze from the ocean, casting the lines, and boating. But one never catches enough fish to eat or feed his family. The other is extremely successful, eating his fill, feeding his family, and trading the excess for other goods ("extrinsic" reinforcers). Natural and operant selection hold that only the individual whose fishing behavior is reinforced will survive. The other who loves to fish for "the inherent satisfaction," but receives no reinforcers for fishing will have to learn another trade or die.

In terms of operant selection only the fishing behavior of the successful fisherman will be selected. "Intrinsic motivation" *is dependent on reinforcement!* The other failed fisherman may well say, "there is no sight so sore nor smell so foul as the fishing boats coming to dock." The differential consequences of competent fishing and incompetent fishing will differentially select fishing with only the successful ones finding fishing "intrinsically" or naturally reinforcing. *All behaviors whether they are called "intrinsically motivated" or "extrinsically motivated" are a function of their consequences, whether they are natural or contrived consequences.* (The problem is how to ensure that productive, socially appropriate behaviors can be developed and maintained with natural reinforcement when it is not possible to maintain them with contrived reinforcement).

Many behaviors are a function of both contrived and natural reinforcers. A child may fish because she enjoys the various sensory stimulation fishing provides (sensory stimulation is a primary reinforcer, see Baldwin & Baldwin, 2001) and eats the fish caught (natural reinforcers). The child may also be praised for her fishing skill and sell most of the catch (contrived reinforcers). Opponents of the use of reinforcement would argue that the praise and the profit from the fish, the contrived reinforcers, will undermine the natural reinforcers, because supposedly "all expected tangible rewards made contingent on task performance do reliably undermine intrinsic motivation" (Ryan & Deci, 2000, p. 70). The opponents of reinforcement procedures have invented the misleading concept of intrinsic interest that posits that because the behavior was reinforced, the behavior is no longer "self-determined" or "autonomous" and thus the intrinsic interest is undermined. How can selling excess fish or being given praise "undermine" the natural reinforcing sensory stimulation of fishing? Another child may read because he enjoys adventure stories and learning the outcomes of sporting events (natural reinforcers for reading). The child may also be praised for his reading and earn two dollars for each book read (contrived reinforcers). Opponents of the use of reinforcement would

argue that the praise and the profit from the reading, the contrived reinforcers, will undermine the natural reinforcers, "undermine intrinsic motivation." How can being paid to read a book or praise for reading
"undermine" the enjoyment of adventure stories and learning the outcomes
of sporting events? The reality is that the extrinsic, contrived reinforcers
add value to the behavior. Extrinsic, contrived reinforcers do not undermine behavior.

FEELING FREE VERSUS BEHAVING FREELY

You may throw this book off a bridge; its pages will flutter and some may
rip. How it will flutter and rip I cannot tell you. Its fall to earth may be
described as a "free fall," that it "fell freely to the ground." However, a
physicist given the proper knowledge may reply that "although the book
appeared to fall freely, *given* the angle it was thrown, the wind currents, the
height of the bridge, the mass of the book, the ridgedness of the spine, and
all other physical characteristics of the book and environmental conditions
current at the time; given all the relevant *natural* variables, while the book
appeared to fall freely, it fell the only way possible." *The fall appeared free
but was 100 percent determined.* Of course, human behavior is much more
complex and dynamic than the behavior of a book thrown off a bridge;
nevertheless this analogy applies to human behavior. "A deterministic position . . . holds that behavior is *lawful* and its causes can be identified in
environmental events. . . . Human behavior is subject to lawful prediction.
People do things, or decide to do things, because of past events and present circumstances" (Alberto & Troutman, 1999, p. 39). The feelings of
"self-determination" and "autonomy" are products of past events and present circumstances, primarily of positive reinforcement and a lack of coercive control (negative reinforcement and punishment).

It is obvious that behavior is not free when it is under the control of
aversive consequences: punishment and negative reinforcement. The conception and importance of feelings of freedom and self-determination are
largely a consequence of the contrast between behavior controlled by aversive contingencies; negative reinforcement and punishment, and behavior
controlled by positive reinforcement. "We feel free and happy when we
behave one way rather than another." argues William M. Baum of the University of New Hampshire, "not because the unchosen action is punished,
but because the chosen action is more positively reinforced" (Baum, 1994,
p. 155).

If a prisoner of war must sign a declaration against his home country
or have his compatriots and himself killed, then it is obvious that his
behavior, signing the confession, has been coerced; there was no "free will."

But someone who migrates to a new country for work (positive reinforcement) may "freely" renounce his citizenship to his former country.

When people argue for the importance of "free will" and "self-determination," they are (usually) really arguing against the use of coercion. "The history of civilization is a continuous story of the abuse of power. . . . The effect of this tradition has generally been to increase the reinforcements occurring to the more powerful at the expense of those occurring to the less powerful" (Martin & Pear, 1999, pp. 388–389). The United States of America considers itself "the land of the free" because it eliminated many of the coercive contingencies, taxation without representation, imprisonment without trial, government search and seizure without warrant, and other aversive contingencies imposed by British colonial rule. Invariably, whenever a country or people "win their freedom" it means that the ruling force's coercive control over behavior has been removed. The people and their behaviors may now be free of coercive control (or at least from one source of coercion).

B. F. Skinner argued that "in one way or another intentional aversive control is the pattern of most social coordination—in ethics, religion, government, economics, education, psychotherapy, and family life" (Skinner, 1971, p. 26). In some religions, people are preached to "do this and don't do that or burn in hell *forever!*" In government and economics, people are ordered, "don't do this or be fined; do that and be imprisoned." The history of education is no different: "visit one of these colleges when the lessons are in progress; you hear nothing but the cries of children being beaten and of masters drunk with anger" (Montaigne, 1580/1958). In many families the situation is similar: "finish you dinner and help your mother or get a spanking." As a product of this aversive control, aggression and violence increase (Sidman, 1989; Straus, 1994). Because this aggression occasionally removes or reduces the aversive control, "people tend to act aggressively or to be reinforced by signs of having worked aggressive damage" (Skinner, 1971, p. 27).

"Being free" or "self-determined" from this perspective, then, means to be free from aversive control, punishment, and the threat of punishment, free from coercion. However, this "literature of freedom" has been *over*-generalized by some to the point that all control and all attempts to control are viewed as evil. "Those who manipulate human behavior are said to be evil men, necessarily bent on exploitation. Control is clearly the opposite of freedom, and if freedom is good, control must be bad" (Skinner, 1971, p. 38). Of course, this position is untenable given the insurmountable evidence that *human behavior is controlled and this control allows successful functioning of society and man.* People are never completely free, but always constrained by their environmental circumstances. In the United States I am not free to drive on the left side of the road, stop at green lights, and go at red lights. I am not free to work as a nuclear engineer or to teach chemistry or physics classes. I am only "free" to teach certain courses in behavior analysis and psychology. What courses I do teach and when and where I teach them are further controlled by a number of constraints and contingencies.

But, it is this very lack of freedom in driving any which way that allows me to arrive safely to work and prevents injuries to myself and others. My lack of freedom to work as an nuclear engineer or in many other potentially dangerous jobs protects many lives. My lack of freedom in teaching whatever and whenever prevents me from teaching subjects I am unqualified to teach, but ideally what I do teach will be accurate and useful to the students in my courses. "What is overlooked [by the proponents of freedom] is control which does not have aversive consequences at anytime" (Skinner, 1971, p. 38).

What is also overlooked is that the opposite of planned control is not freedom but anarchy. Without civil control, "the life of man" would be "solitary, poor, nasty, brutish and short" (Hobbes, 1651/1997). The problem is not control, but coercive control. "Feeling free" occurs when behavior is under the control of positive reinforcement. "Operant behavior under positive reinforcement is distinguished by the lack of any immediately antecedent event which could plausibly serve as a cause, and as a result it has been said to show the inner origination called free will" (Skinner, 1974, p. 197). This, of course, means that when Deci and Ryan claim that intrinsically motivated behaviors "stem from the self" they are referring to behavior under the control of positive reinforcement! Operant behavior is selected by past behavior-environment interactions. Therefore, as argued by philosopher Bruce Waller, freedom cannot refer to an absence of environmental control:

> If freedom required escaping environmental control (or escaping the potential knowledge of that controlling environment) there would be no freedom, since there is no escaping environmental contingencies. But such escape would not be freedom in any case; to the contrary, the escape would condemn one to isolation and ineptness. (Waller, 1999, p. 203)

A USEFUL DEFINITION OF FREEDOM

If it is impossible, save by death, to ever be free of reinforcing and punishing environmental contingencies, then the very existence of freedom is called into question. To be clear, if freedom is taken to mean action taken free of, independent of, environmental contingencies then there is no such thing as freedom. *However,* the concept of freedom can remain useful if freedom is given a functional definition, as Waller does: "Freedom is in the capacity and opportunity to respond effectively to our environment with a rich range of behavior that has been shaped for success in that environment" (Waller, 1999, p. 203).

Waller's definition of freedom suggests that rather than avoid the use of positive reinforcement as the proponents of the myth of undermining intrinsic interest argue, positive reinforcement needs to be used to maximize freedom, the feeling of free will, and feelings of self-determination. "To make the social environment as free as possible of aversive stimuli we do not need to destroy that environment or escape from it; we need to redesign it" (Skinner, 1971, p. 39).

REINFORCEMENT INCREASES FREEDOM

By increasing the options available to an individual, reinforcement actually increases an individual's freedom. Regardless of whether behavior is purely a product of reinforcement contingencies or of "free will," one can only engage in those behaviors one is capable of. For example, other than engaging in self-injurious behavior to escape task demands, many individuals with severe developmental disabilities have no functional communication skills. These people have no freedom; they are at the mercy of their caretakers. Fortunately, now that reinforcement procedures are widely utilized with individuals with developmental disabilities, many can learn communication skills such as sign language. Once these people learn communication skills they are "liberated" in a very real sense because now they can communicate their wants and needs in a fashion that is much more likely to be reinforced. Furthermore, through such procedures as shaping by reinforcing successive approximations, people with developmental disabilities are taught numerous independent living skills such as dressing, bathing, housekeeping, and even toileting skills. Contrived reinforcement is often necessary initially to shape these skills, but as the skills are mastered the natural contingencies usually trap the behaviors. With each new skill that is shaped with reinforcement, the individual's freedom increases because her dependence on her caretakers decreases. The more behaviors that are shaped, such as cooking or dressing and choosing what outfit to wear, the more one is "free to do for oneself." Indeed, reinforcement procedures, applied behavior analysis, is recognized by the scientific community and most parents of autistic children as the *only* effective treatment for autism. In fact applied behavior analysis is so effective that some studies (e.g., Lovaas, 1987) show that individuals can have a complete recovery from autism (e.g., Maurice, 1993) and the demand for people properly trained in behavioral analytic reinforcement methods has "far outstripped supply" (Newman, 2000, p. 56). An autistic child with no social skills, no communication, no responsiveness is "free" to do little else than sit in twenty-four-hour custodial care. Conversely, a child recovered from autism, through the reinforcement of successive approximations of functional behaviors, in a regular classroom, is "free" to do everything that every other child in the classroom is free to do.

Similarly, a juvenile who does not know how to read or do basic math is not "free" to do very much. An illiterate is not "free" to attend college, much less the college of one's choice. If one can't read, one is not "free" to read. If one cannot do basic math one is not "free" to correctly charge customers; collect fees; calculate expenses, profits, or savings. One who cannot read street signs is not even "free" to legally drive on the road. But once these skills are taught, perhaps at a teaching-family group home, or in the context of another token economy-based program, the juvenile's freedom increases dramatically. Once basic skills are taught, a juvenile can hold down a job delivering newspapers, as a carpenter's helper, cashier, or delivery person, just to name a few possibilities. *The more one is reinforced, the freer one becomes.* "Freedom, then, lies not in escaping but rather in enhancing environmental control and the range of behavioral responses. . . . [That is,] freedom is found in the capacity to respond to a rich range of environmental contingencies with an effective repertoire of responses" (Waller, 1999, p. 203). Furthermore, the more one is reinforced, the more one *perceives* one's actions to be autonomous and self-determined (e.g., Eisenberger et al., 1999; Overskeid & Svartdal, 1996). To the extent that society can be designed to maximize the use of positive reinforcement, the perceptions of freedom, autonomous action, and self-determination can be maximized.

NON-COERCIVE BUT EXPLOITIVE CONTROL

Unfortunately positive reinforcement can provide the perception of freedom, yet simultaneously exploit the reinforced (yet it is a falsehood that all use of reinforcement is exploitative as Kohn [1993] and Ryan & Deci [2000] maintain). Coercive control produces escape and aggression. Therefore, many agents involved in the control of human behavior employ measures that rely on positive reinforcement but are nevertheless exploitative because the controlling agent gains at the expense of those controlled. People "feel free," but the costs outweigh any reinforcement. As opposed to an overtly coercive relationship such as between a government and citizens where taxes must be paid or citizens are punished, government lotteries and church bingo nights are two examples of covertly exploitative relationships. People do not feel they pay taxes out of "free will," "autonomy," or "self-determination"; they feel coerced. So

> as an alternative, the government organizes a lottery, and instead of being *forced* to pay taxes, the citizen *voluntarily* buys tickets. The result is the same: the citizens give the government money, but they feel free and do not protest in the second case. Nevertheless they are being controlled, as powerfully as by a threat of punishment, by that particularly powerful (variable-ratio) schedule of reinforcement . . . the effect of which is all too clearly shown in the behavior of the compulsive or pathological gambler. (Skinner, 1974, p. 198, emphasis in original)

(In variable ratio schedules reinforcement is contingent on a variable, unpredictable number of responses; see Appendix II in this book.)

Lotteries are additionally exploitative because they are disproportionately played by working- and lower-class citizens, and each ticket bought by a low-wage earner taxes a disproportionately large amount of their earned income relative to that of moneyed class citizens. (I have heard lotteries referred to as "taxes on the poor," "taxes for people who can't do math," and less politely as "a tax for being stupid.")

Churches that raise money through bingo or "poker nights" are likewise exploiting the very people they purport to help. Rich parishioners do not attend bingo: working- and lower-class citizens do. Bingo also pays off on a variable ratio schedule. The more one plays, the more likely one wins, and wins are not predictable from previous wins or plays. Thus bingo produces persistent, high-rate behavior (many bingo players play several cards simultaneously). But the net utility is negative. In the long run the poor always pay more than they win in bingo. (Jesus overturned the tables of the money changers. What would he have done to the bingo tables?)

The control of the variable ratio-like schedules of reinforcement that games of chance have over gambling behavior is admitted by those who have "hit bottom." Before they hit bottom, they say they do not have a problem, that they are "in control," that they have not lost their "self-control." But when they hit bottom, they rightly admit that they have "no control," and clearly see that their behavior is controlled by the selective consequences of gambling (but they may not see that the net utility is negative). When does the gambler's *perception* go from having "self-control" to "no control"?

Many people are lifelong gamblers without "hitting bottom." Non-problematic gamblers have many other sources of reinforcement available to them for behaviors other than gambling. They receive reinforcement for behaviors related to work, social, and family activities. They are *free* in Waller's sense of the term. However, other gamblers do not have as many sources of potential reinforcement. Thus, they are "driven to gambling" by gambling's powerful reinforcement contingencies and by the relative lack of other sources of reinforcement in their environment. They are not "free" according to Waller's definition. The more they gamble, the less reinforcement received for other behaviors (because gambling is occurring instead). As gambling increases, reinforcement available from jobs, spouses, and friends decreases and becomes lost. At first they "freely" gamble, but soon "gambling controls them." In reality, all the while the relative rates of available reinforcement were controlling all of the gambler's gambling and nongambling behaviors.

Those with environments rich in sources of reinforcement for various behaviors engage in a rich array of behaviors. Those in environments poor in sources of reinforcement engage in a limited range of behaviors that more clearly "control" them. This analysis does not apply only to gambling behaviors. During the Vietnam conflict, many U.S. infantrymen were regular heroin users. However, only some of those continued to use heroin when they returned to the United States. Those who stopped returned to environments rich in sources of reinforcement. Those who continued drug abuse behaviors generally returned to situations with a relative lack of reinforcing opportunities (e.g., Franken, 1998, pp. 185–186; McKim, 2000, p. 109). Drug abuse behaviors share some similarity to gambling behaviors in that when the addict "scores" (gets and takes his drug of choice) or the gambler wins, the reinforcement is immediate and intense, but in both cases the reinforcement is brief, and in the long run the net utility is negative.

Thus, lotteries, bingo, and drug abuse all exploit the already exploited. The exploited have "no control" because there are no, or few, other sources of reinforcement to select other behaviors such as the nonexploited have. Or if reinforcers are in the environment, the exploited lack the necessary skills to obtain the possible reinforcement. People become "addicted" to drugs and gambling for the same reason; the environment selects the behaviors. If more sources of reinforcement were made available to the exploited for behaviors other than drug use and gambling, then other, possibly beneficial, behaviors would be selected.

According to Skinner and Baum, one may be a "Happy Slave" when behavior results in immediate positive reinforcement, but the ultimate result is exploitation (Baum, 1994, p. 180; Skinner, 1971, p. 36). Child labor in the nineteenth century; children who receive food, presents, and affection from parents only after performing sexual acts or begging; and citizens "addicted" to the lottery or bingo are all examples. This exploitation of the Happy Slave may be what is really feared by those who claim "extrinsic reinforcement undermines intrinsic motivation." Positive reinforcement provides the perception of freedom and self-determination, yet the reinforced are exploited (one doesn't *have* to play the lottery after all).

CONTINGENCY TRAPS

More generally, positive reinforcement may result in detrimental, ultimately maladaptive situations known as contingency traps. "One problem with positive reinforcement . . . is that it can be used abusively. Small, conspicuous reinforcers delivered immediately can be so powerful that people sacrifice long-term welfare for short-term gain. Such situations are known as contingency traps" (Baum, 1994, p. 157). People caught in contingency traps are said to "act impulsively," "be possessed," and lack "self-control" and "will." But "recognition of the aversive consequences of impulsiveness explains why people caught in contingency traps are unhappy and do not feel free" (p. 159).

Contingency traps reveal that impulsiveness is not a function of a "lack of will" but a function of the powerful effects of immediate reinforcement. *At the moment* of nicotine deprivation, nicotine and social reinforcers for smoking are more powerful than the long-term health benefits of not smoking that are hard to discriminate and experienced only over an extended period of time. While the reinforcement for smoking is immediate, the punishers for smoking—cancer, heart disease, and emphysema—while much larger than the reinforcers, are long delayed. This is the nature of all contingency traps. Overeating, drunkenness, and even nightly extended long-distance phone calls, all produce immediate positive reinforcement, but delayed punishment. Further compounding the problem of contingency traps is that while the ultimately maladaptive behavior produces immediate positive reinforcement, the aversive effects are only *cumulatively* significant. Smoking one more cigarette does not produce cancer. The next extra dessert by itself does not produce obesity. One long-distance phone call does not result in a bill that cannot be paid. The aversive effects of contingency traps are only cumulatively significant.

In sum, positive reinforcement *can* be used "abusively." Positive reinforcement *can* be used to exploit people. But it is simplistic to claim that just because reinforcement can be used abusively to exploit, the systematic use of reinforcement should be avoided. Electricity can be, and is, used "abusively" in many ways (from playing music "boom" boxes full volume at 2:00 A.M., to electricity's use in systematic torture). Nor should we ignore the exploitation of the environment for cheaply produced electricity. In fact, the exploitation of the environment for cheap energy can usefully be conceptualized as a contingency trap. Strip mining, blasting away mountains, and drilling in fragile ecosystems to harvest energy sources all produce relatively immediate reinforcement for the energy companies, but the long-term punishers for such action in the forms of toxic, polluted land, air, and earth are yet to be fully experienced.

But to argue that because electricity can be used abusively and for exploitation, the systematic use of electricity should be avoided is absurd. The same argument holds for all technologies, including applied behavior analysis—the technology that uses positive reinforcement as its primary tool. To argue against the systematic use of positive reinforcement of human behavior because it compromises the sanctity of free will is to plead for ignorance. "In its conflict with determinism, godly or natural, free will seems to depend on ignorance. Indeed," argues Baum, "free will is simply a name for ignorance of the determinants of behavior. The more we know of the reasons behind a person's actions, the less we are likely to attribute them to free will" (Baum, 1994, p. 13). But, to maximize the *feeling* of freedom and the *feeling* of autonomy, the use of positive reinforcement to control behavior needs to be maximized. When several reinforcing alternatives are available, and aversive consequences are lacking, the feeling of freedom and autonomy are maximized. Nevertheless what behavior occurs has been selected by past consequences of similar behaviors in a similar context. The person feels free and autonomous but the behavior has been selected, determined by past reinforcement contingencies.

You may "freely" decide to go to a concert rather than a movie. *Why* did you "freely" chose to do this? Perhaps you have heard the musicians before and found listening to them reinforcing and your friends are going to an action movie while you prefer romances. Whatever the *reasons*, once they are known it is clear that while you felt free to go to the movie or concert, and you were free in the sense that there was no coercion, going to the concert was nevertheless selected, determined by selective forces of past-reinforcing consequences of similar actions. Behavior exists in, is a function of, affects, and is effected by the environment. Behavior is selected by past consequences of similar behaviors (operants). When behavior appears to be "autonomous," to "stem from the self," and to be "intrinsically motivated," the truth is that the observer (the observed may be another person or oneself) is simply ignorant of the causes of the behavior, and/or that the behavior may be maintained on an intermittent schedule in which the behavior is only infrequently reinforced.

5

THE REALITY OF
EXTRINSIC REWARDS AND
INTRINSIC MOTIVATION

When the claim that "all expected tangible rewards made contingent on task performance do reliably undermine intrinsic motivation" (Ryan & Deci, 2000, p. 70) is rephrased as "all expected tangible *contrived reinforcers* do reliably undermine natural reinforcers," the absurdity is apparent. In fact, the opposite is true—*expected tangible contrived reinforcers set the conditions where behavior may come under the control of natural reinforcers.* As Paul A. Alberto of Georgia State University and Anne C. Troutman of the University of Memphis argue in their textbook for teachers, the astute teacher, parent, or behavior analyst maximizes the use of contrived reinforcers ("tangible rewards") to bring important behaviors, such as reading, under the control of natural reinforcers:

> Although many appropriate behaviors are maintained by naturally occurring reinforcers, this natural process may be insufficient to maintain all desirable behaviors. Teachers often find students for whom naturally occurring reinforcers currently fail to maintain appropriate behavior. Some students may see little immediate benefit from learning plane geometry or applied behavior analysis. Some students may be motivated by stronger competing reinforcers than those being offered by the teacher. These students may find the laughter of other students more reinforcing than the teacher's approval. Some students may not value the reinforcers the teacher offers. Grades, for example, may have little meaning to them. In such instances, the teacher must

develop a systematic, interim program to arrange opportunities for students to earn reinforcers they value. When naturally occurring reinforcers are not sufficiently powerful, the wise teacher looks for more powerful ones. (Alberto & Troutman, 1999, pp. 220–221)

The promoters of the myth that extrinsic rewards undermine intrinsic interest would argue that the teacher is shortsighted, not wise. Fortunately, there is strong and more than ample evidence supporting Alberto and Troutman's argument for contrived reinforcement programs. The evidence further shows that contrived reinforcers do more than simply supplement natural reinforcers for desired behaviors; these reinforcers set the conditions where natural reinforcers gain control over desired behaviors. That is, stated with the myth's jargon, "expected tangible rewards made contingent on task performance enable development of intrinsic motivation for the task." (Objectively, while the task may appear to be undertaken out of "intrinsic motivation," it must be recognized that a natural science account holds that task engagement is a function of the current situation and the selective forces of past-reinforcing consequences of similar actions, not due to something "inside the person.")

A prototypical "tangible expected reward" system, or contrived reinforcement system is the Book it! reading program (introduced in chapter 1 of this book) where children's reading behaviors are reinforced with free personal pan pizzas when they meet individualized monthly reading goals! An investigation of the effects of the Book It! program provides a critical test between the competing assertions—one claiming that "all expected tangible rewards made contingent on task performance do reliably undermine intrinsic motivation" (Ryan & Deci, 2000, p. 70), and the other assertion, the assertion of this book, that contrived contingent reinforcers facilitate task engagement where the desired behavior may come under the control of the behavior's natural reinforcers. My youngest brother (a Ph.D. in quantitative psychology from the University of North Carolina), and I conducted just such an investigation. In addition to investigating the effects of Book It! on reading we investigated the effects of being paid for reading during childhood on reading habits of college students.

During the 1995–1996 school year over 22 million children in Australia, Canada, and the United States participated in the (Book It!) program. If rewards undermine intrinsic interest, then during the 1995–1996 school year, the reading habits of over 22 million children were aversely affected. If reinforcing reading sets the conditions where intrinsic interest in reading may develop (Flora, 1990), then Book It! may improve childhood and subsequent adult literacy. Likewise, parents who pay their children to read may be either harming or helping their children's possible interest in reading depending on the truth or falsity of the myth that rewards undermine intrinsic interest. (Flora & Flora, 1999, p. 5)

Our results did not support the myth that rewards undermine intrinsic interest. "Neither being reinforced with money or pizzas [during childhood] increased or decreased the amount college students read nor influenced their intrinsic motivation for reading" (Flora & Flora, 1999, p. 3). Our results did support the assertion that contrived contingent reinforcers facilitate task engagement where the desired behavior (reading) may come under the control of the behavior's natural reinforcers.

Answers to direct questions about Book It! and parental pay for reading suggest that when a child is extrinsically reinforced for reading, the child will increase the amount read, enjoyment of reading may increase, and if they do not yet know how to read fluently, the programs may help the child learn to read. . . . Extrinsic rewards for reading set the conditions where intrinsic motivation for reading may develop. Any concerns that reinforcement programs for reading will decrease later reading behaviors are unfounded" (Flora & Flora, 1999, p. 3).

An earlier study of Book It! by the Institute of Human Science and Services of the University of Rhode Island reached the same conclusion. Surveys from 2,741 teachers representing 16,130 students reported that Book It! improved attitudes toward reading and enjoyment of reading, and the longer the children were in the program the more their reading level rose and enjoyment increased. According to the report, "the basis behind the program was to offer *immediate positive* reinforcement to reward *individual accomplishments*" (Institute, 1985, p. 17, emphasis in original).

The beneficial effects of contrived reinforcement to eliminate illiteracy are also seen in the Earning by Learning program that pays academically at-risk children two dollars for each book they read (also introduced in chapter 1 in this book). Using both pretest/post-test measures and comparisons against nonparticipating controls, participating in the Earning by Learning program was found to increase total positive attitudes toward reading, attitudes toward recreational reading, and attitudes toward academic reading (McNinch et al., 1995). When contrived positive reinforcement is used to increase reading, it also increases reading level and increases positive attitudes toward academic and recreational reading; when contrived reinforcement increases the amount children read, increases their enjoyment of reading and facilitates their learning to read, how can that be called "abusive"? How do these reinforcement programs "exploit" children? Clearly, contrived reinforcement is not abusive, does not exploit, and does not "undermine intrinsic interest," but does just the opposite. Tangible rewards, contrived reinforcement, promote the development of intrinsic interest.

Children who do not read or do not know how to read fluently have no "intrinsic interest" in reading that could possibly be undermined in the first place. The problem is how to get children to read so that the natural reinforcers for reading, all the intrinsically interesting phenomenon reading reveals, will maintain and increase reading. Contrived reinforcement solves this problem. Children from professional homes are likely to have copious age appropriate reading materials available and receive copious reinforcement for prereading and reading behaviors. Children from such environments may not require highly salient contrived reinforcers for reading because reading behaviors will have been selected in the home environment and maintained by the natural reinforcers for reading. However, children who come from educationally impoverished environments may require highly salient contrived reinforcers for reading. Again: "In such instances. . . . When naturally occurring reinforcers are not sufficiently powerful, the wise teacher [or parent] looks for more powerful ones" (Alberto & Troutman, 1999, pp. 220–221). Such programs not only select reading but make reading enjoyable, and once the program is completed there is no undermining of interest in reading (e.g., Flora & Flora, 1999).

BUILDING ACADEMIC INTRINSIC MOTIVATION IN "AT-RISK" CHILDREN

Over the last quarter century, Harve E. Rawson, Ph.D. has studied the effects of behavior modification programs within short-term residential summer school programs on academic achievement and behavior problems of "at-risk" boys, all of whom have some combination of learning disabilities, behavior disorders, adjustment problems, and are from low socioeconomic backgrounds, broken homes and are considered culturally and socially deprived (McIntosh & Rawson, 1988; Rawson, 1973a, 1973b, 1992; Rawson & Cassady, 1995; Rawson & McIntosh, 1991; Rawson & Tabb, 1993). These programs that rely heavily on contrived reinforcers or "extrinsic rewards," have been found to produce increases in self-esteem, decreases in anxiety, increased perceived internal locus of control, and decreased levels of depression. Harve E. Rawson specifically investigated the effects of the intensive short-term remediation program on academic intrinsic motivation. The foundation of the remediation program was contrived reinforcement.

> The program featured . . . use of a *token economy* system where coveted "fun" activities were earned through appropriate academic performance and classroom behavior, [and] working up to individual ability levels. . . . All teachers involved in the remedial program consistently employed the following teaching techniques regardless of the learning situation: *frequent verbal praise*; . . . continual *physical gestures of approval* and affection . . . for socially appropriate behavior; frequent episodes of personal success in *"earning" coveted program activities* by individually programming activities where each child is sure to succeed; . . . *public ceremonial awards* (three times a day) for personal successes and achievements. (Rawson, 1992, p. 277, emphasis added)

If one believes that extrinsic rewards undermine intrinsic interest, the remedial program was designed nearly perfectly to *undermine* or reduce academic intrinsic interest. Conversely, the program was also well designed to *facilitate* the development of academic intrinsic interest if contrived reinforcers (e.g., points in a token economy and ceremonial awards) set the conditions where the natural reinforcements for academic activities can gain control over academic behaviors.

Comparisons of pretest and post-test scores on the Children's Academic Intrinsic Motivation Inventory found that *the program did indeed increase academic intrinsic motivation. Significant gains in intrinsic interest were found* for reading, math, social studies, science, and general interest in academics. That intrinsic academic motivation increased as a result of the summer program is especially encouraging because "learning disabled children frequently *decline* in academic motivation over the summer months" (Rawson, 1992, p. 281, emphasis in original). Informal observations also revealed that the academic behaviors, initially selected with contrived reinforcers, came under the control of the naturally occurring reinforcers for learning:

> Since many rewards [contrived reinforcers] for good academic performance were built into the remediation program, extrinsic academic motivation would be expected. But learning for its own sake [intrinsic motivation] or for the joy of learning was often evident in the program. Children often stayed in class to ask more questions when contingent rewards were not available; children frequently asked questions of their peers who were not giving

tangible reinforcements; and long-term parental feedback most frequently stressed that observable change in a child's wanting to learn because he now knew he could learn. (Rawson, 1992, p. 282)

That is, as a product of the contrived reinforcement program, learning became a naturally reinforcing process. Further results suggested that these improvements in intrinsic academic motivation were lasting. "A four-month follow-up study . . . reflected significantly higher academic grades for the average remediation program participant. . . . Of the 42 participants, 29 [69 percent] were reported by their teachers to be 'doing markedly better in class'" (Rawson, 1992, p. 283).

These results conclusively refute the myth that extrinsic rewards undermine intrinsic motivation. The results instead strongly argue that contingent reinforcement programs are a powerfully beneficial tool that can evoke academic and other socially useful behaviors so that they occur at a sufficiently high rate so that the natural reinforcers for the behaviors can gain functional control over the behaviors. That is, extrinsic reinforcers set the conditions where intrinsic interest may develop.

INTRINSIC INTEREST AND GRADES: PAY NOW, PERFORM NOW AND LATER

Once contrived reinforcement has increased the rate of the desired behaviors sufficiently for natural reinforcers to gain control of the behaviors, once extrinsic rewards have occasioned the development of intrinsic motivation for desired behavior, the beneficial gains persist. Students in junior level college courses were asked if they enjoyed college (a bare bones assessment of intrinsic interest); if their parents (or other guardians) ever paid them money for good grades while they were in school; if their parents rewarded them for good grades in other ways; and if they were paid for grades, or rewarded for grades in other ways, to give any comments they had concerning how it affected them (Flora & Popanek, 2001). The students' college grade point averages (GPAs) were also obtained.

Almost all of the students reported that they enjoyed college. Being paid in childhood for earning good grades did not undermine college students' intrinsic interest in college. Almost all of the students, paid and not paid for grades, reported that they were rewarded in other ways, usually with praise, for good grades. That is, virtually every student reported receiving some sort of extrinsic reward, contrived reinforcement, for earning good grades. If extrinsic rewards undermine intrinsic interest these students should not enjoy college and the rewards would undermine their enjoyment of school, but the opposite result occurred. Almost without exception students who had been rewarded for good grades reported that they enjoyed college. Contrived reinforcers, extrinsic rewards, for academic achievement increase intrinsic interest in academic achievement.

Most strikingly, students who had been paid money for good grades had significantly *higher* college grade point averages, approximately half a letter grade, than students who had not been paid for good grades during childhood. This finding contradicts the myth that contrived reinforcement undermines intrinsic interest. If it were true, then being paid for good grades would undermine students' interest in earning good grades, and, as such, paid students would have lower GPAs than students who were not paid for earning good grades.

However, the finding that students who had been paid money for good grades during childhood had significantly *higher* college grade point averages than students who had not is exactly what is predicted by reinforcement theory in general and Robert Eisenberger's Learned Industriousness Theory (e.g., Eisenberger, 1992) in particular. The contrived reinforcers, money, for earning good grades become differentially associated with earning good grades. This process adds value to earning good grades. Because earning good grades is associated with valuable consequences such as parental praise and affection in addition to money, earning good grades becomes valuable behavior for the student.

Furthermore, earning good grades often entails effortful, sometimes dull and repetitious work. According to learned industriousness, the reinforcement of the high effort necessary to earn good grades would condition reward value to high effort. This process of reinforcing high effort to earn good grades in childhood generalizes so that high grades are worked for in college. Reinforcement for earning good grades with money, praise, or other reinforcers during childhood directly contributes to the development of an "industrious college student." Indeed, to excel in almost any endeavor, repetitive dull work is usually required even in highly interesting, exciting activities. Thousands of free throws must be practiced before an individual is likely to earn the chance at a game winning shot. The same pass route must be run hundreds of times in practice before a receiver is likely to be thrown a pass in a critical game situation. A surgeon must dissect and operate on numerous animals and cadavers before she is allowed to operate on a live human. Therefore, as argued by Eisenberger, even with "intrinsically interesting," naturally reinforcing activities, the contrived reinforcement of effort is a prerequisite for skillful performance.

Most academic subjects involve a combination of tasks with varying degrees of intrinsic interest and difficulty. Even if a student

finds that an academic subject is generally interesting, the acquisition of a good understanding of the subject matter requires the
study of some topics found to be dull and repetitive and other
topics that, although interesting, are discouragingly difficult to
master. An increased secondary reward value of high effort may
encourage selection of, and persistence on, difficult academic
tasks. Reinforced high effort on dull, repetitive tasks can even be
used to increase subsequent effort in intrinsically interesting
tasks. For example, preadolescent children who had been
rewarded for accuracy on a monotonous pronunciation task produced more accurate subsequent drawings and stories than did
students who had been rewarded for simply completing the pronunciation task. (Eisenberger, 1992, p. 263)

Paying children for goods grades is *not* the optimal way to arrange
reinforcement contingencies for children to *learn the subject matter* per se.
(The education section in chapter 10 in this book, describes how reinforcement should be arranged to maximize learning.) But, as suggested by
Eisenberger's findings and arguments, reinforcement for earning good
grades in subjects that may require dull, repetitive, and discouragingly difficult work, selects persistence on dull, repetitive, and discouragingly difficult work. Persistence is a prerequisite for success. If persistence is not
selected, individuals are much more likely to cheat or quit. Paying children,
or providing children with other tangible rewards for good grades, teaches
them a valuable life lesson. Hard work pays off. Furthermore, argues
Willard Stawski, author of *Kids, Parents & Money: Teaching Personal
Finance from Piggy Bank to Prom,* paying children for good grades models
the economic world they will enter when schooling ends.
    "As a parent of five boys, I have no problem with a monetary 'atta-boy'
for a job well done," argues Stawski who pays five dollars for each A; "Our
society and economy are based on negotiated compensation for directed
effort. I want my boys attention on the job at hand—quality schoolwork—
without distraction." Other parents quoted in the advice column *Parent to
Parent* (Mills & Flagler, 2000) agree with Stawski:

"I'm a unionized employee at a large telecommunications company," says a mother of five . . . who has received gift certificates
and lunch as perks. "Cash incentives accurately reflect what a
high achiever can expect to find in the work-a-day world."
[Another mother] who has been in education for 40 years, agrees:
"I think children should get paid for their work just like their parents do. It does teach them responsibility." Valerie Balester of

Bryan, Texas, a college professor, used to get $5 for every A. "I felt like it was just something to look forward to, and it gave me an extra little push when I was between a B and an A" she says. Another [parent's] step children were given $500 for each semester they made straight A's. 'It's not a matter of swapping money to learn responsibility. It's major discipline they teach themselves and goals they set to get that reward."

In short, paying children for good grades, or giving them other tangible rewards for academic work is commonplace, teaches important life lessons, and *increases intrinsic academic interest* (Flora & Popanak, 2001; Flora & Flora, 1999; Rawson, 1992). For children who already find a behavior naturally reinforcing, or "intrinsically interesting," there is *no evidence* that tangible rewards have an aversive effect. Contrived reinforcement adds to the total reinforcing value of an activity (there is no mathematically logical way that *added* contrived positive *reinforcement* could *subtract* from the *total reinforcing* value of any task). In the Flora and Flora Book It! reading study, no respondent indicated aversive effects of extrinsic reinforcers. Responses only indicated no effects or beneficial effects: "'Money had no influence— I love reading.'" and "'I believe that being rewarded for reading showed me how much an education pays off. It has provided me with a motivation to study and pay attention in school that I still have today'" (Flora & Flora, 1999, p. 11). Responses to the survey (Flora & Popanak, 2001) on being paid for good grades also indicated only beneficial effects. For example, one student responded that being paid for grades "supported a motivation for good grades at a time when good grades weren't as much a priority as friends." Given the powerfully beneficial effects and the lack of aversive effects of reinforcement programs in developing literacy and academic achievement generally, arguing against, or attempting to prevent the systematic planned use of contrived reinforcers to promote reading and academic achievement is elitist at best, if not outright discrimination against the educationally impoverished.

A CASE STUDY IN CONTRIVED
REINFORCEMENT FOR READING

For a "shaping project" requirement in my applied behavior analysis class, an adult female student attempted to improve the reading level of her daughter who was in special education classes. My student's daughter, "Amy," a sixth grader, did not want to be teased, picked on, and alienated by her peers for being in special education classes when she was to start junior high school the following school year. According to Amy's school district's Individualized Educational Plan (IEP), she suffered from "low-learning ability," and at the end of the sixth grade was "reading at the third-grade level." She had been receiving "learning support and adapted instruction" from a "learning support teacher" in reading and spelling for 2 1/2 years.

For the project, Amy's reading deficiency was attacked with a widely available commercial computer software reading program. The program provided subtle and obvious contingent, automatic, frequent immediate reinforcement for correct reading. For example, hearing a spooky, silly, Dracula-like voice reinforced correct sentence completion. A "mystery mode" reinforced activity completion with clues to solve the mystery that in turn allowed advancement to the next level. Dynamic computer animation and "headline news articles" featuring Amy also reinforced correct answers that depended on reading. Completing a level was rewarded with printable certificates, original stories, and humorous animations by the computer program. The printable certificates were "expected tangible rewards made contingent on task performance" (Ryan & Deci, 2000, p. 70). Amy's mother also provided reinforcers in the form of teen magazines and a new computer-assisted tutorial for advancement through the program. Computer animation and silly voices are also contrived "extrinsic" consequences that do not normally occur contingent on reading. Therefore, according to the myth that extrinsic rewards undermine intrinsic interest, due to the project, Amy's interest in reading should have decreased and her reading level should have remained the same or decreased because of this project.

Rather than undermining Amy's intrinsic motivation for reading, however, *the program increased Amy's reading ability three grade levels in two months*! After completing the program Amy scored 95 percent correct on a sixth-grade reading comprehension test. Just two months prior, her school's IEP said she "was reading at the third grade level." Following the shaping project, Amy's mother fought the school district to have her daughter placed in regular classes instead of special education for her first year of junior high. Amy responded by passing, with work in regular classes, including a mainstream English class with the same requirements and no more in-school help than the "average" students had. Amy advanced to the next grade level. The university funded Amy's mother so that she could present her results at the annual conference of the International Association for Behavior Analysis (Davidson & Flora, 1999). Following the mother's college graduation, Amy and her mother moved to Baltimore, Maryland, so that Amy's mother could take a job using her applied behavior analysis skills. After one year in the school system with the standard school curriculum, Amy excelled and was offered a spot in a *magnet school for the gifted and talented*!

Amy's intrinsic interest in reading was not undermined. Amy continues to enjoy reading teen magazines and young adult novels. The "expected tangible rewards made contingent on task performance" in reading did not "reliably undermine intrinsic motivation" but promoted an intrinsic interest in reading for Amy. In addition once her reading skills were developed, other behaviors that Amy excels in were able to bloom. When Amy was reading-deficient, these talents were hidden under the false label of *low-learning ability*. Reinforcement of reading increased Amy's freedom.

Amy's case illustrates the importance of promoting the use of systematic contrived reinforcement for desirable behaviors (reading, basic math, social and self-help skills, etc.) when the natural reinforcers for such behaviors are insufficient to develop and maintain those desired behaviors. To function effectively in human society, and especially to excel, one needs to know how to read, write, and do basic math. If one has no "intrinsic interest" in developing these behaviors, as many children from educationally impoverished background claim, then society has three options. One, the "uninterested" can be taught these skills through coercion with aversive contingencies. But this program has a number of undesirable side effects including teaching violence as a means to control, increased truancy, and increased risk of depression (see chapters 11, 12, & 13 in this book).

The second option is to use systematic contrived reinforcement as advocated in this book. Even if tangible rewards did undermine intrinsic interest, although clearly they do not, the systematic, science-based application of reinforcement principles can be efficiently used to teach necessary skills such as reading and basic math. One can try to beat a child until the child reads (the stick), or improvements in reading can be reinforced (carrots). Even if the reinforcement did somehow undermine interest in reading, one still needs to read to function successfully in society. Whether one likes to read or not, one needs to read maps, road signs, instruction manuals, job descriptions, and so forth. Even if the contrived reinforcers Amy received for reading had undermined her intrinsic interest in reading (they did not), Amy still would need to know how to read at grade level to pass her history, science, and other classes in which reading is a prerequisite skill.

One of the intrinsically reinforcing things about reading is that effective reading makes other reinforcers available for other behaviors. Effective reading increases freedom. A child who can read instructions will have more success, and receive more reinforcement for building model cars than a child who does not, or cannot read the directions, *whether or not he "likes" to read*. But successful model assembly will in turn make reading more interesting due to the contingent consequences reading enables. Likewise, an adult who reads the owner manuals to appliances will receive more reinforcement from the appliances, and they will last longer on average than those of the adult who does not read the manuals, *whether or not the adult claims an intrinsic interest in reading.*

If one objects to carrots as well as to the stick, the final option is to leave the "uninterested" to "their own devices," where the prevailing environmental contingencies will haphazardly select a wide range of unpredictable and predictable (e.g., criminal behavior and drug abuse) behaviors. Such a program is very costly because the prevailing contingencies in educationally impoverished environments favor the selection of behaviors that are harmful to society's well-being. The cost of education from Head Start all the way through graduate school is far less costly than keeping an adult in prison.

If literacy is not reinforced, illiteracy occurs by default. If "healthy living" is not reinforced, the population becomes unhealthy and the ever smaller proportion of literate, healthy people must bear the cost. The reinforcement for healthy eating and lifestyle behaviors are often only cumulatively significant. Overeating fat or sugary foods, drug abuse, smoking, and television "channel surfing" while lying on the sofa produce immediately reinforcing consequences with little effort for the person who engages in those behaviors (the educationally impoverished). The reinforcing consequences of "healthy living" are often not immediately powerful, if they occur at all, and the naturally reinforcing consequences may take time to develop. For example, beginning runners often state that they "hate running" but start because of certain consequences running produces (weight loss, decreased blood pressure, and increased lung capacity). Usually, only those who have been running for a while (often years) claim to run because they "love to run." If Amy had not been reinforced for reading, then she would have remained in special education classes and she would have continued to be teased and picked on. Instead of developing an interest in school, it is likely that Amy would have terminated her education as soon as possible as a result of being misplaced in special education classes, teased, and picked on.

To do nothing is to court anarchy, disease, and death, but out of unwarranted fear of "undermining intrinsic interest," doing nothing is apparently what the opponents of reinforcement programs are advocating. The most ethical course of conduct is to acknowledge the ubiquitousness of reinforcement; that reinforcement contingencies exist on a continuum from contrived to natural; that reinforcement contingencies can be arranged that are coercive and exploitative; but also that reinforcement contingencies are most often in no way coercive or exploitative; that positive reinforcement increases perceived autonomy and perceived self-determination; that contrived reinforcers can occasion behaviors that will then come under the control of natural reinforcement, or said differently, that extrinsic rewards develop intrinsic interest; and that the careful, planned use of reinforcement is the most powerful tool available to better the human condition and should be used to do so.

6

REINFORCEMENT
CRUSHES CREATIVITY

Unfortunately, not only is it falsely argued that reinforcement undermines intrinsic interest, but it is also argued, largely by the same antagonists to reinforcement (e.g., Kohn, 1993), with essentially the same arguments, that reinforcement is detrimental to creativity. This myth is also widespread. The previously mentioned National Education Association primer on promoting classroom creativity (chapter 7 in this book) argues under "How to Kill Creativity," that "an expected reward . . . makes [students] much less likely to take risks or to approach a task with a playful or experimental attitude" (Tegano et al., 1991, p. 119). One frequently cited review concluded that rewarded work is "more stereotyped and less creative than the work of nonrewarded subjects working on the same problems" (Condry, 1977, pp. 471–472).

Using rewards, "extrinsic motivators," or more accurately, the purposeful use of contingent, contrived reinforcers, is said to make behavior simply a "means to an ends," which supposedly decreases the probability of creative performance. For example, Teresa M. Amabile of Harvard University and Jonathan Cheek argue that expectation of reward causes a task to be "defined more narrowly . . . simply as a means to an end rather than as an opportunity for exploration and play" (Amabile & Cheek, 1988, p. 60). Berry Schwartz of Swarthmore College has argued that it is not possible to increase creativity with reinforcement because "reinforcement seems ineffective at producing anything but stereotyped repetition of what works" (B. Schwartz, 1982, p. 57), and that "token reinforcement interferes with the development of creative problem-solving ability" (B. Schwartz & Robbins, 1995, p. 202).

ROUSSEAU'S ROMANTICISM

According to Robert Eisenberger, the philosophical objection to reinforcement with regard to intrinsic interest, self-determination, and creativity is
based on the work of French philosopher Jean-Jacques Rousseau's "romantic interpretations of creativity [that] stress interest in a task for its own
sake (intrinsic motivation) and freedom from social constraints. Jean-
Jacques Rousseau . . . believed that creativity depends on the free exploration of imagination and the pursuit of momentary whim; he argued that
limitations concerning whether, when, or how a person is allowed to carry
out a task interfere with the spontaneity required for creativity (Eisenberger et al., 1999, p. 309).

In "The War Against Boys," Christina Hoff Sommers argues that the
increase in school shootings, the decreases in morality, ethics, and even
academic achievement of American males is directly traceable to the philosophy of Rousseau. The "progressive-education theorists . . . advocated
abandoning the traditional mission of indoctrinating children in the 'old
morality.' They succeeded in persuading the American educational establishment to adopt instead the romantic moral pedagogy of Rousseau"
(Sommers, 2000, p. 199). The progressive-education theorists took
Rousseau to be against all social constraints. "In his [Rousseau's] view, the
goal of moral education is defeated when an external code is imposed on
children . . . 'Let us lay it down,' [argued Rousseau] 'as an incontestable
principle that the first impulses of nature are always right.' . . . Rousseau's
followers," Sommers continues, "go further by regarding 'directive' moral
education as an assault on a child's right to develop freely" (p. 190). The
adoption of Rousseau's philosophy by humanists and progressive-education theorists has resulted in advocacy against all constraints in education,
including explicit reinforcement contingencies.

Because "the educational philosophy of Rousseau inspired the progressive movement in education, which turned away from rote teaching
and sought methods that would free the creativity of the child" (Sommers,
2000, p. 192), the implications for developing creativity per se are clear.
According to the Rousseau-inspired progressive movement, any supposed
constraint, including a teacher-supplied contrived reinforcement contingency, on a child would necessarily be detrimental to the creative process.
Indeed, that reinforcement contingencies are a constraint inherently detrimental to the creative process is exactly the argument of Amabile and Alfie
A. Kohn. "'Do this and you'll get that' makes people focus on the 'that'
[reward], not the 'this' [creative behavior]" which is, argues Kohn, "about
the last strategy we ought to use if we care about creativity" (Kohn, 1993,
p. 67). Amabile argues that "the more single-mindedly an external goal is
pursued, the less likely . . . that creative possibilities will be explored"

(Amabile, 1988, p. 144). Indeed, the interpretation of Rousseau's philosophy of being against all constraints and contingencies is clearly echoed by Kohn when he writes:

> What rewards and punishments do is induce compliance, and this they do very well indeed. If your objective is to get people to obey on order, show up on time and do what they're told, then bribing or threatening them may be sensible strategies. But if your objective is to get long-term quality in the workplace, to help students become careful thinkers and self-directed learners, or to support children in developing good values, then rewards, like punishments, are absolutely useless. In fact, as we are beginning to see, they are worse than useless—they are actually counterproductive. (Kohn, 1993, pp. 41–42)

In short, the Rousseauian, Kohnian, romantic stance on behavior generally, and creativity specifically, is that behavior is optimal and best when behavior freely *originates* in a creating individual. If this is so (it is not), then *any* environmental influences, inducements, be they punishers or reinforcers, would be inherently detrimental to the creative process.

Conversely, the utilitarian, or reinforcement, perspective holds that if creativity is reinforced, creativity will be selected. Simply, either stereotyped behavior or creative behavior can be selected depending on which type of behavioral repertoire is reinforced. In "Creating the Creative Artist," B. F. Skinner summarizes the romantic stance and the reinforcement-based view and hints at the potential and more promising possibilities of the reinforcement-based account:

> If art springs from an inner life which is truly original, in the sense that it *begins* with the artist, then there is nothing to be done beyond giving the artist an opportunity. It is much more promising, however to argue that the achievements of the artist can be traced to the world in which he lives, for we can then begin to examine that world not only to explain the achievements but also to find the means of taking practical steps. . . . Artists paint pictures *because of the consequences*. (Skinner, 1970/1999, p. 380, emphasis in original)

CREATIONISM VERSUS SELECTIONISM

The difference between the romantic notion of creativity and the utilitarian, reinforcement position on creativity is virtually identical to the difference between fundamental religious beliefs of a *creator* versus the scientific position of *evolution by natural selection* (see Skinner, 1970/1999 for a similar discussion). Briefly, the creationists believe that all living things are the result of an intelligent design, by a creator (God) who was the originating (original) locus of all existing life. God, the originator, *creates* life. God is *creative*. Conversely, evolution through natural *environmental selection* holds that the selection of random variations is responsible for all existing life. Those variations that were advantageous to survival were selected and retained. Through the process of variation (through random genetic mutation, sexual reproduction, etc.), and selection by consequences (some variations are disadvantageous to survival and die out; some are advantageous and are retained), all existing life came to its present form.

Like creationism, the romantic notion of creativity holds that the creator is the originator. Creativity comes from within. As God is seen as the creator of all life, the individual is seen as the originator of creativity, void of any external causal influence. For example, in defending the miracle-working self, philosopher Charles A. Campbell defines "creative activity" as activity "in which (as I have ventured to express it) nothing determines the act save the agent's doing of it" (Campbell, 1974, p. 177). Be it God or man, creativity *originates* with the creator.

Conversely, like evolution through natural selection, a deterministic position holds that creativity is the result of selection of advantageous behavioral variations. In "A Lecture on 'Having' a Poem" (1971/1999) Skinner notes that in Charles Darwin's *Origin of the Species*, "Novelty could be explained without appeal to prior design if random changes in structure were selected by their consequences. It was the contingencies of survival which selected new forms" (p. 399). This is also true for novel behavior. Novel behavior is explained without appeal to an originating agent because random changes in behavior are selected by their consequences. It is the contingencies of reinforcement that select creative behavior.

PESSIMISTIC CONCLUSIONS
AND PARLOR GAME PSYCHOLOGY

Consistent with the romantic worldview of creativity as originating with the individual and most likely when the individual is unfettered by any environmental influences, such as a reinforcement contingency, so that "playful attitudes," "freedom," and "exploration" can be maximized, when the intellectual descendants of Rousseau, the opponents of applied reinforcement, study creativity, they find environmental factors, especially reinforcement, to be detrimental to creativity. Of course, without any environmental factors there is nothing for the creative person to explore or be playful with. However, the opponents of reinforcement seem unconcerned with this basic fact. Indeed, if virtually all environmental influences undermine creativity, a fatalistic, pessimistic conclusion is all that remains for the so-called romantics. "Although this certainly was not my initial aim," bemoans Amabile, "most of my research has uncovered methods of destroying creativity . . . [one possibility is that] creativity *cannot* be enhanced, that the most one can do is avoid undermining [it]" (Amabile, 1983, p. 189). Make no mistake, reinforcement is counted among the methods of destroying creativity.

This pessimistic conclusion logically follows from the myth that intrinsic interest can be undermined with reinforcement. The argument that reinforcers are bad for creativity is based on unrealistic, highly contrived experiments that lack any similarity to situations where meaningful creative achievement takes place (e.g., in science, technology, manufacturing, or the fine arts). Jock Abra of the University of Calgary, Canada, notes that these experiments generally "lack face validity, being more of the . . . parlor game than creative variety" (Abra, 1993, p. 323). Like many of the experiments on the effects of rewards on intrinsic interest, many of the experiments on the supposed effects of reinforcement on creativity bear little relation to how reinforcement programs are administered outside the laboratory. Instead, the experiments are designed to confirm the researcher's already formulated conclusions.

Typically, subjects—children or college students—are simply given a little task, told to do their best and that they may be rewarded for a good job. As opposed to actual reinforcement of behavior, "the majority of . . . studies," note Eisenberger and Judy Cameron, "like studies of the effects of reward on intrinsic motivation, incorporate the promise of reward or a single pairing of performance with reward" (Eisenberger & Cameron, 1996, p. 1160). Furthermore, "investigations of the effects of reward on creativity have typically *eliminated instructions concerning any requirement to engage in novel performance*" (Eisenberger et al., 1999, p. 309, emphasis added). Not surprisingly, when subjects were not told that creativity was in any way important, researchers have reported that promised reward reduced creativity (e.g., Amabile, 1983, 1996). It is the frequent, repetitious, and *actual* receipt of reinforcers contingent on behavior that select the contingent behavior in the reinforcement process. In the creativity investigations, reinforcement is never frequent and often does not even occur. Using these studies to make decisions about creativity would be like studying oceans to make recommendations on mountain management. For these studies, which do not even use reinforcement, conclude that reinforcement destroys creativity.

DEFINING CREATIVITY: CONVENTIONAL
PERFORMANCE VERSUS NOVEL PERFORMANCE

It is not surprising that creativity does not increase in experiments when subjects are offered a reward for completing a task but given no instructions to be creative or any contingency for creativity. It may not be clear, however, why creativity might decrease on such tasks. Fortunately, when the selective nature of reinforcement is understood, this puzzle is solved. First, an operational definition of creativity is necessary to study creativity objectively. If creativity is defined as "creative action originating in the individual," independent of the environment, then in addition to its being a naturalistic impossibility, it would be impossible to reinforce creativity. Fortunately, "creative action originating in the individual," is not really what most mean by creativity and an acceptable, pragmatic widely agreed upon definition of creativity is available: "Creativity involves the generation of novel behavior that meets a standard of quality of utility" (Eisenberger et al., 1999, p. 308). In addition, Abra argues that most definitions of creativity include *novelty* (or infrequency of occurrence) and *quality* or usefulness (e.g., Abra, 1993, p. 293). Given a working definition of creativity as behavior that is novel and useful and a basic understanding of reinforcement, it becomes possible to understand why creativity might actually decrease in some studies reputedly designed to understand creativity.

By the time an individual reaches grade school, he or she has an extensive history of reinforcement for behaving conventionally, not creatively. *Throughout childhood and into adulthood*, for almost every behavior from language to lettering and drawing, *conventional performance is differentially reinforced relative to novel or creative performance.* As most children learn, after language has been shaped, only proper conventional requests are likely to be reinforced relative to nonconventional requests. When a five-year-old is capable of asking, "May I please have some ice cream, Mom?" asking "cre, cre, mee, mee, plea, plea" although cute and creative is not likely to be reinforced with ice cream. The conventional request is more likely to be reinforced. In most homes and preschools, coloring within the lines, standing in line, stopping at red lights, crossing streets with the light and in the crosswalk, copying letters and numbers the same way they are printed, building conventional block structures, saying the alphabet from A to Z (vs. Z to A, or saying letters randomly), stating one's parent's name, address, and phone number in the correct (conventional) sequence, dressing conventionally (e.g., shoes over socks and not vice versa), and counting, are all differentially reinforced for being performed in their conventional, correct manner relative to nonconventional variations. In short, a lot, perhaps most of what is expected and reinforced in early childhood centers on behaving in socially approved, standard, conventional—that is, noncreative—ways.

If this learning did not occur, society would not be able to function. Society cannot have creativity in how and when pedestrians cross the street ("I cross when the light is yellow and stop when it's green"), in spelling ("The fone kaw aint four u"), or in counting ("1, 3, 5, 8, 2, 9, 10!"). Families must have certain conventions shaped and reinforced to function properly. (Children's "'no' means 'yes'" game is usually tolerated for only a short time, if at all, by most parents.) In short, much of our early life is spent learning how to behave conventionally and having conventional behaviors reinforced. As a result of this reinforcement process, conventional performance is differentially selected relative to nonconventional or creative performance. Given this reinforcement history, when subjects are given no indication to perform otherwise, it is not surprising that conventional, not creative, work is produced in typical experimental tasks supposedly designed to test creativity.

Not only is conventional, rather than creative, behavior differentially reinforced in childhood, but conventional behavior is more likely to be considered "good work" and "correct." Creative counting and spelling are "wrong," and not reinforced. Conventional spelling and counting are "correct," "good work," and reinforced. While some parents may attempt to reinforce creative artwork in their children, peers and siblings are more likely to reinforce conventional performances and tease or punish creative work. (The more my motorcycle drawings looked like real motorcycles the more compliments I got and the more my friends wanted a copy—which was very reinforcing. If my drawings were unrealistic I was teased.) By the time children reach grade school, conventional work is "correct," "good work." An art teacher who was my former student said that when her students make pictures of monsters, the first graders' work is very creative and original. But by the time children reach the fourth or fifth grade their work is very stereotyped and conventional. She finds it next to impossible to get these children to make monsters that do not resemble the conventional media monsters. Reinforcement of conventional behavior has selected conventional behavior. A "good monster picture" will resemble the monsters seen in the media; other monsters will be considered stupid or worse by one's peers. Given this standard history of reinforcement for conventional behavior and the equating of conventional work with "good work," it is not surprising that Amabile found that children who were given positive evaluations for paintings later made collages judged to be less creative but more organized than those of children given no evaluation (Hennessey & Amabile, 1988). Indeed, as Eisenberger and his colleagues argue, "These children may have concluded they were being evaluated positively for conventional performance and may have generalized this learning [to behave conventionally]" (Eisenberger et al., 1999, p. 312). "Decremental effects of reward on creativity appear to occur primarily when individuals do not discriminate the dependence of reward on creative performance and therefore respond conventionally" (p. 320).

Reinforcement does not automatically decrease creativity, but reinforcement selects whatever behavior(s) have produced reinforcing consequences in past similar contexts. In a context where a child's behavior is evaluated—a testing context—conventional behavior, not creative behavior, usually produces reinforcing consequences such as verbal praise ("That's right Honey"), other affection, high grades, tokens, or other conditioned reinforcers. Because, in the past, conventional behavior has been reinforced in evaluative contexts (testing situations), conventional behavior, not creative behavior, comes under the discriminative control of evaluative contexts (this is what is meant by the phrase "force of habit"). Experimental contexts are evaluative contexts (testing situations); therefore in experimental situations, conventional behavior, not creative behavior, is usually the result.

7

REINFORCEMENT
CREATES CREATIVITY

The analysis of both conventional and creative behavior as being cases of selected operant behavior, implies that given the proper reinforcement history, reinforcement would select creative behavior rather than conventional behavior if, in the past, creative behavior rather than conventional behavior had been reinforced.

As the phrase "starving artist" suggests, many artists do not receive much, or any, monetary compensation for their creative work, yet they continue in their creative endeavors. It is a mistake however to claim that these artists persist despite the lack of any reinforcement. Their creative work *is reinforced.* Monetary compensation is just one type of conditioned reinforcement. At the bare minimum, when a painter has a blank canvas and paints a picture, the picture painted is a consequence of painting. If, as a result of that painting, the painter paints on more canvases, then the picture was a *reinforcing consequence* of painting. Likewise, sound is a consequence of the behaviors of singing or playing a musical instrument. If the sounds produced by the singing or playing cause the singer or musician to make more sounds, then the sounds produced by the behaviors were reinforcers. This is true "intrinsic reinforcement." No contrived reinforcement is given. However the reinforcement does not "come from within" but is an *environmental consequence of the behavior-environment interaction.*

For even very successful artists, most paintings or songs may not result in reinforcement, contrived or natural. Yet the artist persists. Just as intermittent reinforcement produces highly persistent gambling behavior, if creative work is intermittently reinforced, the artwork is likely to persist despite many unreinforced attempts (see intermittent reinforcement in appendix 2 in this book). A pathological gambler continues to gamble although most gambles go unreinforced. The occasional reinforcer, a "win," maintains gambling in spite of many unreinforced gambles. Likewise, an artist may appear to be "addicted" to his craft, persisting even though most creative attempts are unsuccessful. If creative works are reinforced only after an unpredictable, variable number of attempts, the occasional reinforcer, a beautiful painting or song, will maintain the behavior despite many unreinforced attempts. Thus, while any particular creative attempt may not produce reinforcement, reinforcement nevertheless maintains the creative behaviors.

Unfortunately, for many artists, the natural consequences of their artwork is too intermittent and insufficient to maintain artistic behavior. No matter how beautiful a painting or how thrilling a story, if one cannot receive contrived reinforcement, that is, if one cannot sell one's work, one cannot be an artist for a living. "Starving artists" do not enjoy starving. Almost without exception, artists want enough compensation, contrived reinforcement, from their work to make a living. This "extrinsic reinforcement" does not "undermine intrinsic reinforcement" but adds to the total reinforcement for creativity. How can being paid a million dollars for a novel or a painting make the novel less thrilling or the painting less beautiful to look at? It doesn't! The contrived reinforcement further motivates creative work.

In an early demonstration that creativity could in fact be increased as a function of reinforcement, Elizabeth M. Goetz and Donald M. Baer (1973) showed that social reinforcement given contingent on constructing new forms, increased creative block construction. Social reinforcement for repeating forms decreased novel constructions. That is, reinforcement of creative performance increased creative performance; reinforcement of repeated forms, sameness, decreased creativity. Andrew S. Winston and Joanne E. Baker reviewed twenty studies that "treat creativity as operant behavior" (Winston & Baker, 1985, p. 191) and concluded that "taken together, the results of the studies reviewed here leave *little doubt* that behavioral [reinforcement] procedures can *effectively* alter a wide range of creative products with varied age groups" (p. 200, emphasis added).

Despite theses strong findings, Winston and Baker cautioned,

> the wider community may still object to the use of reinforcement training for creativity. The notions that creative activity must be "intrinsically motivated" and unconstrained by external evaluation are deeply held in our culture. If creativity is generally viewed as spontaneous "self-expression," then the notions of creativity and training through reinforcement may be seen as antithetical by educators and others involved in the supervision of children's creative activities." (Winston & Baker, 1985, p. 202)

Winston and Baker's caution is well founded. Indeed, in making the case for competition as a primary motive for creative action, Jock Abra noted that the humanists have the same concern: "The humanists' version has most influenced such domains as education. Creativity is a natural, healthy metaneed that everyone can, should and will achieve by actualizing their unique potentials, which are subtly voiced by intuitive impulses, . . . uninhibited spontaneity will bring out creative proclivities . . . environments presumably can only inhibit, not enhance it, by stifling impulse expression" (Abra, 1993, p. 323).

Conversely, in "Creating the Creative Artist," B. F. Skinner (1970/1999) saw the illogical implications and the ultimately pessimistic and fatalistic conclusion of the romantic humanist position. Skinner took the position that increasing creativity with reinforcement is promising, productive, and pragmatic:

> To become an artist [to become creative] is a form of learning. The "instruction" responsible for it may be entirely accidental. Can it be deliberate? Can we teach a person to be an artist? So far as technique goes, the answer is yes. And the fact is relevant to the present issue. The more competent the artist, the more reinforcing his work is likely to be. . . . [But Skinner asks rhetorically] can we actually teach an artist how to discover or invent new forms of beauty in the sense of new kinds of reinforcers?
>
> The easy answer is "no," and it is usually given by those who continue to regard artistic achievement as the expression of an inner life. Such a life is not directly within reach of a teacher; genius must be left to work its way out. *And if that is the nature of art*, then, apart from technique, *the teacher cannot teach*. . . . Moreover, he must think twice about teaching technique lest he interfere with untaught creative expression. *The position has the support of many educational philosophies* outside the field of art where *subject matter is abandoned* in order to strengthen an inquiring spirit. *The position is in essence a renunciation of teaching*[!] . . . But we do not need to abandon subject matter in order to teach. . . . It is not true that if we fill the student's head with facts he will be unable to think for himself. (Skinner, 1970/1999, p. 384, emphasis added)

Indeed, the more facts learned and the more material the student has to think with, the more his freedom to think for himself is increased with each new fact.

> Learning the techniques of others does not interfere with the discovery of techniques of one's own . . . on the contrary, the artist

who has acquired a variety of techniques from his predecessors is in the best possible position to make truly original discoveries. *And he is most likely to be original if he has been taught to do so.* (Skinner, 1970/1999, p. 384, emphasis added)

Skinner acknowledges the conflicting implications between the romantic, humanist position and the deterministic, reinforcement position:

The very assignment of producing a creative artist may seem contradictory. How can behavior be original or creative if it has been "produced"? Production presupposes some form of external control, but creativity, taken literally, denies such control. [It has been argued that] a behavior analysis of creativity is not only impossible but ludicrous, since novelty cannot arise in a "mechanistic" system. [But] A creative mind explains nothing. It is an appeal to the miraculous; mind is brought in to do what the body cannot do. But we must explain how the mind does it, and if we accept that assignment, we discover that we have merely restated our original problem in much more difficult terms. (Skinner, 1970/1995, p. 385)

The solution to the creativity problem is selection by reinforcement, selection of variations by the differential consequences produced by those variations. Painting on various types of media (e.g., paper, canvas, or wood); with various types of paint (oil, water, or acrylic based); using various types of brushes (horse hair, sponges, or fingers); and with various types of brush strokes (swift, narrow, broad, etc.) all are capable of producing a virtually infinite number of variations with different consequences for those variations. Indeed, just the combinations and permutations of these factors result in several dozen variations and the subject of the painting hasn't even been mentioned! The consequences of some variations will be more reinforcing than the consequences of other variations, and the artist will tend to make future works of art that are similar to the more reinforcing variations.

The reinforcing consequences of different variations select the artist's "style." If the creative artist were to remain indiscriminately variant, unaffected by the differential consequences of different variations, then it is unlikely we would call the work "creative," much less "important," or "significant." Instead the work is likely to be called "scattered," or "confused." Only novelty, not the criteria of utility, would likely be met. If creativity were not a function of reinforcement, then the cubism of Pablo Picasso, impressionism of Claude Monet, or stoicism of Hemingway would not be recognizable as such. Instead their cubism, impressionism, or stoicism would exist as a single variation among many variations, and subsequent works of creative activity would be unaffected by the consequences of previous creative activity. As a result, the work of any artist would be unrecognizable as the work of that artist (other than by signature). If creativity were not a function of naturalistic environmental consequences, but instead originated solely within the creator, then it is just as likely that a cubist work of art would have been produced by Ernest Hemingway or even Skinner as by Picasso! But each of these artists found that reinforcement within their respective creative domains and creativity is a function of reinforcement. The cubism of Picasso, impressionism of Monet, and stoicism of Hemingway are recognizable as such. Variations in their creative work exist within their cubism or impressionism or stoicism. Subsequent works of creative activity are affected by the consequences of previous creative activity.

Nevertheless, it could be argued that the more entrenched the artist becomes in his style, the more works can be identified as being produced by the particular artist, the *less creative* the artist becomes. The reinforcing consequences of working within a particular style restrict the creative artist from creating in other styles (e.g., maybe with environment independent creativity—an impossibility—Hemingway would have painted great works of art!). So, it may be argued, reinforcement undermines creativity after all. But, this predicament is resolved by recognition that creativity can be selected as an operant response class, that some "arena" or context (e.g., a vocation or hobby) of behavior must be selected and conventional behavior within that arena must first be selected, and often mastered, before meaningful creativity can occur, and by recognition that each individual has a unique reinforcement history.

THE OPERANT SELECTION OF CREATIVITY

Reinforcement can select creativity *as operant response classes*. In addition to the twenty studies evaluated by Winston and Baker (1985) that leave little doubt that reinforcement can increase creativity, recent findings by Robert Eisenberger and his co-workers strongly support the conclusion that creativity as an operant is selected by reinforcement contingencies.

In Eisenberger's prototypical creativity experiment (e.g., Eisenberger et al., 1999; Eisenberger, personal communication), children are reinforced (typically five cents for each correct response) for giving either conventional uses for common objects or unusual, creative uses for common objects. For example, a child in the conventional uses group would be shown a paper clip and asked to give the usual use for a paper clip, and verbal responses indicating that paper clips are used to clip papers together would be reinforced. But in the creative uses group, the child would be shown a paper clip and asked to give an unusual use. Answers indicating clipping papers together would not be reinforced. But all answers that indicated a creative use, such as "wear it as an earring," "pick a lock," or "use it as a mouse's antenna," would be reinforced. In other experiments, creativity training is conducted by reinforcing the generation of multiple words from strings of letters (e.g., Eisenberger & Selbst, 1994). Generating five different words requires more creativity than generating the same word five times.

The test phases of Eisenberger's experiments show that individuals reinforced for giving creative responses show increased creativity in completely unrelated tasks. Children are given a paper with circles on the paper. One circle may make the outline of a "happy face." The children are then asked to make pictures using the circles, and told that they can make other faces (conventional behavior) or other drawings. This test is adapted from the Torrance Tests of Creative Thinking (Torrance, 1965; see Eisenberger et al., 1999), and is widely recognized as a test of creativity by teachers.

Children given unusual uses training make more creative drawings. That is, children who have been reinforced for giving creative verbal responses make more creative drawings (Eisenberger & Armeli, 1997; Eisenberger et al., 1999; Eisenberger & Selbst, 1994). Children who were reinforced for giving conventional uses were more likely to draw more happy faces, sad faces, and so forth. But, children who were reinforced for giving unusual, creative uses for common objects were more likely to make pictures other than faces with the circles; for instance, eyeglasses, flowers, screwdriver tops, cups, spaceships, battle tanks, lamps, cars, and motorcycles.

In sum, Eisenberger's creativity research clearly shows that when creativity is reinforced, it is selected *as a generalized operant*. When creativity is reinforced in one context, it increases in totally new contexts. The practical implication of the reality that reinforcing creative behavior selects creativity is clear: If you want people to behave more creatively, reinforce creativity!

PARLOR GAMES VERSUS REALITY

This research could be criticized on the same grounds used to argue that reinforcement is inherently detrimental to creativity. That is, it could be argued that Eisenberger's creativity research is not a convincing demonstration that reinforcement can increase creativity; instead it is little more than a "parlor game." (I maintain that Eisenberger's work is a convincing demonstration that reinforcement can be used effectively to increase creativity. But readers are encouraged to read the primary source and come to their own conclusions.) Fortunately, Abra's and others' analyses of nonlaboratory creativity and Eisenberger's more recent research all point to the same conclusion: Creativity is a function of reinforcement. When creativity is reinforced, creativity is selected.

Eisenberger and Linda Rhoades (2001) found that reinforcing creative performance for one task (giving unusual uses) increased children's creativity in generating movie and short-story titles. This finding generalizes Eisenberger's results beyond the circle picture test to other completely different tasks. They found the same result with college students, thus showing that the conclusion that creativity can be selected with reinforcement applies to the behavior of young adults as well as children.

In the workplace as well as in the schoolhouse, reinforcement is positively related to creativity. Hundreds of employees of a large electronics and appliance chain were evaluated by Eisenberger and Rhoades and a positive relationship was found between reward for high performance (e.g., reinforcement contingent on productivity) and creativity at work. Furthermore, reinforcement, or pay contingent upon high performance, increased workers' perceived self-determination and intrinsic interest as well as creativity! "Contrary to the assertion that reward generally decreases intrinsic task interest, a positive relationship was found between performance-reward expectancies and creativity, as mediated by intrinsic job interest. . . . These findings are consistent with the view that extrinsic motivation in the form of expected reward for high performance leads to greater perceived self-determination over one's actions, contributing to intrinsic task interest and creativity" (Eisenberger & Rhoades, 2001, p. 735). In sum, employees who are reinforced for high performance are more interested in their jobs and more creative on the jobs. This reality is exactly what would be expected from a naturalistic, determinist understanding of reinforcement.

NECESSITY IS THE MOTHER OF INVENTION: THE CONTEXT OF CREATIVE BEHAVIOR

In his defense of competition as a motive for creative behavior, Abra points out that "great achievement" occurs within a field or discipline. Great achievement is almost invariably creative. If the work were not quality and were not novel, but just repetition of prior achievements, the work would not be called "great" or an "achievement." Therefore, as suggested by the phrase "standing on the shoulders of giants," *meaningful creativity* almost always occurs within a discipline where the conventional, existing, phenomenon of the discipline must first be mastered, or in the creator's repertoire, prior to any creative achievements. In such contexts, competition and reinforcement contingent on creativity are "omnipresent when creative work involves not parlor games played by students but professional prides *and livelihoods*" (Abra, 1993, p. 312, emphasis added). That is, "necessity is the mother of invention." Real-life, meaningful creativity is a function of reinforcement contingent upon professional-, or reputation-, based achievement. Furthermore, notes Abra, "a society that failed to recognize [reinforce] excellence would be both uncreative and boring" (p. 303).

Great creative achievement occurs not in a context-free, consequence-free environment for uninhibited "exploration and play," as advocated by Teresa M. Amabile, Edward L. Deci, Alfie A. Kohn, Richard Ryan, and the other romantics. Instead great creative achievement occurs in domain specific, demanding, consequence-contingent environments. This means that often a copious repertoire of conventional behavior and facts must be learned before any creative achievement occurs. Before creative achievement can occur in chemistry, physics, behavior analysis, or in any area, much of the existing knowledge must be mastered, and expertise in the standard, conventional, experimental methods must be mastered, or at least be familiar. Before advances in creative "experimental science" occur, the scientist must know the facts and procedures in the established, conventional, "textbook science."

Innovation requires knowledge of the conventional. I have a picture of a clown on my wall. It's a print of a painting by Picasso. It is not a "cubist" painting that Picasso is famous for, but is a realistic portrait of a man who is dressed as a clown and is holding a mask. He has a bittersweet, somewhat melancholic expression on his face. Before Picasso developed his cubist innovations, he mastered conventional painting.

A prerequisite for meaningful creativity, that is, creativity that advances a discipline or produces more and/or different reinforcers than previously experienced by the individual, is industriousness. As Eisenberger noted: "An increased . . . reward value of high effort [through reinforcement of effort] may encourage selection of, and persistence on, difficult academic tasks. Reinforced effort on dull, repetitive tasks can even be used to increase subsequent effort in intrinsically interesting tasks" (Eisenberger, 1992, p. 263). As Eisenberger's more recent research on creativity and Stephen King's life (see the next section) attest, these statements apply directly to creativity.

ACHIEVEMENT, INDUSTRIOUSNESS, AND CREATIVE GENIUS: PRODIGIES AND THE MYTH OF "NATURALS"

The popular belief that people are "naturals" that geniuses are born not made, is a myth. As Thomas Edison's quote, "genius is ten percent inspiration and ninety percent perspiration" suggests, great achievement of any type—including creativity—requires not context-free, consequence-free "uninhibited play," but *hard work*. Jazz great Charlie "Bird" Parker spent between eleven and fourteen hours a day during his adolescence practicing (National Public Radio interview played November 14, 2000). A great myth of creativity is that "beat" novelist Jack Kerouac wrote *On the Road* in three weeks during April 1951. The reality is quite different. "Kerouac was a fastidious, old-fashioned *craftsman*. For every day he spent "on the road" during his lifetime, gathering material, he toiled for a month in solitude" (Brinkley, 1998, p. 51, emphasis in original). No basketball player ever worked as hard in practice as Michael Jordan (Smith, 1999). Francis Crick and James D. Watson's discovery of the structure of DNA was a highly competitive race that required maintaining a brutal work schedule for years (Watson, 1968). Bruce Lee, who revolutionized the martial arts film industry and was known for his creative moves, would practice for over eight hours a day. Lee's *routine* included throwing 1,000 of the same basic straight punches each day. Current acrobatic martial arts film star Jackie Chan's training routine also included 1,000 punches and 500 kicks *daily* (Buchalter, 2001).

THE EXTRAORDINARY REQUIRES MASTERING THE ORDINARY

Before one can make creative innovations in a discipline, one must first master the existing conventional work of the discipline. This takes hard work and effortful persistence. It is an insult to say that great achievement and creative innovations "just come naturally," or that someone achieves because "he is a natural." Performance appears natural when performance is fluent. Fluent behavior is accurate high-rate behavior, and fluency is obtained by reinforcing repetitious responding (see chapter 1 in this book).

Before a diver, dancer, gymnast, or ice skater can make an innovation, a new creative skill, they must first master the existing skills. First a flip must be learned, then a double flip, in pike position, in layout position, and so forth. Not until contentional skills are fluent is the performer likely to produce an innovation. Creativity depends on mastery of the conventional. This is true for nonathletic behavior as well as athletic performance. Before an architect can produce innovative, creative buildings (ones that can stand, last, and have functional space at least), the architect must have working knowledge of geometry, physical engineering, and other prerequisite knowledge. Before a doctor can perform innovative, creative operating procedures, the doctor must first be fluent in conventional operating procedures. The doctor must know what are the strengths and weaknesses of the conventional procedures. It is unlikely that a patient would allow a doctor to attempt a creative procedure unless the patient was confident the doctor was fluent in the conventional procedures.

Once a creative innovation occurs, the *creative becomes the conventional*. Once the 'triple lux' was a creative innovation in figure skating. Now the 'triple lux' is a conventional move that must be mastered to reach the top level of the sport. Once artificial insemination was a creative innovation for fertility doctors. Now it is part of the conventional repertoire of all fertility doctors. Once only a few "creative" people, "wiz kids," were familiar with computers, the Internet, computer software, and computer programming. Now computer use is considered to be almost as vital in basic education as reading, writing, and math. Computer literacy is considered conventional knowledge. As more creativity occurs, more becomes conventional. The best way to obtain both conventional and creative performance and knowledge is with systematic reinforcement programs that utilize both natural (intrinsic) and contrived (extrinsic) reinforcement including copious praise and affection contingent upon effort and achievement.

PRODIGIES

Without many repetitions Jordan probably would have been able dunk a basketball. But millions of American kids can dunk a basketball. Dunking is ordinary. What made Michael Jordan *Michael Jordan* was his *constant, consistent* effortful persistent reinforced practice (D. Smith, 1999). Without his work ethic, which was developed with reinforced effort, Jordan would have been just one of millions of people who can dunk a basketball. There were hundreds of naturalists, but what made Charles Darwin *Charles Darwin* was his constant, consistent, effortful, persistent reinforced work (Desmond & Moore, 1991). What made George Patton a great general, what made Henry Ford a creative industrialist was consistent, effortful, persistent reinforced work (Eisenberger, 1989).

Prodigies are made, not born. Michael J. A. Howe of Exeter University, England, spent over seven years studying "innate" talent, especially in musicians. But ironically, he found NO evidence of innate talent or creative genius. Instead he found that it takes "thousands of hours of lonely, boring, solitary concentration to become a good musician. That is not something children and teenagers are naturally keen to do." The most critical factor in becoming a good musician, according to Howe's research findings, is parental support and encouragement (praise and reinforcement). Indeed, usually the fast progress of career concert pianists is a product of "vigorous encouragement." Likewise, mathematicians show "very few early signs of exceptional promise prior to deliberate parental encouragement" (Howe et al., 1998, p. 404). Without parental encouragement, creative success early in life, much less during childhood, is very unlikely. Howe and his co-researchers found that "even among highly successful young musicians, the majority freely admit that without strong parental encouragement to practice they would never have done the amounts of regular practicing needed to make good progress. *Strong and sustained parental encouragement to practice was evident in virtually all successful young musicians*" (p. 406, emphasis added).

Howe's research over the last decade involving hundreds of "gifted" children, teenagers, and their parents, examining the factors responsible for high achievement and creative genius has produced results that support the reinforcement account of creative achievement, not the romantic account. High achievement requires *technical* practice. Formal effortful practice determines musical achievement (Sloboda et al., 1996). Most gifted students did not show any particular signs of promise, but their parents took an active role in *supervising* and *encouraging* progress (Sloboda & Howe, 1991). "Effortless" performances are the result of years of hard work (Howe, 1990). There is no evidence of natural ability, and no one has ever obtained great achievements without a long period of intense and careful preparation (Howe, 1990).

Case in point—contrary to popular belief and portrayals, *Mozart was no "natural."* Furthermore, both Mozart and the Beatles' (Paul McCartney and John Lennon) "creative" music writing and performance came only after years of practicing existing conventional music. According to Robert W. Weisberg of Temple University, Mozart's first seven works produced between the ages of 11 and 16 were not actually Mozart's but arrangements of others' works. The first "masterwork" (No. 9) was written years later. "Mozart, then 21, had been immersed in music for 16 years, and had worked in the genre for 10 years. Thus, in Mozart's case," says Weisberg, " the preparation years were filled with learning from practice, in the sense of immersion in the works of others, rather than the simple out flowing of innate talent" (Weisberg, 1998, p. 430). Similarly before the Beatles' first song, Lennon and McCartney had put in over 1,200 hours in performance alone, augmented by practice sessions. "In addition," says Weisberg, "the performances themselves were much like practice, because their early repertoire consisted mainly of very faithful cover versions of works of other performers" (p. 430). Through repetitive practice, the Beatles mastered the conventional before the creative.

In an interview on National Public Radio (1997, September 23) celebrating Ray Charles's fifty years in recording, interviewer Robert Siegel asked the acclaimed artist, "You practice a lot?" Charles answered, "Whenever I can. . . . I don't practice as much as I would like to. . . . I practice things like scales and chords and movement of my hands and things like that. . . . What I'm practicing for is to try to improve what I might play." The extraordinary requires mastering the ordinary.

Uninhibited opportunities for exploration and play in context-free, consequence-free situations, in addition to being a realistic impossibility, do not produce achievement or creativity as the romantics and humanists argue. In fact, children who are not given boundaries and limits on their behaviors are at risk of developing anxiety problems (Heckhausen, 1967). The reality is that early praise, encouragement, and supervision emerge as powerful determiners of future achievement and creativity. (But adults who did not have a supportive childhood, given the proper circumstances, are still capable of creative achievements [Howe, 1990].) The power of praise cannot be overly stressed because the effects of praise on shaping behavior are immense.

Theodore Roosevelt's childhood sickness, his recovery, and his subsequent lifelong quest for physical conquest are directly traceable to the influence of early affection, praise, and encouragement from his parents, particularly from his father. Roosevelt suffered from childhood asthma and his "parents tried everything they could think of. . . . When the fits came, the only thing they could do was hold him, walk him around, and try to comfort him . . . this chore fell to his father," according to biographer H.W. Brands. "As a result," Brands continues, "the boy came to associate the attacks—unconsciously, to be sure—with a opportunity to receive his father's undivided attention" (Brands, 1997, p. 10). That is, Roosevelt's childhood asthma attacks were positively reinforced with his father's attention. "It definitely didn't escape his notice that during his attacks he became the center of his father's world. [The other children] could wait. . . . His father would bundle him in blankets and take him for a fast ride through the darkened streets of Manhattan—a thrill the young child could appreciate" (p. 11). When asthma attacks are reinforced with a very busy, but very loved parent's undivided attention and affection, all other things being equal, the attacks increase in frequency. Because Roosevelt's father reinforced his asthma attacks with attention and affection, not only did the attacks increase, but the reinforced response (sickness) generalized to other ailments—toothaches, headaches, and intestinal problems (p. 23). Roosevelt also noted that his sisters became sicker when being sick was reinforced with parental attention. "Conie was sick but her sickness always decreased when Mama was out of the room and she could not be peted (sic)," Roosevelt wrote in his journal (from Brands, p. 23).

To clear Teddy's lungs, Roosevelt's father would take him for walks in the fresh air and would praise and encourage him to keep up. Thus, Roosevelt's father also began to encourage and praise his son's physical accomplishments. "'Theodore' [his father said], 'You must make your body. It is hard drudgery to make one's body, but I know you will do it.' The young boy, adoring his father and naturally craving his approval, responded to the challenge. 'I'll make my body,' he vowed. So began a course of physical exercise that continued for the rest of Roosevelt's life" (Brands, 1997, p. 26). As Roosevelt's childhood story illustrates, if parental attention occurs only as a consequence of childhood sickness, then increased sickness is a probable result. But equally important and more promising is that parental encouragement and praise for achievement and effort can help produce great achievement.

Indeed, adult attention and praise was in no small part responsible for Charles Darwin's career as a naturalist that culminated in his theory of natural selection. "Charles's education began at home, with his sister Caroline . . . taking charge. He competed for her affection. . . . He was an attention-seeker; *he wanted praise*," according to biographers Adrian Desmond and James Moore (Desmond & Moore, 1991, pp. 12–13). "He was an inveterate collector and hoarder—shells, postal franks, birds' eggs, and minerals. They were trophies, *piled up for praise*" (p. 13, emphasis added). Had Darwin received disapproval for his trophies, or had they gone ignored, he may have never collected the necessary evidence for the theory of natural selection. Darwin's early collecting behavior was a successive approximation, reinforced with praise and attention, of his later scientific behavior. Had the former not been reinforced, the latter would not have been possible. Darwin would "do anything at school 'for the pure pleasure of exciting attention & surprise'. . . . He told tall tales about natural history, reported strange birds, and boasted of being able to change the color of flowers" (p. 13). Darwin "relished his father's approval" (p. 21) and worked hard to receive it. As Darwin matured, in addition to his collecting, he became an avid hunter—keeping track of the number of kills and the variety of game shot for the admiration of others. The praise Darwin received for his early natural science endeavors encouraged further work. At a meeting of the Wernerian Natural History Society, while still a student, Darwin unraveled the mystery behind black bodies in oyster shells, correctly identifying them as eggs from leeches. This finding was published by one of Darwin's early mentors who "congratulated his 'zealous young friend Mr. Charles Darwin' for his discovery" (p. 37). Thus, further approximations toward great scientific achievement were reinforced with praise and recognition. As Desmond and Moore's biography documents, Darwin's great works—*On the Origin of the species by Means of Natural Selection* (1859); *The Expression of Emotions in Man and Animals* (1872); and *The Descent of Man, and Selection in Relation to Sex* (1871); just to name a few—did NOT originate within a creator or as products of uninhibited exploration and play acting on momentary whims. No, Darwin's great works were a product of reinforcing successive approximations of scientific behavior with praise during childhood and a lifetime of painstaking effortful detailed, environment-contingent hard work.

While often not recognized as such, several of today's business practices, both those hated and those admired, were once *creative innovations* of John D. Rockefeller Sr. Like those of Roosevelt and Darwin, Rockefeller's adult endeavors and achievements are directly traceable to early childhood encouragement and attention. Microsoft's attempt to bundle its Internet Explorer with its Windows operating system, found guilty of violating anticompetitive laws, was just a mild imitation of Standard Oil's horizontal and vertical monopoly of the oil industry. Without Rockefeller's *creative* innovative methods of eliminating competition—secretly owning "competing" companies, selling product below cost to bankrupt the competition, merging with competition to cooperatively manipulate the market, "kickbacks," or forming trusts "in the restraint of trade"—many of today's antitrust laws and regulations would not be in existence according to biographer Ron Chernow. For Rockefeller's father taught him "that you were entitled to outwit the other fellow by any means, fair or foul" (Chernow, 1998, p. 25).

Developed to govern the immense trust and shield the plutocracy from personal legal accountability, the executive committee and subcommittee structure standard in business today was a creative innovation of Rockefeller and his cronies at Standard Oil. "The committee system was an *ingenious* adaptation" (Chernow, 1998, p. 229, emphasis added). Furthermore, while the trust eliminated competition between companies, Standard Oil's committees ensured productivity by reinforcing competitive gains of its units. "The committees encouraged rivalry among local units by circulating performance figures and encouraging them to compete for records and prizes [reinforcers]" (p. 229).

Rockefeller's interests were money and serving the Baptist Church, both shaped in early childhood by parental encouragement and supervision. Also because of parental encouragement, Rockefeller saw these interests, not in conflict, but as complementary. His mother "*encouraged* the children to drop pennies into the collection plate: Rockefeller later cited his mother's altruism as the genesis of his philanthropy. Early in life *he learned* that God wanted his flock to earn money and then donate money in a never-ending process. *"I was trained* from the beginning to work and save,'" Rockefeller explained. "I have always regarded it as a religious duty to get all I could honorably and to give all I could. *I was taught* that way by the minister when I was a boy." The low-church Baptists didn't prohibit the accumulation of wealth" (Chernow, 1998, p. 19, emphasis added). Rockefeller's father once gave John five dollars to read the Bible, "creating an early association between god and money" (p. 18).

Rockefeller's parental encouragement and "extrinsic" reinforcers did not undermine his interests but only magnified them, as would logically be expected to occur:

> Even as a boy, he bought candy by the pound, divided it into small portions, then sold it at a tidy profit to his siblings. By age seven, encouraged by his mother, he was dropping gold, silver, and copper coins that he earned into a blue china bowl on the mantel. John's first business coup came at age seven when he shadowed a turkey hen as it waddled off into the woods, raided its nest, and raised the chicks for sale. To spur [reinforce] his enterprise, Eliza [his mother] gave him milk curds to feed the turkeys, and the next year he raised an even larger brood. As an old man, Rockefeller said, 'To this day, I enjoy the sight of a flock of turkeys, and never miss an opportunity of studying them.' (Chernow, p. 17)

These experiences did not undermine Rockefeller's interest in business or even in turkeys as the opponents of reinforcement would claim. Instead these events increased his enjoyment and interest in both business and turkeys (even as an "old man")! Likewise, work did not undermine Rockefeller's freedom but increased his feelings of freedom. At his first job Rockefeller found that "Work enchanted him, work liberated him, work supplied him with a new identity" (Chernow, 1998, p. 47). Work increased Rockefeller's freedom.

The early association between money—"extrinsic reward"—and the church never undermined Rockefeller's interest in the Baptist Church. Instead, the church provided Rockefeller with other important reinforcers. "The church gave Rockefeller the community of friends *he craved* and the respect and affection *he needed*" (Chernow, 1998, p. 51, emphasis added). Rockefeller's childhood training in giving was a successive approximation of lifelong philanthropic activities. At his first job "the young clerk donated about 6 percent of his wages to charity" (p. 50). Spelman College, the first black female institution of higher education in Georgia, was made possible by donations from Rockefeller. In fact, the founders offered to name the college after Rockefeller. But he insisted that it be named after abolitionist Lucy Spelman. Similarly, the University of Chicago would never have come into existence if it were not for the philanthropic donations from Rockefeller. Even today, much of what is seen on public television is "made possible by a grant from the John D. Rockefeller Foundation." Indeed, charitable foundations are another *creative innovation* of Rockefeller. He wanted to give his money systematically and objectively to causes that would result in the most long-term good. But, besieged by requests, it became impossible for him to study the merits of each cause. Thus, *out of necessity*, not a momentary whim, or exploration and play, the creative solution of systematic giving by foundations was developed.

Like the lives of Darwin and Roosevelt, Rockefeller's life reveals that early reinforcement of particular behaviors—in Rockefeller's case making money and philanthropy—shape lifelong behavioral tendencies. This knowledge is neither good nor bad, but reality. But like other knowledge, it can be used for good or evil. If the knowledge that early reinforcement of particular behaviors shapes lifelong behavioral tendencies is used to develop philanthropy and altruism, most argue that is good. But early training can also be used to shape behavioral tendencies, such as theft and deceit, which most hold as evil. Nevertheless, once these behavioral tendencies have been shaped, *creative* innovations occur when the situation demands them and the innovations result in reinforcement. Creative innovations do not occur in times of uninhibited play in a context-free, consequence-free environment. In such situations there is no need to be creative or innovative.

CREATIVITY CONCLUSION: THE STRANGELY ORDINARY CASE OF STEPHEN KING

Stephen King is the best-selling author of over thirty-five novels and numerous shorter pieces—thrillers, horror stories, science fiction, and tales of boyhood friendship. Many of King's works have been made into blockbuster movies—*The Shining* (starring Jack Nicholson), *The Green Mile* (starring Tom Hanks), *The Running Man* (starring Arnold Schwarzenegger), *Carrie*, and *Stand by Me*, to name just a few. It would be hard to find anyone who has produced more prolifically, originally, or *creatively* than Stephen King. His book *On Writing: A Memoir of the Craft* (2000), both a memoir and writing instruction-suggestion book provides an opportunity to examine the effects of contrived reinforcers—"extrinsic rewards"—and intrinsic interest on creative output, the effects of contingent praise on creativity, and to weigh the relative truth of the romantic-humanist account of creativity versus the pragmatic behavioral reinforcement account.

Intrinsic Rewards

Romantics may point to the concluding comments of King's book to argue that, for King at least, writing is a product of intrinsic interest, not extrinsic rewards or contrived reinforcement:

> *Do you do it for the money honey?* The answer is no. Don't now and never did. Yes, I've made a great deal of dough from my fiction, but I never set a single word down on paper with the thought of being paid for it. . . . I have written because it fulfilled me. Maybe it paid off the mortgage on the house and got the kids through college, but those things were on the side—I did it for the buzz. I did it for the pure joy of the thing." (King, 2000, pp. 248–249, italics in original)

No clearer statement for intrinsic interest could be made. However, much in the preceding 248 pages of King's book contradicts this claim. When millions have already been made and any work is guaranteed to earn millions of dollars, it may be easy to say it is not the money. But before the millions came, as King earlier reveals, money was much more than "on the side." To be sure, money is just a token, worthless in and of itself. But because money is a generalized, conditioned reinforcer, exchangeable for an infinite variety of backup reinforcers, money becomes a very valuable token. So, if we take King's statement to be true that he did not write for the money, he may have written and in fact did write for other reinforcers that money is associated with (praise, attention, and acclaim) or exchangeable for (health care, medicine, and food).

To summarize the romantic humanist viewpoint: *all* external constraints and influences hamper creativity. Free exploration, uninhibited play, and momentary whims—all consequence free—are necessary to maximize creativity. Work, effort, repetitions, and punishing or reinforcing consequences of any type damage creativity. And of course, "all extrinsic rewards undermine intrinsic interest." Conversely, the behavioral reinforcement viewpoint holds that creativity is a product of reinforcement of creativity, that creativity comes after mastery of the conventional that is a function of effort, practice, and reinforced repetitions. As revealed in "On Writing," *Stephen King's creative life is the prototype of the behavioral reinforcement account.*

Work

According to King, creative writing is a product of work, of effort, of practice. Creative writing is a "learned skill." "At its most basic we are only discussing *a learned skill*, but do we agree that sometimes *the most basic skills can create things* far beyond our expectations?" (p. 137, emphasis added). In describing a poem by his soon-to-be wife, King claimed there was "a work-ethic in the poem that I liked, something that suggested *writing poems (or stories, or essays) had as much in common with sweeping the floor as with mythy moments of revelation* (King, 2000, p. 65, emphasis added). Indeed, persistence, dogged determination, is necessary for creative work. Because even if there is "intrinsic interest" in the work generally, to produce creative works, it is often necessary to suffer through periods when the work is not enjoyable. This happened to King several times while working on *Carrie*, the novel that would transform his life. According to King, "Stopping a piece of work just because it's hard, either emotionally or imaginatively, is a bad idea. Sometimes you have to go on when you don't feel like it, and sometimes you're doing good work when it feels like all you're managing is to shovel shit from a sitting position" (pp. 77–78). Effort, practice, and mastery of the conventional are necessary for creative writing, according to King: "Good writing consists of mastering the fundamentals" (p. 142). "If you don't want to work your ass off, you have no business trying to write well. . . . You have to do all the grunt labor" (p. 144). "If you want to be a writer, you must do two things above all others: read a lot and write a lot. There's no way around these two things that I'm aware of, no shortcut. . . . There is a learning process going on" (p. 145). Creative writing is "just another job like laying pipes or driving long-haul trucks" (p. 157). "You can only learn by doing" (p. 173). "The skill necessary [for creative work] comes from *years of practice*; the art comes from a creative imagination which is *working hard* and having fun" (p. 185, emphasis added). For good storytelling "practice is invaluable" (p. 195). The extraordinary requires mastering the ordinary.

Reinforcing Successive Approximations with Praise and Money: "Extrinsic Rewards"

King's opinions and suggestions come from his life experiences that reveal that the practice—the hard work—necessary for creativity is shaped and selected by a lifetime of reinforcement for that work. As a sick child, spending most of a year in bed, King read "approximately six tons of comic books" (King, 2000, p. 27). Then he "began to write [his] own stories. *Imi-*

tation preceded creation; I would copy comics . . . word for word" (p. 27, emphasis added). Thus, just like those of Mozart and the Beatles, King's creative behaviors started as mere copying of others' work. This noncreative, very unimaginative behavior was nevertheless a successive approximation of mastering the conventional and becoming creative. Additionally, King's copying resulted in very powerful social reinforcement, praise from his mother. "Eventually I showed one of these copycat hybrids to my mother, *and she was charmed*—I remember her slightly amazed smile . . . *and I absolutely loved it"* (p. 28, emphasis added).

However, when she learned that the stories were merely copied, some of her affection was withdrawn and she suggested that King write his own stories. Thus King's creative writing began with a prompt—parental encouragement—not as a momentary whim during a period of uninhibited play and exploration. Furthermore, the resulting creative writing resulted in very powerful extrinsic reinforcers, parental attention, praise, and *money*! "I eventually wrote a story about four magic animals who rode around in an old car, helping out little kids," writes King. "When I finished, I gave it to my mother, who sat down in the living room, put her pocketbook on the floor beside her, and read it all at once. I could tell she liked it—she laughed in all the right places" (King, 2000, pp. 28–29)—immediate parental attention, a powerful positive reinforcer. King's creative writing was further reinforced with praise. "She said it was good enough to be in a book. Nothing anyone has said to me since has made me feel any happier." Proof that this praise functioned as a positive *reinforcer* for creative behavior is seen in King's next statement. "I wrote four more stories about Mr. Rabbit Trick and his friends" (p. 29).

These stories were also reinforced with money. "She gave me a quarter apiece for them and sent them around to her sisters. . . . Four stories. A quarter apiece. That was the first buck I made in the business" (King, 2000, p. 29). Thus, although he claims he never wrote for money, it is clear that for King from an early age, money functioning as a *conditioned* reinforcer was strongly associated with attention, praise, and love. Clearly these reinforcers produced "joy" and "buzz" for King. Both praise and money continued to reinforce successive approximations toward successful creative writing. Although many of King's early submissions of stories to magazines were rejected, handwritten notes, praise from editors, reinforced his efforts. "This is good. Not for us, but good. You have talent. Submit again," wrote one editor. "Those four brief sentences," explained King, "brightened the dismal winter of my sixteenth year" (p. 41). King "came to relish any little personal dash [reinforcing attention and praise] on these printed pink-slips. They were few and far between, but when they came they never failed to lighten my day and put a smile on my face" (p. 222).

In addition to his creative attempts, through uncreative plagiarism and newspaper reporting, King continued to master the conventional—reinforced all the while with money and praise. After viewing a horror movie, King simply typed out a "novel version" of the book and *sold it* at his high school. Earning nine dollars, quite a lot at the time for a high school student, King "was walking around in a kind of dream, unable to believe [his] sudden ascension to previously unsuspected realms of wealth" (King, 2000, p. 49). If money was not a powerful reinforcer, if money didn't matter, if extrinsic rewards undermined intrinsic interest, if conventional behavior prevented later creative behavior, then King never would have plagiarized the movie in the first place, much less sold copies at school. Undoubtedly, the fact that his high school peers bought the book shows that the writing was reinforced with peer attention that further strengthened the association between money and social reinforcement.

Not surprisingly, plagiarizing a horror movie and selling copies at school was not viewed favorably by school officials. Nevertheless, they further reinforced King's writing efforts by helping him land a job reporting sports at the local newspaper. The editor "promised me a wage of half a cent a word. It was the first time someone had promised me wages for writing" (King, 2000, p. 56). This "expected reward" did not undermine King's interest in writing as opponents of systematic reinforcement would suggest. Far from it. Instead, he attributes his work at the newspaper as some of his most important training (pp. 56-58). The creative comes from mastering the conventional. Ernest Hemingway also honed his craft writing for a newspaper, *The Kansas City Star*. In addition to writing for the local newspaper, King and his brother as children produced their own newspapers at home that *they sold* to neighbors, relatives, and friends. Beat writer Jack Kerouac did the same. Thus, some of the most creative writers of the twentieth century shaped their craft by writing conventionally on conventional topics for which they were paid money—a contrived, extrinsic reinforcer.

The conditioned reinforcer, money, continued to select King's creative writing as he matured. Following high school, still writing for the newspaper for money and working in a textile mill, King heard about rats that were "big as cats" that he turned into a story that sold for two hundred dollars. In "a single stroke. It took my breath away, it did. I was rich" (King, 2000, p. 60). Money reinforces creative writing. While money is a vital conditioned reinforcer, direct praise and encouragement from loved ones is also sometimes necessary to sustain work, necessary to reinforce effort. King received this social reinforcement first from his mother, then his wife. "My wife made a crucial difference. . . . Her support was a constant. . . . Writing is a lonely job. Having someone who believes in you makes a lot of difference" (pp. 73–74). Indeed, King had given up on *Carrie*, throwing away what he had written. However, his wife retrieved the papers from the trash and reinforced his creative efforts. "She wanted me to go on with it. . . . She had her chin tilted down and was smiling in that severely cute way of hers. 'You've got something here,' she said, 'I really think you do'" (p. 77).

While praise and support is vital, selling the creative work, making money is the big deal behind creative writing. Not the money in and of itself, but money as the conditioned, generalized reinforcer. Money that means the behavior is approved. Money that is and always has been associated with praise and affection. Money that can be exchanged for other valuables. Money that can pay the bills. King also suggests that money, as a reinforcing consequence of writing and selling stories resulted in sexual intimacy with his wife—a powerful reinforcer for most men. When King sold a story that he didn't believe he would be able to sell, "the check was for five hundred dollars, easily the largest sum I'd ever received. Suddenly we were able to afford not only a doctor's visit and a bottle of THE PINK STUFF [Peptol Bismol], but also a nice Sunday-night meal. And I imagine that once the kids were asleep, Tabby and I got friendly" (King, 2000, p. 71). Money, money, money, a powerful generalized reinforcer. Very useful in selecting creative work. When King's wife told him that *Carrie* had been sold for $2,500, she was "out of breath but deliriously happy" (p. 83). Selling novels for money did not undermine King's or his wife's intrinsic interest in writing; no, it added value to writing. When *Carrie* sold as a paperback for $400,000 both King and his wife were overjoyed, speechless, and cried tears of joy—intrinsic interest intact.

External constraints and influences did not hamper King's creativity but occasioned his creativity. Free exploration, uninhibited play, and momentary whims consequence free did not result in creativity. Work, effort, repetitions, and reinforcing consequences are responsible for King's creative writing. Clearly, "extrinsic rewards" added value to King's "intrinsic interest" in creative writing. There is absolutely *no* suggestion that the millions earned, the "extrinsic rewards," in any way undermined intrinsic interest. King's creativity is a product of reinforcement of creativity; it came after mastery of the conventional, which is a function of effort, practice, and reinforced repetitions.

Finally, it is obvious that the money did not undermine King's intrinsic interest in creativity. While King may not write for the money as he claims (and contradicts), in describing the fictional case of "Frank" a beginning writer, compiled from three nonfictional friends, King makes it clear that money is in fact a powerful reinforcer for creative writers, largely owing to its association with social reinforcement—praise, attention and acclaim:

Frank gets his first acceptance letter—oh happy day. . . . For twenty-five dollars plus a dozen cc's—contributor's copies. Frank is of course, delirious; way past Cloud Nine. . . . Twenty-five bucks won't pay the rent, won't even buy a week's worth of groceries for Frank and his wife, but it's a validation of his ambition, and that—any newly published writer would agree, I think—is priceless: *Someone wants something I did! Yippee!* Nor is that the only benefit. It is a *credit*. (King, 2000, p. 241, emphasis in original).

Money reinforces successive approximations of creativity. There can be seemingly magical outcomes of hard work but other than the magic of positive reinforcement, there is nothing magical about the process.

8

THE MYTH THAT IMITATION AND INSTRUCTION FOLLOWING INVALIDATE REINFORCEMENT THEORY

Particularly popular among college psychology instructors is the myth that the existence of imitation or "observational learning" (also referred to as "social learning theory") invalidates reinforcement theory or at the very least proves that reinforcement is unnecessary for observational learning. Because the myth that reinforcement is not involved in, or important for imitation is often presented as fact, usually during students' first exposure to the concept of reinforcement, this myth may be particularly damaging to both the advancement of psychology as a science and to students' understanding of observational learning or understanding reinforcement itself. In introductory psychology textbooks the chapter on learning almost always follows the same general format. A few introductory remarks emphasize the importance of learning in psychology. At this point there is little disagreement that almost all behaviors, from taking an exam, to driving, to sex, to shoplifting, to the binge-purge behaviors of bulimics, all involve learning. These remarks are followed by a discussion of classical, respondent, or Pavlovian conditioning (although very important, this form of learning is not the subject of this book). The section on classical conditioning is usually followed by coverage of operant conditioning or reinforcement theory, followed by observational learning or "social learning theory." The textbook may then present information on how these three classes of learning—classical conditioning, operant conditioning, and social learning—are interrelated in many cases of actual behavior (e.g., seeing a sign for a steak house increases my insulin release and salivation, which is classical conditioning. I see others going into the restaurant and leaving the restaurant looking content, which is involved in observational-social learning. And in the past, eating at that restaurant was enjoyable or reinforcing. As a product of these three factors I go to eat in that restaurant).

However, in virtually every textbook, the sections on social learning argue that because people can learn by observation when reinforcement is *supposedly* not operating, reinforcement is unnecessary, or not involved at all in observational or social learning. This is wrong. The myth is typically supported either by studies showing animals that may imitate without apparent reinforcement, or by studies showing children imitating without apparent reinforcement (e.g., Bandura et al., 1963). While this approach is typical and may be sufficiently convincing evidence to present in an introductory textbook, it is actually wrong to do so because limited evidence is used to present an erroneous conclusion. Furthermore, readers who conclude that reinforcement is unnecessary for observation learning and attempt to teach using observational learning may have disappointing results.

The natural history—the evolution—of an organism is a process of selection of advantageous variations. Often, an organism that would imitate the behaviors of a conspecific or other similar species would have an evolutionary advantage over organisms that did not tend to imitate. For example, a wild dog that imitated other wild dogs that ran away from lions and ran after new born zebras to eat would be at an evolutionary advantage over a wild dog that did not imitate running in these situations. To the extent that "the ability to imitate" a particular type of behavioral flexibility can be genetically represented, over successive generations wild dogs that imitated would be differentially selected. Thus, the *tendency* to imitate may be selected. This analysis may also suggest that reinforcement is unnecessary for observational learning. Similarly, numerous studies with children and college students study imitation without apparent reinforcement, suggesting that reinforcement is unnecessary for observational learning.

Indeed, I start my lectures on *imitation as a generalized operant response* by making circles with my thumbs and first fingers; then I invert my hands and place the circles over my eyes making a very silly-looking face. Then I ask the students to do the same. Most do; most imitate. Then I ask how many have ever done that before. Most have not. The students just learned to make a new silly face by imitating without apparent reinforcement.

However, the students imitated only because they have a *history of reinforcement for imitation*. Beginning in infancy and continuing throughout their lives, almost all children are reinforced for imitating their parents and teachers—from learning to speak, to forming letters, to shooting basketballs, to heating compounds in chemistry class. In the game "follow the leader," for example, children are also reinforced by peers for imitating and probably the earliest reinforcement of imitation is the infant game of peek-aboo! Thus, by the time people reach college they have been reinforced thousands of times for imitating, particularly for imitating their teachers. Therefore, although a particular instance of imitation may occur without being reinforced, imitation occurred only because *in the past imitation has been reinforced.* Imitation is selected as a generalized operant response.

Because many different behaviors are modeled, imitated, and subsequently reinforced, rather than the particular behaviors imitated, *imitation per se is selected as an operant.* For example, when a parent shows a child how to wipe the table and kisses the child when he imitates wiping the table both wiping the table *and imitating have been reinforced.* When a child watches his brother turn on the television and later does the same and is reinforced by the programs watched, then turning on the television *and imitating have been reinforced.* After thousands of these instances, imitation becomes a very strong operant, and because imitation per se, not just the particular behaviors imitated, is selected, imitation becomes a powerful way to teach and learn new behaviors. Because of this history of reinforcement for imitation, as is the case with partial reinforcement generally, it is not necessary for each instance of imitation to be reinforced. Thus, it may appear that imitation was not reinforced, and it may not have been, in that instance. But that does not mean that there isn't a lifetime's history of reinforcement for imitation (there almost always is).

Furthermore, imitation as an operant comes under strong discriminative stimulus control. For example, during my lectures if a class "trouble-maker" had made a silly face, it is unlikely that most of the class would have imitated and made the same face. Imitation in the classroom usually is under stimulus control. Teacher behaviors are often imitated (especially when accompanied by instructions to do so), because *in the past, imitating instructed teacher behaviors has been reinforced.* Because in the past imitating troublemakers has not been reinforced, or has been punished, imitation of troublemakers is less likely to be reinforced.

In an early experimental demonstration of imitation as an operant, Neil Miller and John Dollard (1941) showed that when a child "follower" was reinforced by finding a piece of candy where another child, the "leader," found a piece of candy, the follower imitated the leader. When a follower was not reinforced, found no candy where the leader had found a piece of candy, the follower child stopped imitating. Miller and Dollard's simple experiment clearly shows an important point: when imitation is reinforced, imitation occurs; when imitation is not reinforced, imitation extinguishes. Imitation is an operant response, just as saying "please," or pressing a lever may be operant responses. Yet because different particular behaviors may be imitated, including those that the imitator have never seen or performed before, imitation is a particularly powerful and useful operant response.

Males are more likely to imitate males and females are more likely to imitate females. Imitators are more likely to imitate a model that was reinforced than a model that was not reinforced or that was punished. Social learning theorists make the false claim that reinforcement cannot account for these observations (see Mazur, 1998 for a summary of this argument, and a clear presentation of imitation as operant behavior). But, in fact, reinforcement, or more specifically differential reinforcement, is the reason for these observations.

When an individual is initially learning to imitate the behaviors of others, imitating models who are reinforced, imitating models who are punished, and imitating models who were not obviously reinforced or punished for their behavior, may all be equally likely. However, in all but the most bizarre environments, an imitator is most likely to be reinforced when imitating a model who was reinforced. An imitator is least likely to be reinforced when imitating a model who was punished. As a result of *the imitator*'s history of reinforcement for imitating models who are reinforced, and history of nonreinforcement for imitations of nonreinforced models, whether or not imitation occurs depends on the consequences received by the model.

For example, before imitating comes under the discriminative control of the consequences to the model, a child may watch his older sibling throw mud on the wall and receive a time-out. The child may imitate mud throwing and also receive a time-out as a consequence of imitating the behavior. The child may see his older sibling clean his room and be reinforced with a hug and other affection. The child may then imitate this behavior and also receive reinforcing affection. Eventually, after more instances similar to these, when the child sees his older sibling perform a behavior and receive a time-out for the behavior, the child will be less likely to imitate the behavior modeled by his older sibling. Similarly, when the child sees his older sibling perform a reinforced behavior, the child will be more likely to imitate the behavior modeled by his older sibling. Imitation is more likely when the model's behavior is reinforced because in the past when the imitator has imitated a model's reinforced behavior, the imitator's behavior was also reinforced. In an operant reinforcement analysis, the consequences to the model are important only to the extent that they are discriminative for the probable consequences of the imitator's behavior.

Differential consequences, *to the imitator* are also a major reason why same sex imitation is more likely than imitating the behaviors of a member of the opposite sex. With the increasing acceptance of women in the workforce and in athletics the previous statement may be less true for girls than for boys. But in the stereotypical family, a boy who imitated his mother, wore a dress, put on lipstick, and sewed would likely be teased by other children and reprimanded or worse by his parents. In short, imitating females would be punished. However, a boy who imitated his father, wore "workingman" clothes, did mechanical work, wrestled, and played football would likely be reinforced both by other children and by his parents. In short, imitating males would be reinforced. As a consequence of this history of reinforcement, sex of the model would gain discriminative control over the imitative behavior of the imitator. The boy would be more likely to imitate males than females. Today it may be more likely that a girl may be reinforced for imitating either gender-typical behaviors such as aggressive play in basketball or cheerleading, but that does not seem to be the case for males. (I am not arguing that reinforcement for imitating same-sexed behavior is the only reason for gender differences in society, only one of several reasons. There are many different hormonal, genetic, and structural [including in the brain] differences between the sexes that an increasingly convincing body of evidence suggests is responsible for different behavioral tendencies. But that is not the subject matter of this book.)

Because some animals, including human infants, have shown an innate *tendency* to imitate that does not mean that reinforcement is not responsible for imitation as a general operant response. An initial imitation may or may not be innate. However, there are consequences for that imitation, innate or not, and all future imitations are influenced by that consequence as part of the cumulative consequences of all previous imitations. For example, a wild dog may have an innate tendency to imitate other dogs that run after newborn zebras. But if after seeing other dogs run after zebras, this dog runs after a zebra that kicks it, knocking out several teeth, or that turns and bites the dog, then it is likely that this dog would stop chasing zebras, and it is less likely that this dog would imitate the other dogs. Likewise, if a human infant was hit every time he imitated his caregiver's smile or other facial movements, then this infant would not continue to imitate. Fortunately, almost all infants are reinforced for imitating, and, as a consequence of this reinforcement, imitation as an operant is selected. Sounds are imitated and this imitation is reinforced and language is learned. If imitating sounds were not reinforced, then language could not be learned. Once a behavior occurs, an imitation or otherwise, there is some sort of consequence for that behavior. If the consequence is reinforcing then the behavior will be selected. In short although the tendency to imitate may be innate, whether or not imitation occurs is a function of the past consequences of imitative behavior. Similarly, whether or not instruction following occurs is a function of the past consequences for this behavior.

INSTRUCTION FOLLOWING

Parents or teachers may make the claim that they don't use reinforcement; they just instruct, or tell their children or pupils what to do and the children do it. Indeed, this often occurs. But people follow instructions because of a history of reinforcement for this behavior. Instruction following is selected as an operant response class. It is incorrect to claim that reinforcement is not involved in instructional controlled behavior that has no overt reinforcement built into the instructions. Reinforcement is the reason for all instruction following.

Frequently, especially early in life, modeling and instructions occur simultaneously. A caregiver instructs: "open wide; open wide," and simultaneously opens his mouth wide. If the child follows the instruction and imitates mouth opening, then the behavior will likely be reinforced with a bite of food and affection. When a caregiver instructs: "Say 'Mama'; say 'Mama,'" and the child imitates and follows the instruction, the behavior of saying "Mama" will likely be reinforced with affection. In instances such as these not only are the particular behaviors that were imitated and instructed reinforced, but *imitation and instruction following were reinforced as generalized operants*. Thus, initial instruction following may capitalize on a possibly innate tendency to imitate, but due to the consequences of this behavior, instruction following becomes a generalized operant response.

Eventually instruction following is uncoupled from imitation. When instructions such as "When you clear the table and wipe the counter, then you can watch TV" and "After you finish your homework, then you can play outside" are reinforced with the reinforcers explicit in the instructions (watching TV and playing outside), then not only have clearing the table, wiping the counter, and finishing homework been reinforced, but following instructions in general has been reinforced. For most individuals, after thousands of instances such as these, instruction following becomes a very powerful operant.

Instruction following is not automatic. For it to occur it must be reinforced. This fact comes as a surprise to many new teachers. Paul A. Alberto and Anne C. Troutman note that teachers may make the assumption that students' behavior is under stimulus control of "follow instructions." But "do not be surprised if students fail to follow your instructions. . . . Many students do not follow instructions as any experienced teacher will attest" (Alberto & Troutman, 1999, p. 339). Alberto and Troutman then suggest that teachers provide students with instructions and "reinforce following instructions to the most specific detail" (p. 339). "For students whose behavior is not under the control of rules [instructions], systematic efforts must be made to establish a relationship between following rules [or instructions] and positive reinforcement. . . . The teacher must continue to provide consistent reinforcement for following [instructions]" (p. 468). Indeed, it is unrealistic to expect a youth who has no history of reinforcement for rule following (rules are instructions), to follow the instructions of authority figures. One reason why a youth may be "unruly" is because following rules has never been reinforced!

NEGATIVE REINFORCEMENT AND IMPLICIT REINFORCEMENT FOR INSTRUCTION FOLLOWING

The reinforcement critic may remain unconvinced: "I never provided any positive reinforcement for following instructions but my kids all follow my instructions, and they'd better well had, or else! Furthermore, I have to follow instructions all the time and no one reinforces me for it." The critic's comments reflect that instruction following may be a function of negative reinforcement in addition to positive reinforcement and that the reinforcers for this behavior are often not explicit in the instructions but occur as an automatic consequence of following the instructions.

Often children are given instructions and expected to follow them. When they do, following the instructions is not necessarily positively reinforced. But aversive consequences occur if instruction following does not occur; they may be spanked or lose privileges. A parent may explain, "I don't reinforce following instructions. Children should know to do that. But because they know they should follow my instructions, I punish them if they don't." In everyday language the meaning of this statement is understandable. But technically, this parent is not using punishment, but negatively reinforcing instruction following (refer to Appendix II in this book for definitions of punishment, negative reinforcement, and positive reinforcement). In this example, instruction following *avoids aversive consequences* and *escapes the threat of aversive consequences*. Following instructions to avoid aversive consequences that occur if instructions are not followed is negative reinforcement of instruction following. This behavior increases (reinforcement), to escape or avoid (negative) aversive consequences. In such cases, although it may not be obvious to the person giving instructions, instruction following is as strongly reinforced as in cases where it produces overt positive reinforcement.

While using threats and aversive consequences for not following instructions may be effective in inducing instruction following, it is well established that using such aversive techniques produces a number of usually unwanted side effects (e.g., Sidman, 1989; Straus, 1994). One relevant behavioral by-product of using aversive techniques is that it creates escape tendencies on the part of the person receiving the aversive stimulation. Thus, if a child is following instructions to escape the threat of pain or not breaking rules to avoid the aversive consequences that breaking the rules produce, then the child is at increased risk to avoid or escape the entire instructional environment. That is, the child who is made to follow rules by aversive, coercive means is at increased risk of running away from home, skipping school, or dropping out. If following rules and instructions is negatively reinforced, the student may very well follow the rules and instructions to avoid the aversive consequences of not following the rules and instructions. But, another way to avoid the aversive consequences would be to avoid school entirely. Conversely, if a child is following instructions to obtain positive reinforcement then the child is more likely to seek out and stay in the instructional environment, more likely to happily do chores, more likely to come to school and stay in school, and more likely to request instruction from instructors. To have behaviors positively reinforced, one must be in an environment where positive reinforcers are possible.

Like increased escape tendencies, another usually unwanted by-product of behavior controlled by aversive consequences is increased anxiety. Thus, the person who follows rules because rule following is negatively reinforced is more likely to suffer from anxiety and from all of the behavioral deficits, such as depression, aversively impacted by anxiety. A child whose instruction following is positively reinforced will be less likely to suffer problems of chronic anxiety because there is no constant threat.

Most children learn to follow instructions by some mix of positive and negative reinforcement. For example, not following the instruction, "do not hit your sister" may result in a time-out. The intention of the time-out is to punish (decrease) sister hitting, and to negatively reinforce (increase) instruction following. The same child may also be told, "if you help your sister clean, then you can have some cookies." Here the cookies would positively reinforce (increase) both cooperation and instruction following.

The individual who knows that behavior is a function of its consequences, primarily a function of reinforcement, is more likely to shape rule following with positive reinforcement. When following rules and instructions is reinforced then this behavior will be selected. Breaking rules and not following instructions are a product of the rule breaker's past history of reinforcement (or lack of reinforcement) and current environmental circumstances. Rather than punish, the person who believes in positive reinforcement is likely to ask, What behaviors have been selected by this individual's history of reinforcement that are competing with rule following? Is this individual lacking a history of reinforcement for instruction following? If so, the process of selecting instructional control with reinforcement needs to begin. What in the current environment more strongly reinforces the behavior(s) that occurred instead of instruction following? How can the environment be arranged to occasion and positively reinforce instruction following so that behavior comes under the stimulus control of rules and instructions now and in the future? In short, positive reinforcement is used to select desired behaviors.

Often instructions, directions or assembly instructions, for example, contain no overt indication of reinforcement. However, reinforcement is a natural consequence of following such instructions. Following driving directions is reinforced by arriving at the desired location. Following assembly instructions is reinforced by a correctly assembled product. Following instructions known as cooking recipes is perhaps the most common example. When the instructions for cooking a soufflé, for example, are followed the result is usually much more reinforcing than attempting to make a souffle without following the recipe very closely. Following instructions for automobile care and maintenance is reinforced by properly functioning and longer-lasting automobiles. In short, if following instructions did not produce reinforcing consequences, then this behavior would extinguish.

As humans mature and rise in educational level, less and less behavior is shaped directly by immediate reinforcement contingencies. Learning by instruction is increasingly relied on. However, it would be a mistake to conclude that reinforcement is not operating. While the reinforcement may not be as obvious to the casual observer, reinforcement is implicit in every instruction. At a minimum, the implicit reinforcement in educational instruction is better grades and brighter job prospects. Similar to reading (of course much instruction is read), perhaps the greatest source of reinforcement for following instructions is that it usually increases an individual's repertoire of potentially reinforcing behaviors. Instruction following increases freedom. As long as sufficient instructional materials are available, for instance, cookbooks, a cook who follows cooking instructions has greater freedom in cooking than a cook who learns to cook only by trial and error.

Like imitation, instructions allow people to learn from others' past experiences. As such, imitation and the ability to follow instructions have allowed the rapid advancement of human society. We can repeat the successes of others and avoid the failures. These forms of learning from others are possible by the power of reinforcement, by the selection by consequences. When imitation and instruction following are reinforced, they are selected; when they are not reinforced they extinguish *in the behavioral repertoire of the individual.* Observational learning and instruction following are not examples of learning without reinforcement. Observational learning and instruction following are confirmations of the power of reinforcement.

Part II

FOR BETTER OR WORSE.
IN SICKNESS AND IN HEALTH:

Reinforcement in Action

9

REINFORCEMENT OF ACHIEVEMENT AND UNDERACHIEVEMENT

All parents and teachers want their children to be successful, to achieve. People who have high-achievement motivation desire accomplishment, can work independently and rapidly; they work to overcome obstacles to obtain a high standard of excellence and to surpass the success of others; they are ambitious and competitive (S. B. Klein, 1982, p. 353). In the first generation in the history of the United States when children are expected to have a *lower* standard of living than their parents, development of achievement motivation cannot be overemphasized. People who score high on achievement motivation are more likely to attend college, earn higher grade point averages, have higher job status, work harder in their career, and have higher expectations of future success than people who score low on achievement motivation. More successful entrepreneurs score higher on achievement motivation and earn more money than less successful entrepreneurs (McClelland, 1961, 1985).

Just as reinforcement creates creativity, positive reinforcement is the most important factor in the development of achievement motivation. Parental encouragement, support, and praise for achievement select the behavioral characteristic of high-achievement motivation. In a classic study of achievement motivation, when blindfolded boys were asked to build block towers, mothers of boys scoring high in achievement motivation had higher expectations, showed more positive emotions, and were more reinforcing—hugging and kissing—following success than were mothers of boys scoring low in achievement motivation (Rosen & D'Andrade, 1959). Achievement motivation develops when achievement is associated with positive affect—positive reinforcement.

Also importantly, boys with high-achievement motivation had fathers who showed *less* dominating involvement than boys with low-achievement

117

motivation. Negative reinforcement (threats, intimidation) and punishment (yelling, spanking) produce behavioral inhibition, fear, and anxiety—not achievement. Positive affect, positive reinforcement for success, selects high-achievement motivation.

But positive affect does not mean "anything goes" or that all behaviors are acceptable. Mothers of children with high achievement have high expectations and set standards and limits for their children that must be met before reinforcement occurs. For example, Stephen King's mother gave King affection for writing a story but withdrew this affection when she learned he was simply copying stories from comic books (see chapter 7 in this book). But by encouraging him to write his own stories, she set a higher standard of achievement. When King met this standard by writing his own stories, his mother reinforced his writing—reinforced his achievement—with attention, affection, and money. Standards without reinforcement will not work, and reinforcement without standards does not work either.

DISCIPLINE AND SELF-DISCIPLINE

Discipline and self-discipline—following the rules, completing tasks independent of constant supervision, working independently toward a distant goal or as a valued and cooperative "team-player"—are achievement-related behavioral characteristics desired by parents, educators, supervisors, and managers. However, "discipline" does not mean punishment, and "self-discipline" does not mean behavioral inhibition. "Discipline" has the same root as "disciple" that means "to follow." This suggests that having self-disciplined role models is an important factor in the development of self-discipline.

For example, in a classic observational learning experiment (Bandura & Kupers, 1964), children watched adults play a bowling game in which adults could score up to thirty points. Some children saw adults reward themselves by taking candy from a bowl only when they met a high self-imposed standard of 20 points or more. Other children saw the adults reward themselves when they met a low standard, 10 or more points, and still other children saw adults eat the candy regardless of their score. When the children were given the opportunity to play the bowling game themselves with a bowl of candy available, and *no* instructions concerning scoring or eating candy, the children tended to adopt the standards set by the adult model they had observed. Children who saw an adult model display self-restraint and set high standards of achievement before eating candy, ate candy themselves only when they obtained a high score. Children who saw the adults set low or no standards, set low or no standards for themselves and ate candy regardless of their performance.

When adults model the self-discipline necessary for achievement and reinforce children for imitating approximations of this self-discipline, children will develop discipline and achievement. Teaching discipline does not mean punishing; it means setting an appropriate example and reinforcing appropriate behavior. None of the world's great religious figures—Jesus, Buddha, or Mohammed—beat their disciples. Instead they set appropriate examples, and encouraged and reinforced appropriate behavior by their disciples. If they had relied on beatings or other punishment, it is unlikely that they would have had any disciples.

Those schooled in the western traditions of punishment may point to the biblical passage "spare the rod and spoil the child" as justification for the use of punishment. However, a good shepherd does not use the rod to beat his sheep. No, the rod is used to beat that which is bad for the sheep, specifically wolves and foxes. If the shepherd beat the sheep, the sheep would run away just as children are more likely to do when they are beaten (Straus, 1994). It is the curved staff that is used on the sheep to *gently* pull them back into the flock.

Punishment *can* be used to inhibit behaviors. But, at best, punishment teaches what not to do. Punishment does not teach what to do (Martin & Pear, 1999, p.171). Punishment does not teach what behaviors are appropriate nor what behaviors will produce positive reinforcement. Theoretically, punishment may prevent individuals from breaking laws, rules, and social conventions. But partly because punishment elicits aggression from the punished (Azrin & Holz 1966; Sidman, 1989) ultimately the punishment will backfire. If punishment is relied on excessively, it will result in aggressive, dishonest, law-breaking individuals suffering from depressive symptoms (e.g., Straus, 1994). The very behavioral inhibition produced by punishment precludes the punished from developing into high achievers, can-do, go-getters characteristic of the "self-disciplined." The more punishment is used, the less likely a child (or anyone punished) is to try novel behaviors because in the past these behaviors have more frequently produced punishment than positive reinforcement.

Like punishment, *negative* reinforcement is *not* likely to produce high achievement. Negative reinforcement occurs when the rate of a behavior increases because an aversive event or stimulus is removed or because behavior prevents an aversive event from occurring in the first place (see appendix 2 in this book). Because negative reinforcement depends on the possibility of an aversive consequence for the nonoccurrence of the target behavior, its use has all of the disadvantages and aversive side effects of punishment, such as increased aggression and increased probability of depression and other psychological problems. Furthermore, negative reinforcement results in behavior "just good enough to get by"—the minimal amount of behavior necessary to avoid the aversive consequence. On the other hand, *positive* reinforcement typically results in more than the minimal amount of appropriate behavior necessary. Positive reinforcement produces *discretionary effort* (Daniels, 1994, p. 28). Positive reinforcement produces achievement. A child required to work in the family business to avoid being grounded and beaten (negative reinforcement) is likely to do just enough to avoid the aversive consequences of not working. But the child who works in the family business to receive part of the profits or other incentives such as praise or being paid for completing various chores is more likely to exceed performance requirements and to find additional ways to improve the business. Similarly an employee who works to avoid being fired or reprimanded by management (negative reinforcement) is likely to work *just enough* to avoid the aversive consequences of not working. But an employee motivated by incentives—pay raises, access to the executive washroom, performance contingent company paid vacations or bonuses—an employee motivated by positive reinforcement will work at more optimal levels. Punishment and negative reinforcement do not result in achievement but in underachievement of the possible.

REDUCING PUNISHMENT AND AVERSIVE CONSEQUENCES

The most effective way to avoid the use, and (falsely) perceived need to use punishment, or aversive consequences of any sort, is to increase the use of positive reinforcement. An individual is capable of only so much behavior during any given period of time. If appropriate, useful, socially productive behavior is occurring, there is less time available for inappropriate behaviors. The best way to increase appropriate behavior, the best way to maximize performance, the best way to produce high achieving individuals is with positive reinforcement.

Children who receive copious amounts of praise and other reinforcers for drawing, painting, working on computers, playing board games or sports, playing with blocks or dolls, riding tricycles and bicycles, listening to and telling stories, "helping" parents clean and cook, and looking at and reading books, by definition of reinforcement, will be engaging in these appropriate behaviors. Therefore they will have less time available that might be occupied with destructive or other inappropriate behaviors.

Children who do not receive sufficient reinforcement for appropriate, productive behaviors will find other behaviors to gain attention, including destructive and other inappropriate behaviors. Indeed, often the very attention meant to decrease the inappropriate behavior is the consequence that is maintaining the unwanted behavior. When a child is being spanked at the very least the child is being paid attention. Many teachers will attest that if misbehavior is the only way a child can receive attention then that child will misbehave in order to receive the attention. When teachers attempt to reduce the number of disapprovals they give and increase their approvals, they often find that their disapprovals for inappropriate behaviors were what had been maintaining the inappropriate behaviors in the first place. This typical observation was noted by one teacher who reported: "While I was increasing my approvals, I needed to use disapprovals less" (from Flora, 2000, p. 68). Similarly, University of Kansas researchers Lori Greene, Debra Kamps, Jennifer Wyble, and Cynthia Ellis found that training parents of young children with behavior problems to increase parental rates of praise for appropriate behavior improved child compliance *and decreased inappropriate child behaviors* (Greene et al., 1999). If positive reinforcement is appropriately used, punishment is not needed. But, if beatings are the only form of attention a child receives, then the child will misbehave in order to be beaten. One crack-cocaine and heroin dealer claimed, "The only one that ever hit me, was my grandmother, but I liked'ed it. . . . She hit me, and it'd be funny. . . . I liked to get hurt. . . . I mean *I was always looking forward to getting beat down* by [my grandmother]. Sometimes she'd even throw a punch. And she would hit hard" (from Bourgois, 1996, pp. 184–185, emphasis added). If this individual had received attention for appropriate behaviors and had productive skills reinforced and shaped with praise, perhaps he would have ended up in a different career than illegal-drug dealing.

The way to reduce the perceived need for punishment and the way to reduce illegal and destructive behaviors is to increase reinforcement for achievement. Children and adolescents who are reinforced for reading, computer work, science projects, building models, mechanical work, woodworking, organized sport participation, drama, debate, band, writing, photography, singing, or gardening, to name a few examples, will, by definition of reinforcement, be spending time doing those activities. The reinforcers, just to name a few possibilities, can be some combination of attention, praise, "quality time" spent with a parent or guardian, money, toys, driving privileges, field trips, movies, sleepovers, athletic equipment, CDs, and, of course intrinsic reinforcement resulting from the behavior-activity interaction itself. But regardless of the particular reinforcers used, if children are reinforced for engaging in productive behaviors, *they will be engaging in productive behaviors, not destructive behaviors,* and will have less time for nonproductive behaviors such as hanging out at the local mall or illegal behaviors such as experimenting with illegal drugs.

Children who are not spanked are not "wild," "out of control," and undisciplined. In fact, the more children are spanked, the more behavioral problems they will have (Capaldi et al., 1997; Straus, 1994). Parents who are helping their children develop into productive, high-achieving people don't spank. They don't need to. Because their children are praised for appropriate behaviors and independence is encouraged, their children engage in appropriate independent behaviors. Parents of children with high-achievement motivation are quick to praise and encourage their children in all areas of endeavors. This parental behavioral pattern results in children who are well behaved.

Parents of children with high-achievement motivation do not punish failure, but following failure, encourage and assist their children in finding areas where they can be successful. Failure is punishment enough for failure. A child who strikes out in a little league game does not need to be yelled at by a coach, parent, or teammate. Striking-out is punishment enough. Singing off-key or playing the wrong notes during a performance does not need to result in scolding or reprimands from parents or teachers. The faulty performance is punishment enough. Instead, parents who are helping their children develop high-achievement motivation and high self-esteem will find additional activities that their children may be successful in. Perhaps a child would enjoy track-and-field more than baseball; perhaps another child will find writing stories is more reinforcing than singing or playing musical instruments. Or by reinforcing successive approximations, parents of high-achieving children will assist their children in learning the skills necessary to be successful in the child's chosen activities. A baseball batter may be shown, encouraged, and reinforced for changing his batting stance, "choking-up" on the bat, swinging more smoothly with follow-through, and so on. Following each improvement the child is praised, and ultimately these improvements will result in improved performances that "intrinsically" reinforce the effort.

PERSISTENCE, EFFORT, INDUSTRIOUSNESS, AND ACHIEVEMENT

Even the top batters fail to get on base more often than they have a successful at bat. Even the top musical performers occasionally play off-key or hit the wrong note. Musicians, writers, computer programmers, scientists, and salespeople—virtually all professionals—have just as many failures as successes, and often many more failures than successes. Yet the person who achieves—the person who succeeds—will persist despite these failures. When the going gets tough, the tough—the achievement oriented—get going. The reason why some people persist, put forth high effort, and are industrious despite failure and setbacks is because they have a history of being reinforced for persisting, for putting forth effort. They have a history of reinforcement for behaving industriously. Typically the approximations of the effort needed for great achievement were encouraged and shaped beginning in childhood. The early behavioral psychologist John B. Watson observed that "the formation of early work habits in youth, of working longer hours than others, of practicing more intensively than others, is probably the most reasonable explanation we have today not only for success in any line, but even for genius" (J. B. Watson, 1930/1970, p. 212).

It is *a history of reinforcement* of working and practicing intensively that shapes the work habits of working longer hours and practicing intensively (see chapters 1–9). It is summarized and expanded here to emphasize the relation between achievement and reinforcement. In addition to encouraging and reinforcing independence and achievement directly (e.g., McClelland, 1985; Rosen & D'Andrade, 1959), increasing levels of effort and persistence also need a history of reinforcement to select the persistence and effort necessary to overcome the inevitable obstacles on the path to achievement (if there were no obstacles to overcome, the behavior would not be considered an achievement, but just a simple act that anyone could perform). When tasks requiring high effort are reinforced, the result is greater *generalized* persistence, greater industriousness across behaviors. Children who are reinforced for every five spelling words they have spelled correctly work longer and solve more math problems than children reinforced for each word spelled correctly (Eisenberger & Adornetto, 1986). Indeed, Robert R. Eisenberger's work on industriousness has shown that increasing the required performance for reinforcement on one task results in improvements across a wide range of behaviors including learning-disabled and typical preadolescent students' handwriting, drawing, and mathematics performance, and college students' perceptual identifications, essay writing, anagram solving, and resistance to cheating (see Eisenberger, 1992; & Eisenberger & Cameron, 1996 for reviews). Reinforcement for effort selects effort as a behavioral trait that generalizes across behaviors. The resulting industriousness and persistence is a prerequisite for achievement.

But, increasing the level of effort required for reinforcement must proceed gradually or the behavior is likely to extinguish—the person is likely to quit—before the required effort and persistence have been shaped. To illustrate, if a rat is first shaped to press a lever to receive a pellet of food, then the contingency is abruptly changed so that 100 responses are required for a pellet of food, the rat will quit pressing the lever before it ever reaches 100. But if the reinforcement criterion is *gradually* changed from 1 to 2, to 4 to 8, to 20, to 40, to 80, and so forth, the rat's behavior can be shaped to a high level of effort and the rat will press the lever 100 times for a pellet of food. Likewise, a youth who had received an allowance or was given money without having to earn it by completing a chore is less likely to remain employed in a job where pay is received only monthly than is a youth who had a history of being reinforced immediately for each household chore completed but later found his weekly allowance was contingent upon having completed the required chores the previous weeks and still later his allowance was earned every other week if chores had been completed the previous two weeks. The second youth experienced a gradual increase in effort needed for reinforcement. Similarly, a child first reinforced for learning the alphabet, then reading Dr. Seuss books, then "Goose Bumps" stories, "The Hardy Boys," "Nancy Drew," or "Encyclopedia Brown"; then "Harry Potter," then teen-novels; then Ernest Hemingway or Erica Jong novels is more likely to succeed in college than a child who has never been reinforced for increased reading efforts (for some children the reinforcement for increased reading efforts may be the intrinsic reinforcement received from the reading itself, e.g., Carson, 2001).

Indeed, the lack of reinforcement for *academic* effort and persistence may be one of the major reasons why open admissions universities such as Youngstown State University (my employer) have low academic achievement evidenced by five-year graduation rates of less than 40 percent and why many college freshman do not return for their sophomore year. In typical kindergarten though twelfth-grade classrooms there are at least weekly assignments, if not daily assignments, which provide to students feedback—reinforcement for correct performance. However, in the typical freshman college classroom, the student may have only two or four examinations for the entire course, and the instructor is unlikely to even learn the student's name, much less provide daily feedback on the student's academic performance or efforts. Yet, to prepare for these infrequent, but all important examinations, the student may be expected to read several hundred pages of complex material, learn the definitions of hundreds of new words, or learn dozens of math equations and know under what circumstances to employ each equation. If the college student does not have a history of reinforced persistence for academic efforts, then it is naive, if not absurd, to expect her to succeed in college. Without a history of reinforcement for persistence of academic effort, instead of reading, learning definitions and equations, the student will engage in behaviors that provide more frequent and immediate reinforcers such as working off-campus or drinking and "partying." Conversely, because reinforcement for academic persistence selects persistence on academic tasks, the student who has a history of reinforcement for academic persistence and effort is more likely to do the expected reading and learn the required material necessary for success in college. The reinforcement of academic persistence and effort may be one reason why college students whose parents paid them money for earning good grades during childhood have significantly higher grades than college students who were not paid money for earning good grades (Flora & Popanak, 2001).

BETTER LATE THAN NEVER

Ideally, a childhood history of reinforcement for high achievement, persistence, and effort will select those behavioral characteristics in individuals. However, regardless of one's age, given the proper reinforcement for achievement and effort, these characteristics can be shaped to varying degrees. For example, in a classic study on achievement motivation, David McClelland and David Winter (1969) developed a training program to teach people with low achievement how to have high-achievement motivation. The participants were introduced to the concept of achievement motivation, its relationship to personal success, and how to think and act like people with high achievement motivation, to take moderate risks, to set long-term goals, and to plan the steps necessary to obtain them. Participants were given tasks to perform, required to set goals, and reinforced for meeting the goals. Instituting the program for businesspeople in two Indian cities resulted in their working longer hours, starting more new businesses, making more capital investments, hiring new workers, and significant increases in company profits. In a similar Indian city that did not receive the training program there were no changes in business or economic activity. For the businesspeople receiving the achievement motivation training, the initial successes following training further reinforced their high-achievement oriented efforts creating a positive feedback loop between reinforcement and achievement efforts. For achievement-oriented efforts to be maintained, they must continue to be reinforced.

Galileo's great work *Dialogue*, which led him to be tried and sentenced by the Holy Office of the Inquisition, took years to finish. His efforts needed to be reinforced. According to biographer Dava Sobel, what finally motivated Galileo to finish his great work was competition with peers, the social reinforcement victory would bring, and the old standby "extrinsic reinforcement"—money!

> What a blow to think that [Father Christopher] Scheiner, who had foolishly mistaken sunspots for stars before Galileo corrected him, now stood ready to publish this monumental discovery! The shock *impelled* Galileo back to his unfinished manuscript. If he needed *further incentive*, he could look to the *projected income from sales* of the finished book, for his new daughter-in-law was already pregnant, his son still unemployed, and Suor Maria Celeste [Galileo's daughter] anxious to improve the quality of her life through the purchase of private quarters in the convent. (Sobel, 2000, p. 165, emphasis added)

Sobel also makes it clear that these reinforcements did nothing to undermine Galileo's interest in science as Galileo remained highly involved and productive until his death.

From scientists like Galileo, to musicians and mathematicians (Howe et al., 1998) to writers (e.g., King, 2000) competency and high achievement require thousands of hours of hard, effortful, persistent, often solitary practice (Howe et al., 1998). Musician and songwriter Bruce Hornsby advises aspiring musicians to *"Practice and write all the time.* Like my boyhood hero, Bill Bradley of the Knicks [and U.S. senator] said 'If you're not working on it, someone else is, and when you play them, they will win'" (from Waggoner, 2001, emphasis added). *Practicing and writing all the time* is the very advice Stephen King gives aspiring writers.

Yet, as King also observed, without encouragement—support and praise, that is—without reinforcement, the necessary hard, effortful, long, solitary practice would not be possible. This truth is illustrated by David Al Kolb's (1965) classic study of underachieving boys who were taught achievement motivation while attending a summer camp. The boys all had IQ's of over one hundred twenty but had below average performance in school. Six months after the program all of the boys had significant improvements in their grades. However, after eighteen months only the boys from high socioeconomic status maintained their good grades. As Kolb argued, academic achievement is not as valued in lower socioeconomic classes and it is unreasonable to expect achievement gains to be maintained if achievement no longer produces reinforcement. Indeed, some children of minority status from lower socioeconomic levels who achieve academically are picked on and sometimes even beaten for "acting White" and "articulate." In such cases achievement not only is not reinforced, but achievement is actively punished. As a consequence, not surprisingly, these formerly achieving children start to perform worse in school and their spoken grammar worsens. When underachievement is reinforced, underachievement occurs. When achievement is reinforced, achievement occurs. The environment must encourage and reinforce achievement-oriented behaviors—effort and persistence—for their development and maintenance. Fortunately, such programs as Earning by Learning (e.g., McNinch et al., 1995), Pizza Hut's Book IT! reading program, Harve E. Rawson's (e.g., 1992) remediation program, and the "teaching-family" model of adolescence group homes show that high levels of achievement can be shaped, reinforced, and maintained with consequent reinforcement in traditionally underachieving populations.

10

REINFORCEMENT IN EDUCATION

Although reinforcement and education are not synonymous, successful formal education is virtually impossible without copious systematic reinforcement. For optimal educational results, systematic reinforcement should begin in infancy and continue throughout the entire educational process.

In the United States, there are senators, representatives, cabinet members, doctors, lawyers, CEOs, professors, and other professionals from every socioeconomic and ethnic background. This is evidence that a person from any ethnicity can be highly successful in any endeavor *given* the proper educational experiences. Some of these important educational experiences begin in infancy, and one of the most vital experiences is the experience of reinforcement.

The earlier a child experiences behavior-consequence events the larger a head start the infant will have in education and in life. Learning that behavior produces consequences—experiencing reinforcement, experiencing operant conditioning—is one of the most important lessons children will ever learn. Indeed, in a seminal program to reduce socioculturally caused mental retardation, Craig I. Ramely and Neal W. Finkelstein (1978) of the University of North Carolina Frank Porter Graham Child Development Center, reinforced infant vocalizations with contingent auditory-visual stimulation in the children's homes (e.g., the infants received reinforcing stimulation only after they vocalized). This reinforcement training resulted in improved learning in a completely different setting in the laboratory. Early behavior-contingent stimulation (reinforcement) enhances general learning ability. The effects of behavior-consequence reinforcement influence learning and emotionality in infants as young as three days old (e.g., DeCasper & Carstens, 1981). Infants who have caregivers who are responsive to cries and vocalizations, infants who have mobiles that move and make sounds when they kick or move their arms, infants who have toys that reinforce—toys that respond to the infant's behaviors—will be at an educational and emotional advantage over children who have less responsive care givers and fewer or no toys that produce reinforcing stimulation as a result of the infant's behavior.

Learned Helplessness (discussed in more detail in chapter 13 in this book), one of the major causes of depression, occurs when one learns that one's behavior has no effect on one's experiences. Conversely, *learned optimism* (e.g., Seligman, 1990) can "immunize" one against learned helplessness and occurs when one learns that one's behavior can and does produce meaningful consequences. People learn to be optimistic when their behavior produces reinforcement. Whether one develops optimism or helplessness begins in infancy. When cries are ignored or no one is around to attend to the cries; when cries of hunger do not produce feedings; when cries of discomfort do not produce a change of diapers, clothes, temperature, or stimulation; when smiles, "goos," and "gaas" are not reinforced in return with smiles and baby talk, then there is an increased chance that the child will learn to be helpless. Why cry, smile, "goo," or "gaa"—why behave when behavior is useless? Why behave when behaviors are not reinforced? The infant has *learned* to be helpless—taught to be depressed by a lack reinforcement. But when cries are quickly attended to; when cries of hunger produce feedings; when cries of discomfort produce a change of diapers, clothes, temperature, or stimulation until the discomfort is alleviated; when smiles, "goos," and "gaaas" are reinforced in return with smiles, "goos," and "gaas," then the child will learn to be optimistic. The child's behavior will increase because behavior is useful. The child's behaviors will increase because behaviors are reinforced. The infant has *learned* to be optimistic.

Whether an infant learns helplessness from nonreinforced behavior or optimism from reinforced behavior, will influence later learning in the same respective direction. Compared to a child who learned to be helpless during infancy, preschoolers who as infants had lots of response-contingent stimulation, who learned that their behavior can and does produce reinforcement will be more likely to quickly learn that moving and clicking a computer mouse produces changes in color, sound, and animation on a computer with learning software. Preschoolers who have *not* had lots of response-contingent stimulation, who have learned that their behavior does *not* produce reinforcement will be *less* likely to learn quickly that moving and clicking a computer mouse produces changes in color, sound, and animation on a computer with learning software. Compared to children from a less nurturing environment, preschoolers and kindergartners who as infants were frequently praised, talked to (Hart & Risley, 1995), and had their cries and other vocalizations appropriately responded to by caregivers, that is, infants who had behavior reinforced, will be more likely to attend to their early teachers, respond to, and request help from their teachers; they will be more likely to engage in behaviors that produce adult social reinforcement that will in turn elicit further appropriate behaviors in a positive feedback loop. Conversely, children from a less nurturing environment, preschoolers and kindergartners who as infants were *in*frequently praised, seldom talked to (Hart & Risley, 1995), and had their cries and other vocalizations ignored, or worse punished ("shut up"), will be *less* likely to attend to their early teachers, less likely to respond to and request help from their teachers; they will be less likely to engage in behaviors that produce adult social reinforcement that will in turn result in fewer appropriate behaviors that potentially could be reinforced. A downward spiral of less and less appropriate behavior resulting in less and less reinforcement is likely to result.

The groundbreaking longitudinal work of Betty Hart and Todd B. Risely, revealed that on *average* children from professional homes had larger vocabularies and higher IQ scores than children from working-class homes, who in turn, had larger vocabularies and higher IQ scores than children from welfare homes. *However,* a child's socioeconomic background was *not* the strongest predictor of vocabulary or IQ; parental reinforcement was. Statistically, socioeconomic status accounted for 42% of the variance in children's vocabulary growth and 29% of the variance in IQ scores. But parenting (amounts of praising, prompting, encouraging, vs. punishing and reprimanding) accounted for 61% of the variance in vocabulary growth and 59% of the variance in IQ scores (Hart & Risely, 1995, p. 158). "Feedback tone [the relative amount of parental reinforcement and encouragement] was . . . strongly related to rate of vocabulary growth and general accomplishments estimated by IQ score," wrote Hart and Risely. "The more positive the affect during interaction [the more positive reinforcement], the more motivated the child is to explore new topics, to try out tentative relationships, to listen and practice, to add words to those already accumulated, and to notice the facts and relationships that IQ testers ask about" (p. 155).

Thus, the reason why children of lower socioeconomic status tend to do poorer on average in school relative to children of higher socioeconomic status is *not* because of the lower status in and of itself, but because, for a variety of reasons, caregivers of children of lower economic status tend to provide less positive reinforcement for their children's behavior, especially their language and exploratory behaviors. As Hart and Risley's data illustrated, regardless of socioeconomic status, when children are given the proper amounts of reinforcement, which is a copious amount, they can thrive academically. This suggests that one way to improve the academic performance of underachieving children is with *parent* behavioral training. Indeed, the evidence shows that when parents are taught basic reinforcement procedures the behaviors of their children improve (e.g., Greene et al., 1999; Weirson & Forehand, 1994).

Similarly, in addition to repeatedly finding that couples with low rates of mutual positive reinforcement are likely to divorce, marriage researcher John H. Gottman (e.g., J H. Gottman et al., 1997), finds that, assuming a couple has children, these coercive relationships aversively affect the children's physical, social, and academic growth. Fortunately, the parental technique of "Scaffolding/Praising" can act as a buffer against the harmful effects of living in a household high in marital conflict and low in marital reinforcement. Scaffolding/Praising consists of providing warm encouragement and positive reinforcers including parental attention, responsiveness, praise, and physical affection. When Gottman and his co-workers Lynn F. Katz and Carole Hooven of the University of Washington examined parenting they found that the amount of positive reinforcement the parents gave when children were four and five years old strongly predicted a child's academic achievement at age eight. "Scaffolding/Praising parenting is positively correlated with both mathematics and reading comprehension scores" (pp. 157–158).

Conversely, the more intrusive, critical, and mocking a father was, the lower a child's reading and mathematics achievement was likely to be (Gottman et al., 1997, p. 157). "When parents are intrusive, or mock and criticize their child they are teaching the child something new, they are establishing in the child the idea that the child is inadequate. Furthermore," wrote the researchers, "the child will try hard to live up to their negative image [and underachieve]" (p. 159). Intrusive, mocking, and critical parenting "was related to lower scores on mathematics, reading comprehension, and . . . attentional abilities. . . . [But] parent's Scaffolding/Praising facilitate" the child's progress (p. 159). Positive reinforcement from parents in the form of lots of praise provides a foundation for academic excellence. The lack of positive reinforcement early in a child's life will retard a child's academic progress.

WHAT IS MENTAL RETARDATION AND WHAT IS GENIUS?

One sunflower plant may grow to be over ten feet tall and produce thousands of seeds. Another plant may grow only a few feet, struggle for life, and produce no seeds. One plant flourishes and one plant's growth is retarded. There are two possible reasons for the discrepancy between plants. One is that one of the plants is genetically flawed, aversively mutated. The other, more likely, reason is that the plants received different care. The plant that flourished received the proper nutrients, water, and sunlight. The plant with retarded growth was deprived of nutrients, water, and sunlight and may have been exposed to toxins. These are the same reasons why one child may flourish and another may be retarded. When something is retarded, whether it is a plant or child, the meaning of retarded is that its growth has been inhibited, depressed, or otherwise lessened. "Mental retardation," or more accurately, learning or academic retardation, simply means that one's learning, one's academic accomplishments—one's mental growth—has been somehow retarded, inhibited, depressed, or lessened from what would normally be expected. The label *mental retardation* does not indicate how this retardation came about.

Genetic abnormalities, such as trisomy 21 resulting in Down's syndrome, account for some retardation. Other retardation, such as fetal alcohol syndrome, like that of the plant exposed to toxins, are a result of a toxic, corrosive environment. Still other retardation, "socioculturally caused mental retardation," like that of the plant kept out of the sunlight or not given proper nutrients, results, not from any genetic abnormality or prenatal exposure to toxicity, but from an environment lacking in positive reinforcement or nutrition. But as plants with retarded growth given optimal sunlight, water, and nutrients often begin to flourish, individuals with all types of mental retardation (genetic or environmentally caused), to varying degrees, may flourish given the proper nutrients and positive reinforcement. For example, actor Chris Burke, who has Down's syndrome, starred in the TV series *Life Goes On* and acts as a angel in the series *Touched by an Angel.*

Statistically, scoring 70 or below (2 standard deviations below the average score of 100) on a "intelligent quotient" (IQ) test is said to indicate retardation. Scoring 130 or above (2 standard deviations above the average score) on an IQ test is taken to mean that the test taker is "gifted." Whether stunned by a label of *retarded* or *gifted*, a parent who is told his or her child scored in either the retarded or gifted range is likely to remember it forever, and possibly consider the child to be either retarded or gifted for the rest of the child's life. However the cut-offs of 70 and 130 are *arbitrary*. A child who scores 123 on an IQ test will not be labeled *gifted*, but, given the proper environment, is just as likely to excel in school and life as a child who scores above 130. Similarly, a child who scores 68 on an IQ test will be labeled *retarded*, but given the proper nurturing environment, this child can succeed in school and life. In fact, these children's IQ scores will likely be different the very next time they take this test.

Intelligence is not some mystical entity floating around somewhere inside the skull. Intelligence is simply a shorthand way to summarize behavior. An IQ score is nothing more than a general measure of how one person behaved during a very unusual test at one particular point in time. These tests do not measure any internal, stable quality of a person. In fact, Alfred Binet developed the first intelligence test to identify French children who were underachieving in school so that they could be given the proper nurturing to bring their performance up. That is, the first intelligence test was developed because *intelligence can be changed*. According to Binet, "The intelligence of anyone is susceptible of development. With practice, enthusiasm, and especially with method one can succeed in increasing one's attention, memory, judgment, and in becoming literally more intelligent than one was before" (from Weiten, 2000, p. 255).

Furthermore, in addition to being susceptible to change, specifically improvement, IQ tests reflect only academic performance, not the potential for success. "The IQ test was invented to predict academic performance, nothing else," claims social psychologist Robert Zajonc. "If we wanted something that would predict life success, we'd have to invent another test completely" (Zajonc, 1984, p. 22). A thirteen-year-old who scores 130 on an IQ test is likely to perform well on a math test or perhaps on a crossword puzzle, but the score suggests nothing about the child's behavior at the middle school prom, or on the sandlot ballfield.

As *intelligence* is just a summary word for a person's behavioral tendencies under certain conditions at a certain time, "intelligence" is subject to the same environmental influences, such as positive reinforcement, as other behavioral tendencies. The history of ethic minorities in the United States, particularly the history of African-Americans, and Native Americans, is in large part a history of murdering, lynching, dishonesty, and cheating by White European-Americans. The "African-American shuffle" of deliberately working slowly evolved as an adaptive survival mechanism, via negative reinforcement to avoid, reduce, or escape the brutal and unrealistic work demands placed on African-Americans by the White ruling class. The history of education for both African-Americans and Native Americans has been in large part one of denial, prevention, and punishment for education by the White ruling class. During slavery, African-Americans were beaten or even lynched if they were caught trying to read or learn math. Native American children were forbidden to speak their native language in schools and taken away from their parents and put in boarding schools so they couldn't talk to them. Even today, earning an education may be considered Uncle Tom—"acting white." Given this discrepant history and sociocultural reality, it is no wonder that on average Native Americans and African-Americans score lower on intelligence tests than their generally privileged White counterparts. Fortunately, the proper and consistent use of positive reinforcement can lift the educational achievement of all peoples.

Why work hard, a minority child may ask, on a strange test for a strange White man when there is no reason, no reinforcement for doing so? Often there is no immediate reason, no reinforcers for a Native American or African-American child to put forth any effort on an intelligence test. However, if children of any race with any type of educational background are given systematic reinforcement for correct answers on intelligence tests, their scores significantly improve. Robert Devers, Sharon Bradley-Johnson, and J. C. Merle of Central Michigan University (1994) compared the IQ scores of fifth- though ninth-grade Native Americans under either standardized conditions, or standard conditions with the addition of token reinforcement following each correct response. The tokens were later exchangeable for a variety of backup reinforcers (toys, treats, and activities). The token reinforcement group scored significantly higher than the standard group.

The score-improving effects of token reinforcement for correct responding on IQ tests is not limited to children who initially score low on these tests. If correct responding is reinforced, correct responding increases for initially high-scoring children as well as for low-scoring children. Margaret E. Lloyd and Theresa M. Zylla of Drake University in Iowa (1988) give both high- and low-scoring 4-, 5-, and 6-year-old children IQ tests both without and with token reinforcement for correct responses. Token reinforcement of correct responses increased IQ scores of children in both high and low IQ groups. Similarly, an early study (Edlund, 1972) that examined the effect of reinforcing each correct response with an M&M on the IQ scores of lower-class children in the Head Start program found that the reinforcement raised IQ scores from 82 to 94 on average. The control group's average IQ score remained at 82. Results such as these force one to question how many lower-class children are placed in special education classes, not because they have some special organic, physical, or cognitive disability, but because they simply have never been properly motivated, properly reinforced, to perform academically.

In addition to the current environmental conditions, such as the availability of positive reinforcement for correct responding, an individual's performance on an intelligence test, *just like any other behavioral performance*, is a function of the individual's reinforcement history and past environmental influences. Optimally these influences begin during infancy and continue throughout life. Parents and caregivers who are responsive and provide ample opportunities for infant response-contingent stimulation, who encourage exploration and independence, who are warm and affectionate, who reinforce progress, who encourage questioning, who frequently talk to their infants and respond affectionately to infant vocalizations, and who provide at least five positive reinforcers for every criticism are most likely to have children who are academically successful and score high on any IQ test.

Positive reinforcement for children is analogous to the sunlight a plant must receive for optimal growth. In addition to sunlight, a plant must also have access to proper soil nutrients and water to flourish. Likewise, in addition to positive reinforcement, a child must have access to proper materials and environmental conditions to encourage engagement in positively reinforcing activities and occasion optimal behavioral growth. These materials and environmental conditions include consistent parenting; access to books of all types; art supplies (e.g., pens, paper, paint, and clay); math related materials (e.g., blocks, magnet numbers, and checkers); frequent verbal and language stimulation with verbal responsiveness from caregivers, and being read to and being asked questions about reading. Although to date no systematic studies have been conducted on any advantages they may have, there now exist computer software programs for toddlers that at least provide response-contingent stimulation, and teach colors and sounds. If properly designed to incorporate lots of positive reinforcement and gradually shape pre-academic behaviors, this type of software could prove to be a very useful societal development. That is, if the software were made available to lower socioeconomic status children, it could ameliorate many of the early academic disadvantages they experience.

Researcher Joy K. Galentine's study of 24- to 30-month-old toddlers' prereading behaviors led her to conclude that "like learning oral language, literacy development begins with gross approximations of the adult model, becoming more refined with experience. And *it is a child's early exposure to literacy that affects his or her future success in reading and writing*" (Galentine, 1996, p. 255, emphasis added). This is exactly what the mother of Ben and Curtis Carson realized. Ben, a graduate of Yale University and the University of Michigan Medical School, is the chief of pediatric neurosurgery at Johns Hopkins Children's Center, and Curtis is an engineer. But when Ben, an African-American, was in the fifth grade with "miserable" grades, living and going to school in the rundown inner-city of Detroit, his mother, who herself was at the time illiterate and working as a maid, "noticed something in the suburban houses she cleaned—books," wrote Ben. "So she came home one day, snapped off the TV, sat us down and explained that her sons were going to make something of themselves. 'You boys are going to read two books every week,' she said. 'And you're going to write me a report on what you read.' . . . She explained that we would go where the books were: 'I'll drive you to the library'" (Carson, 2001, pp. 33–34). Fortunately, beginning with the first book Ben read, *Chip the Dam Builder*, the intrinsic reinforcers for reading began to occur to Ben almost immediately: "For the first time in my life I was lost in another world. No television program had ever taken me so far away from my surroundings as did this verbal visit to a cold stream in a forest. . . . And I discovered something much more important: not only did I like to read, but I could absorb more information, more quickly, through the printed word than I ever did from sounds or images [on TV]" (pp. 35–36). The intrinsic reinforcers for reading led to other reinforcers as well. "Along the way a funny thing happened: I started to know things. Teachers started to notice it too. It got to the point where I couldn't wait to get home to my books. . . . But I know when the journey began—the day Mom snapped off the TV set and put us in her Oldsmobile for that drive to the library" (p. 36). Ben's story illustrates that for educational success, children must have access to, and encouragement to use educational materials.

POSITIVE REINFORCEMENT AND EDUCATION AT SCHOOL

While many educators blame parents for sending children to school unprepared for formal instruction, many parents argue that the public school systems in the United States are failing to educate their children. School personnel are often correct that the children are sent to them unprepared to learn. Fortunately, beginning in infancy, the use of positive reinforcement can prepare children for formal schooling as we have seen. The more parents adopt positive reinforcement-based parenting techniques, the better their children will be prepared for school. However, the parents' belief that the schools are failing them is partly correct. Laws require children to be in school a minimum of 6 hours a day, 180 days or more a year. A lot of learning can, should, and, by and large, does occur during this time. While "there is no bigger room than the room for improvement," and despite criticisms, the U.S. educational system is generally successful and remains the envy of most of the world. Many of the existing problems can be corrected and the successes can be increased with the optimal use of positive reinforcement in the school. For educational achievement to be optimal, reinforcement contingencies must be taken into account at the level of the individual lesson for the individual student (including computer use); for classroom management; for teacher performance; and for entire school systems.

Individual Lessons

Although studied and discussed as discrete, distinct, separate phenomenon, *behavior and reinforcement exist in a dynamic ever flowing stream of interaction*, ideally, in a seamless manner. Positive reinforcers typically facilitate the flow of the behavioral stream, while punishment acts as a boulder or dam to inhibit the behavioral flow. Behavior is constantly being reinforced or punished, often in subtle, unnoticed ways. Consider the following three hypothetical teacher-student interactions:

1. Teacher: "Spell 'cat.'"
Student: "*k - a - t.*"
Teacher: "No, wrong."

The teacher not only punished the incorrect spelling, but also punished the attempt, *punished the effort*. If the child is only told that he is wrong when he is putting forth effort, putting forth effort is likely to extinguish. The child becomes at risk for developing learned helplessness.

2. Teacher: "Spell 'cat.'"
Student: "*k - a - t.*"
Teacher: "Nice try! That is *very* close! Please try again."

In this case the teacher has correctly identified the incorrect spelling, but *reinforced effort*. The child is likely to try again. However, the teacher has not identified what part of the child's attempt is incorrect. Depending on the child's letter knowledge, the next attempts may very well be "*k - a - c,*" "*c - e - t,*" or "*k - a - f.*" Such results slow progress and often frustrate both the student and teacher.

3. Teacher: "Spell 'cat.'"
Student: "*k - a - t.*"
Teacher: "Nice try! That is *very* close! Can you think of another
    letter that makes the 'ka' sound?"
Child: "*c?*"
Teacher: "That's right! Now, spell 'cat'"
Child: "*c - a - t!*"
Teacher: "Super! Now spell 'cat' again."
Child: "*c - a - t.*"
Teacher: "Great! '*C - a - t*' spells cat. Give yourself another point."

In this final example, in sequence, the teacher's behavior first prompted the child to spell, then identified the incorrect spelling behavior but reinforced the child's effort, then identified the location of the error and prompted error correction, then reinforced error correction and prompted spelling again, then reinforced correct spelling and prompted and reinforced a repetition of correct spelling, and finally the teacher himself gave the correct spelling. As this example illustrates, even teaching the spelling of a simple word may require many embedded instructor-provided reinforcers. Effective teaching of any subject requires copious reinforcement embedded in the lesson coupled closely to student behavior.

The profound effects of systematic reinforcement programs on academic gains were demonstrated in an early prototypical study "Systematic Reinforcement: Academic Performance of Underachieving Students," by Bruce A. Chadwick and Robert C. Day at Washington State University (1971). The students in the study were 25 underachieving African-American and Mexican-American children between 8 and 12 years of age whose average California Achievement Test score was 1.5 letter grades below the norm and whose average grade point average was 1.47 (D). Their parents' education averaged 7 years. In the study there were 3 weeks of nonintervention to establish a baseline, 6 weeks of a systematic token reinforcement program plus teacher-mediated social reinforcement (praise and affectionate attention), followed by 2 weeks of social reinforcement without the token program.

During the token phase, points (i.e., the "tokens") were earned for academic work (reading, math workbooks, etc.) and for social behavior related to academic work such as raising one's hand for attention, or working alone without talking or fighting. Academic work was graded according to a weighted scale that emphasized accuracy (weight = 67%) and speed (weight = 33%). Points earned could be exchanged for lunch (no child ever failed to earn enough points for lunch), candy, clothes, toys, and/or field trips such as boating and swimming.

The results of the program were striking but not surprising for those who understand the power of systematic reinforcement. During baseline, students spent only 39% of the time on academic work, but beginning with the first day of the program the time on academic work immediately increased to average 57%. Problem completion increased dramatically. There was an 83% increase in the completion of math worksheets and a 410% increase in reading laboratory exercises, and, overall, "the level of student efficiency in the seven academic subjects was significantly increasing" (Chadwick & Day, 1971, p. 315). Not only did efficiency increase, but percentage of problems correct, accuracy, that is, *learning* increased during the program at an increased rate. Percent correct went from 50% during baseline to 73% by the end of the program. The children "worked *longer, faster,* and more *accurately* during the tangible and social reinforcement system designed for this study" (p. 318, emphasis in original). The average California Achievement Test score increased .42 years in grade placement as a result of this 11-week summer program. As the reinforcement intervention lasted only 8 weeks, it is likely that if this program had been continued the children's educational achievement would have increased several grade levels in just one academic year! Reinforcement works.

Systematic positive reinforcement increases educational performance both currently and cumulatively. Teodoro Ayllon and Kathy Kelly of Georgia State University demonstrated that both a history of token reinforcement for academic performance and current token reinforcement for correct answers increase standardized test performance of "normal" students on the Metropolitan Achievement Test. In the experimental group, for six weeks correct academic work including spelling, writing, copying, arithmetic, and reading, was reinforced with tokens. The tokens were exchangeable for a variety of enjoyed items and activities. Following the program both the children in the experiment and the control children who were from a normal classroom who did not have a token program for correct academic work took one form of the standardized test. The control children's test scores actually showed an academic decline while the children who had received token reinforcement for correct academic work the previous six weeks scored significantly higher on the standardized test. Next, all of the children were given another form of the test and were reinforced for each correct answer. Reinforcing correct answers on the standardized achievement test, like reinforcing correct answers on IQ tests, significantly increased the scores of both groups. But the effect of reinforcement was even stronger for the children with the history of previous reinforcement for correct academic work. Current reinforcement and a history of reinforcement for correct academic work is necessary for optimal standardized test performance. As the researchers noted, "even with a strong history of reinforcement, contingent reinforcement further augments test performance" (Ayllon & Kelly, 1972, p. 483). Overall the mean standardized test score of the token reinforcement group when tested with token reinforcement for correct answers increased over 50 percent above baseline.

The powerful, beneficial effects of systematic token reinforcement are not limited to standardized tests or to the basic building blocks of academic performance such as basic math and spelling skills. Systematic token reinforcement can also profoundly improve "higher-order" academic skills such as composition. Thomas A. Brigham, Paul S. Graubard, and Aileen Stans of New York University and Yeshiva University argued that "some complex human behaviors can be analyzed in terms of component parts, and these components [are] taught sequentially to produce the complex skill in question" (Brigham et al., 1972, p. 421). In their classic research, they used "reinforcement contingencies to improve and combine current behaviors, thus producing a more complex set of behaviors"

(p. 421). Specifically, male fifth-grade children in a special classroom for behavior problems and academic failure (all students were at least two years behind grade level) were given token reinforcement, points, for general work behaviors, sitting down, finishing work, and so forth; and they received points for the number of words they wrote, points for different words, and points for new words included in written compositions. As a result of the reinforcement program not only did the number of words, different words, and new words that the students used all increase, but the *quality* of the student's compositions improved as well. Mechanical aspects (spelling, grammar, and punctuation); vocabulary (variety and word usage); number of ideas; idea development and internal consistency of ideas all improved. Furthermore, during the program the students' enthusiasm—the students' intrinsic interest—in writing increased. The researchers concluded that the results "support the notion that complex behaviors such as composition may be synthesized by applying specific contingencies of reinforcement to aspects of the behaviors that make up the terminal skill" (p. 427).

Just as the beneficial effects of systematic reinforcement on educational performances is not limited to simple behaviors but improves complex activities, such as composition, the systematic reinforcement itself is not limited to tokens, points, or any specific reinforcer. Systematic use of that powerful social reinforcer praise can also greatly improve educational performances. For example, when Atlanta's Cascade Elementary School that serves a 99% African-American and 80% low-income population went to a three-part-sequence of *immediate personal attention,* testing and basic skills scores greatly increased. The fifth graders' scores went from 44th percentile in reading and the 37th percentile in math on the Iowa Test of Basic Skills to the 82nd percentile in reading and the 74th in math in just four years. Overall the school now averages in the 74th percentile in reading and the 83rd percentile in math. According to Principal Alfonso Jessie, the school's success depends on systematic social reinforcement, contingent praise. "'Children need constant encouragement' Jessie remarks, 'but our encouragement has to be directed at learning.' Cascade's regular testing regime provides the target objectives that the children need to inspire their increased performance. 'We find every opportunity we can to say something positive, but we make sure that we are reinforcing their skill level by doing so'" (Carter, 2000, p. 50). At Cascade Elementary, skill level increases because skill is systematically reinforced. Likewise, when successful remedial techniques for helping students who have fallen behind in their reading were reviewed, the resulting recommendation for remediating reading problems were pause, prompt, and *praise* procedures (Merrett, 1998).

The systematic reinforcing effects of praise can improve educational accomplishments at all educational levels. For example, college students who receive verbal praise for doing homework assignments spend more time completing their assignments (Hancock, 2000). In fact, reinforcing successive approximations with praise may be the fastest way for teachers to build the academic behaviors of their students. As one teacher noted, "When I praised a student that had previously not been completing assignments for having one more assignment completed a particular day than the previous day, that student had even more assignments completed the next day" (from Flora, 2000, p. 68). The critical features of educational reinforcement programs are consistency, immediacy, and frequency of reinforcement contingent on academic and academically related behaviors. The specific form of the reinforcers (tokens, points on a computer, and praise) is not a critical feature. The only critical feature of a reinforcer is that it in fact *reinforces*.

Drill and Thrill

Of course it is difficult for one teacher with over twenty-five students, a too frequent reality, to deliver the proper amounts of reinforcement at the proper moments to individual students contingent on their academic behaviors. Difficult is not the same as impossible, however. Highly effective programs such as Direct Instruction have been developed (e.g., Tashman, 1994) that have frequent reinforcement as a critical feature. However, because these types of instructional programs may depend on highly structured scripts, many teachers argue against their use, claiming that they amount to "drill and kill," and take away from teachers' autonomy to teach as they see best in their classroom. These arguments are without merit.

Giving teachers a completely free hand to teach with absolutely any methods they choose is analogous to allowing doctors to practice medicine with absolutely any methods they choose. For medical doctors this is not only unethical but illegal and should be for teachers as well. Medical doctors are required to give the best treatment possible. Teachers should be required to give the best education possible. When a medical practice is shown to be ineffective or counterproductive it is dropped. When advances are scientifically shown to be effective they replace less effective procedures. To continue to use the less effective procedures would be unethical. Unfortunately there are no such ethical constraints on educators. For example, Project Follow Through was a federally funded study on the effectiveness of different approaches to the Head Start program conducted in the 1970s. Direct Instruction and Behavior Analysis, the two most structured, reinforcement-based approaches were shown to be by far the most effective Head Start approaches (e.g., Berlau, 1998). Unfortunately, and unethically, these results have been swept under the rug, ignored.

In addition to the loss of teaching freedom that high structure of reinforcement programs supposedly cause, these effective approaches are also criticized on the grounds that they amount to "drill and kill," and they turn children into "robots." But whether a lesson is experienced as "drill and kill," or "drill and *thrill*" depends on whether the drill is intrinsically reinforcing or produces instruction-provided reinforcers. There has not been a single case of a reinforcement program reviewed in this book (or elsewhere as far as the author knows) that the recipients of positive reinforcement viewed as aversive. Invariably, structured reinforcement programs increase intrinsic interest. Structured reinforcement programs increase enthusiasm. *Structured reinforcement programs increase the fun in learning.*

Author, and *Psychology Today* book editor, Paul Chance asks, "Where are the robots?" (Chance, 2000, p. 1). Chance argues against the idea that highly structured reinforcement programs that may very well include frequent drilling turn children into robots. He points out that despite years of the educational establishment's chanting this mantra, there has *never been a single case* of a child being turned into a robot. Not a single case of a child having mechanized behavior as a result of these programs. In fact, the opposite occurs. As demonstrated earlier in this book, "the reinforcement of creativity," mastery of the conventional by repetitious reinforced responding lays the foundation for later creative work. Did Mozart, Ray Charles, or the members of The Beatles become musical robots as a result of the thousands of hours they drilled conventional music and standard covers (see chapter 8 in this book)? No, mastery of the ordinary, through reinforced repetitions (drilling) is a prerequisite for the extraordinary. This reality is well understood in the athletic arena. Top performers invariably repeatedly drill the standard basic skills of their sport. If the basics are not mastered, if the basics are not fluent, then any achievements beyond the basic will be impossible.

Self-esteem

In the late 1900s a "self-esteem" movement swept through the educational establishment. The mantra was heard that learning could not occur unless the children first had "high self-esteem." But this claim, untested when first made, is false. Nevertheless, more emphasis was placed on making children feel good about themselves than was placed on learning. A casualty of this poorly conceived movement was that effective reinforced-based approaches were abandoned (Berlau, 1998). Children should not be required to earn tokens, praise, or other reinforcers, it was argued, because it was believed that any failures would undermine their self-esteem. At best the self-esteem movement has only succeeded in making children feel really good about their ignorance. At worst, and the unfortunate reality, is that this movement, by precluding effective highly structured reinforced-based educational approaches, has harmed the educational achievement of countless children (Bereiter & Kurland, 1981; www.uoregon.edu/~adiep/ft/bereiter.htm).

Furthermore, *meaningful* self-esteem is a product of reinforced behavioral performances, not unconditional approval. For example, a child who is told, "that's really great! Keep up the great work. You are super!" for spelling the word *that* as "dat" and *the neighborhood* as "da, hood" may *at the moment of praise* feel good about himself. But the truth is that the child is being cheated by any so-called educator who accepts this spelling. In the long run, if actual literacy is not taught, the victim of this "self-esteem" approach, as an illiterate with few if any employment prospects, will likely live a life in poverty with *low*, not high, self-esteem. In contrast, a child who is gently corrected, has the spelling effort reinforced but is prompted for correct spelling, is, in the long run, more likely to succeed and have high self-esteem. "That's a close try," a teacher might respond, "and that is how many people pronounce the words, but *the* has a 'T-H' sound. Let me hear you say it like that. Good. Now write the word *the* with a *th* ten times, then give yourself a point."

Children who can only spell in "ebonics" or worse, children who are allowed to avoid the sometimes necessary repetitious work involved in learning mathematics to spare their fragile egos, do *not* have high self-esteem. They have been cheated, robbed. Children with high self-esteem are at or above their grade level. They know how to read, how to spell, and know that they can learn and function in the modern world. Children with high self-esteem have learned optimism because their effortful behaviors have been reinforced. Society does not give unconditional approval or reinforcement. Educational practices that do give unconditional approval are misleading, countereducational, and damaging to future success.

The best educational practices all involve structured use of positive reinforcement. Children's behaviors are *frequently* reinforced. Because in effective educational programs, academic and social behaviors are gradually shaped by the method of reinforcing successive approximations, although children do not receive unconditional approval or reinforcers regardless of their behaviors, all children still receive large amounts of praise and affection and their appropriate behaviors are frequently reinforced that builds their self-esteem. When structured positive reinforcement programs are implemented, improved self-esteem is a natural by-product. Children who have their academic achievements shaped with the use of positive reinforcement have increased intrinsic academic interest (e.g., Rawson, 1992), and their enthusiasm for the subjects that produce reinforcement increases (e.g., Brigham et al., 1972). In short when learning is reinforcing, learning is fun.

The Promise of Computers

That today's children are just as smart, just as "quick," and can concentrate just as long as children from any other period can be seen in their skill in computer and electronic games, such as Sega and Nintendo. Children concentrate for extended periods of time and learn very complex material and behavioral skills on electronic games (countless parents have tried and failed to come close to matching their children's performance on computer games). Pioneering reinforcement consultant Aubrey C. Daniels argues that these games provide an effective model of reinforcement delivery for business management. His argument also nicely summarizes what would make an educational lesson effective:

> When you analyze the games, you will see that the player is clear about what is expected of him, that [the] player's behavior is continually measured, and [that] the player is provided with feedback so he knows what the measurements reveal about his performance. Finally, and most importantly, as he plays the game, the player receives high rates of reinforcement which motivate him to play the game over and over again. In fact, reinforcement occurs up to 100 times a minute. (Daniels, 2000, p. 1)

How effective would education be if this structure were adopted for all lessons!

> When you analyze the lessons, you will see that the student is clear about what is expected of him, that the student's behavior is continually measured, and that the student is provided with feedback so he knows what the measurements reveal about his learning. Finally, and most importantly, as he learns, the student receives high rates of reinforcement that motivate him to learn over and over again. In fact, reinforcement occurs up to 100 times a minute.

Effective computer programs are like effective tutors and vice versa. For example, compared to traditional classrooms where a student may go without any feedback or reinforcement for hours on end, effective tutors provide feedback and reinforcement about twice per minute and have a continual rate of interaction, constantly setting the occasions for student responding that is in turn reinforced (Bostow et al., 1995). Relative to the traditional classroom, highly structured approaches such as direct instruction can provide high rates of student responding, feedback, and reinforcement. However, even with these proven approaches a single teacher with twenty-five students is not likely to be able to give optimal feedback and reinforcement to students immediately after each individual responds. However, like "addictive" electronic games, *properly programmed,* learning computer software can provide optimal feedback and reinforcement to individual students. These programs should be clear about what is expected of the student, continually measure performance, and provide immediate feedback and high rates of reinforcement. Additionally, like electronic games where increasing skill permits entry to more difficult levels and "realms," and like all types of effective reinforcement programs in effect worldwide, learning software should *gradually* shape performance to higher and higher academic levels by reinforcing successive approximations. When this approach is followed, learning via computer software is rapid and fun.

To the extent that active responding by the learner receives frequent feedback and reinforcement, effective computer-based learning, or Computer Assisted Instruction (CAI), is effective at all educational levels, from remedial education to college instruction to drug rehabilitation education. A program centered on positive reinforcement and CAI can bring reading levels up years in a matter of months (Davidson & Flora, 1999). Cathy Hall, Thomas Hall, and Judith Kasperek found that "the more time spent on the interactive computer software the higher the course grade" for community-college biology and chemistry students (Hall et al., 1995, p. 967). When general psychology students are required to use computerized study guides that provide frequent and immediate reinforcement for correct answers, their exam scores are approximately half a letter grade higher than when they do not use CAI (Flora & Logan, 1996). A meta-analytic report of research on CAI argued that compared to human teachers with limited patience and energy, "CAI comes into its own with feedback readily available and with an untiring number of examples, encouragement (reinforcement), and challenges for each student no matter what the ability level" (Fletcher-Flinn & Gravatt, 1995, p. 231).

Richard E. Logan's research showed that CAI may also be part of the answer to the puzzle of effective drug abuse rehabilitation. Logan is an African-American retired teamster who began attending college in his mid-forties, graduated with honors, and is earning his Ph.D. in counseling psychology at the University of Akron, Ohio. For his undergraduate honor's project Logan designed a computer program to assist in educating drug treatment clients about the effects of drug abuse. The program was tested, and is still used, in an inpatient drug rehabilitation center. When clients used the computer program, they scored significantly higher on their weekly tests. Former drug abusers who become educated about the effects of drug abuse are less likely to relapse (Logan & Flora, 1997). Therefore, Logan's work demonstrates that the educationally beneficial effects of reinforcement based CAI extend beyond the walls of traditional educational establishments. Again and again it is seen that regardless of the medium delivering the instruction (computer, teacher, parent, or peer); regardless of the form of the reinforcers (praise, tokens, computer points, or candy); and regardless of the individual's present label or situation (college student, infant, retarded, gifted, or drug rehabilitation client) *systematic reinforcement of successive approximations of academic and life goals is the most effective educational approach.*

Classroom Management

Frequent, systematic positive reinforcement of academic activities is also the most effective approach to classroom discipline. When students are working for positive reinforcement contingent on academic behaviors, they will be working on academics, not misbehaving. If the teacher is clear about what is expected of students, continually measures performance; provides immediate feedback, high rates of reinforcement, and reinforces *gradual* successive approximations to shape to higher and higher academic achievement; then the children will be achieving, not misbehaving. If waiting for one's turn, staying in line, and walking in the hall produce positive reinforcement then, *by definition of reinforcement*, waiting for one's turn, staying in line, and walking in the hall, will increase. Going out of turn, breaking in line, and running will decrease by default. If raising one's hand to gain teacher attention, staying in one's chair, working without fighting, or disturbing one's neighbor produce positive reinforcement, then *by definition of reinforcement*, raising one's hand, staying in one's chair, and working without fighting will increase. Speaking without raising one's hand, getting out of one's chair, and fighting will decrease by default.

Indeed, the study "Eliminating Discipline Problems by Strengthening Academic Performance," by Teodoro Ayllon and Michael Roberts from Georgia State University established that systematic positive reinforcement of academic achievement does in fact eliminate discipline problems. At an affluent, upper-middle-class school, the behavior of children in one fifth-grade classroom had become so disruptive that another teacher was added to the classroom. But this had no effect on the disruptions in the classroom. Therefore, to reduce the discipline problems, the researchers developed a token reinforcement system that reinforced reading accuracy, as measured on worksheets based on reading. Problem behaviors were merely noted and recorded. The tokens earned for reading were exchangeable for a variety of activities such as extra recess time. Reading accuracy went from under 50% to 85%. Disruptive behaviors that had been occurring approximately 40% of the time decreased to 5%. Thus positive reinforcement for academic achievement not only increased academic achievement, but drastically reduced problem behavior. "This study is of critical interest to educators," argued the researchers, "because it demonstrates that a positive approach; that is, a focus on academic objectives, rather than on undesirable behavior, reduced problematic behaviors" (Ayllon & Roberts, 1974, p. 75). Positive reinforcement of the good—educational achievement—precludes the bad.

Good teachers do not ever have "bad kids." They have children with different energy levels from different backgrounds who come to them with different levels of academic achievement and different reinforcement histories. But good teachers find effective reinforcers for all of their students and set reinforcement contingencies so that each student can achieve. Like well-designed electronic games that gradually demand more and more skillful performance while all the while providing frequent reinforcement, the skillful teacher gradually changes the reinforcement criteria so that increasingly demanding educational behaviors occur. While very rarely a "time-out from positive reinforcement" may be necessary to eliminate dangerous or extremely disruptive behaviors, the most effective classroom management procedures are centered on systematic positive reinforcement for appropriate behaviors (Alberto & Troutman, 1999; Martin & Pear, 1999; Schloss & Smith, 1998).

Teacher and School System Contingencies

Teaching is behavior. Like all other behaviors, the most effective way to shape and maintain teaching behavior is with systematic positive reinforcement. The most effective, universal, reinforcer for adult humans remains money. Society must sufficiently reinforce teaching to have sufficient teachers. Very few individuals with advanced degrees in math would find teaching intrinsically reinforcing enough that they would leave a business job paying over $100,000 a year to start teaching at less than $40,000. While there will be exceptions, as long as teaching remains one of the most poorly paid professions, teaching will continue to attract only the least accomplished college students into the education major (this is likely one reason why many elite private academies prefer that their teachers have *non*education degrees). The first and easiest way to improve teaching is to improve the pay for good teaching. Teachers need to be paid according to their performance and according to their worth to society. Anyone whose life has been significantly changed by a teacher or by any involved parent will agree that a good teacher is priceless.

But just as good teachers never have a "bad student," effective teachers *never* have students who "can't learn." If there has been no learning, there has been no teaching. It is as simple as that. A teacher cannot claim to have taught if there are no measurable changes in the students' academic behaviors. To say "I taught the material, but the students didn't learn it," is a contradiction of terms, an oxymoron. To say "I taught the material, but the students were not motivated," is just as unacceptable. Learning and performance are inseparable. If the students really learned, then they would have performed. A thought not acted on with overt behavior is functionally the same as no thought at all.

Fortunately, because teaching is behavior, teaching can be taught. The most effective way to teach and maintain effective teaching is with systematic positive reinforcement. This is exactly what Thaddeus Lott did to turn around Weslely Elementary School in Houston, Texas (see chapter 1 in this book). Teachers can be taught and reinforced for learning to establish and reinforce clear student expectations. Teachers can be taught and reinforced for continually measuring student behavior. Teachers can be taught and reinforced for providing feedback so the teacher and students know what the measurements reveal about student learning. Finally, and most importantly, teachers can be taught and reinforced for providing high rates of reinforcement that motivate the students to learn and perform. When Norman L. Breyer and George J. Allen of the University of Connecticut (Breyer & Allen, 1975) praised on-task behavior and ignored off-task behavior, on-task behavior increased. When they started providing tokens for on-task behavior, on-task behavior increased further. But it was not the students' on-task behavior that was being measured and reinforced with praise and tokens, it was the teacher's behavior! Teaching behaviors are a function of reinforcement just like other behaviors.

Of course, it would be impractical, if not impossible, to continuously monitor teachers' daily behaviors so that effective teaching techniques and behaviors could be frequently and immediately reinforced. However, since effective teaching includes frequent, if not continuous, monitoring of student learning and behavior, accurate records of teaching behavior should exist that may also function as conditioned reinforcement for the teacher. The records of the students' improvements and academic achievements are also a record of effectiveness of the teachers' teaching behaviors! Unfortunately, especially in "union shops," the usual employment contingencies for teachers are similar to the contingencies of employees elsewhere. The major requirement is showing up to work on time, and as long as a minimal amount of attempted teaching occurs and as long as there are no major ethical violations, loss of employment can be avoided. Since for most teachers in the United States there is no *systematic positive reinforcement delivered to teachers contingent on student achievement*, there is no motivation to ensure that the children are in fact achieving academically, much less any discretionary effort directed toward the student's learning. Instead the major goal for teachers is "making it till Friday." (This was actually the title of my textbook when I took educational psychology as an undergraduate.) The attitude is, "if the students learned anything, great. If they didn't, well tough. I put in my time."

It does not have to be this way. Performance incentives and other positive reinforcers, effectively improve performance in business (e.g., Nelson, 1994) and could also be used to motivate teaching performance and thus increase student achievement. But, first because teaching is a vital profession, all effective teachers should receive a base pay corresponding to the importance of their job, which would be much more than most teachers currently receive. As long as their students advance educationally at the rate of one grade level per year, teachers should receive this base pay (with cost-of-living and inflation adjustments). However, raises should *not* be based on seniority but on effectiveness. Why should an ineffective teacher be given a raise just because he has been "teaching" ineffectively for twenty years?

Raises, bonuses, and positive reinforcement, should be contingent upon effectiveness that is measured by student achievement. *For example*, a teacher whose students advanced on average 1.0 grade levels over the year would not be given a raise beyond cost-of-living and inflation adjustments. But each tenth of a year average advancement beyond one year could be reinforced with a 2% raise. Thus, a teacher whose students advanced 1.2 grade levels would be given a 4% raise. A teacher whose students advanced 2.0 grade levels would be given a 20% raise and so on. Of course teachers on such a system, or on any other achievement-based compensation plan, may feel pressured to get their students to perform. Surely, that is better than "making it till Friday."

Fortunately, as the evidence shows, the most effective way to maximize student achievement, which is synonymous with teaching achievement, is with systematic positive reinforcement programs. When teaching is based on frequent feedback and reinforcement, high rates of interaction, and frequent student responding that is in turn reinforced, intrinsic interest in academic work increases, enthusiasm increases, and the students have fun. When students are interested, involved in the lesson, enthusiastic, and having fun, teaching is fun and intrinsically reinforcing. Thus, the initial pressure teachers may feel should evolve into enthusiasm. Furthermore, because student achievement measures teaching effectiveness, and teaching effectiveness should be reinforced (financially or otherwise) each measure of student improvement, from individual responses to final exam scores, should function as conditioned reinforcers for the teacher.

Failing Students—Failing Teachers

When students fail to learn, "teachers" have failed to teach. When there is no learning, there has been no teaching. Each student who "flunks" is a failure of the teacher. During his campaign, President George W. Bush repeatedly argued that there need to be "consequences" in education. However, "consequence" is not synonymous with "punishment." As this chapter has argued, the most effective consequence for occasioning educational excellence is positive reinforcement for educationally appropriate behavior.

Yet, the consequence advocated by Bush is to inflict even more disadvantage on failing schools by removing federal funding from schools where the students are not advancing academically. A more effective consequence for failing schools would be to *increase funding contingently*. Because it means their teaching is outstanding, teachers whose students excel academically should be given bonuses, performance-based incentive pay, and other positive reinforcers. These incentives should especially be made available to teachers at generally underachieving schools.

Computers (business "throwaways" could serve the purpose) with positive reinforcement-based learning software (described earlier in this chapter) should be made available to the students at underachieving schools and the teachers should be trained in their use. Connecting all classrooms to the World Wide Web is not what is most needed. Making available to children software that uses positive reinforcement to shape successive approximations resulting in the academic skills of reading, writing, spelling, mathematics, and the scientific method is what is most needed.

Teachers who are ineffective, as measured by the lack of their students' educational achievement, should be *required* to undergo training to develop effective teaching behaviors. Rather than remove funding, funding should be available for this training. Naturally, this training would be centered on the effective use of positive reinforcement. The training should teach teachers to be clear about what is expected of students; to frequently if not continually measure and record student behavior (in part so that student behavior can be frequently reinforced); and to provide the students with feedback so the teacher and students know what the measurements reveal about student learning.

Most importantly, teachers should be trained to deliver high rates of positive reinforcement to motivate the students to learn. Although most teachers believe they deliver high amounts of praise and other reinforcers, they do not (Flora, 2000; White, 1975). Despite the fact, as documented throughout this book that high rates of positive reinforcement—high rates of approval—maximize achievement and development, the reality is that teachers at all grade levels deliver more disapproval than approval (White, 1975; Wyatt & Hawkins, 1987). Fortunately, with proper positive reinforcement the teaching behaviors of even middle-aged teaching veterans with over twenty years of experience can be effectively changed (e.g., Breyer & Allen, 1975). Teachers at all levels of all subjects can increase their rates of appropriate approval and decrease their disapprovals that will invariably result in improved student performances (e.g., Flora, 2000).

Society can go a long way toward ensuring effective teaching, and thus student achievement, by reserving funds for each teacher. Effective teachers as measured by student achievement would receive this money as positive reinforcement for effective teaching. For ineffective teachers, this funding would go toward required reinforcement-based training with some portion given to the teachers for successful completion of the training. Ineffective teachers who refused to undergo the training or to change their classroom behaviors, from whatever they were doing previously to effective positive reinforcement-based instruction should be required to find a new profession.

Standardized Testing, Teaching the Test

The true test of teacher achievement is student achievement. Undoubtably, this is one reason why there is resistance to standardized testing by many in teaching, especially resistance from teachers' unions. Unions of all professions exist to protect their members, their ineffective members as well as their productive members. Teachers' unions are no different. Some educators argue that reliance on standardized testing results in "teaching the test"—as if something were inherently wrong with that. When a skeptic attempts to flush out what protesters mean by this phrase, the usual response is that preparing for the tests takes time away from other activities or prevents the development of vague, touchy-feely, ill-defined concepts such as "holistic growth." The most likely academic source of objections to standardized testing comes from the ultimately harmful romantic and humanistic philosophies of education covered in this book (see part 1). The most likely source of objections to standardized testing by the teachers themselves is the realization that the students' results are also a standardized evaluation of their effectiveness as teachers.

In Ohio, fourth graders are required to pass a standardized reading test to be promoted to the fifth grade. In 2001, in Youngstown Ohio, 44 percent of the children were not be able to pass the test. It is the parents, kindergartner, first-, second-, third-, and fourth-grade teachers who have failed, not the children. The children are the victims. There are effective methods for teaching reading. How can a child who has been in a classroom for 6 hours a day, 180 days a year, for 5 years not know how to read? How can teachers, who have children in their classrooms 6 hours a day, 180 days a year, for 5 years but who do not advance in reading, call themselves "teachers"? These teachers should be required to take, and receive, positive reinforcement for, completing training in positive reinforcement-based teaching procedures and technology. When teachers teach effectively, students achieve. When students achieve, teachers should be amply reinforced. Union or no union, when students do not achieve, teachers should not receive reinforcers such as raises.

The reality is that life is full of tests, and good teaching *always* "teaches to the test." This is easiest to see in athletics and combat. In sports such as football and basketball each game is in fact a test, and is referred to as such by fans, players, and coaches—"Carolina will *test* our speed at the corners, but the *real test* will be in two weeks when we play Michigan." To prepare for these tests, coaches *teach to the test*! Teams have practice squads that exist for the sole purpose of imitating the upcoming opponent, the upcoming test. Competitors learn what the opponents tendencies will be, their mannerisms, what to look for, and what to avoid. If the coach has effectively taught to the test the team will win, pass the test, and be reinforced. Likewise, a boxer's manager will also teach to the test. Mike Tyson would provide a different test, a strong inside fighter, than Lennox Lewis, a tall outside puncher. For a fighter to have a chance against either one of these opponents, a chance to pass the test, he would have to be taught to the test. His sparring partners, his practice opponents, would have to be either stocky and rough, or tall, long, and strong, and he would have to be prepared for what to expect in each type of test. To have a chance of winning, a chance of reinforcement, the fighter's manager would have to "teach to the test."

Teaching to the test has also *always* been a reality in education as well. In Drivers Education, students are taught to drive properly, and the test includes a driving test. Students who cannot drive properly do not receive their driver's license. If they drive properly, learning to drive is reinforced with a driver's license. Students are taught to drive, taught to the test. Would we want people to be allowed to drive who were not taught to the test of driving? Plumbers, electricians, and other professional tradespeople are required to pass tests before they can become licensed. The tests include proving that they can perform their trade correctly and safely. Thus, they are trained to do plumbing, to do safe correct electrical work— they are taught to the test. Would anyone want an electrician to wire their house who had not been taught to the test of proper, safe, electrical work? Would they prefer a "holistic electrician"?

A fourth-grade reading test or high school competency test (which actually measures ninth-, not twelfth-, grade competency) should be no different. Children in the fourth grade should be able to read. People in the twelfth grade should be required to pass a test of basic ninth-grade skills before they are allowed to graduate. If teaching to the test is said to take away from other activities in the classroom, one has to wonder what are these other activities.

Another criticism of standardized testing is that the tests do not measure what they claim to test. If that is true, then that is a correctable problem with the test construction, not a fatal flaw of standardized testing itself. If a so-called reading test does not test reading, then the test needs to be changed. But reading still needs to be tested, and the more frequently the better. Frequent testing serves as an opportunity to provide positive reinforcement for any academic gains, as an important diagnostic tool, and as an opportunity to teach additional topics—an opportunity for meaningful "holistic education."

For example, a standardized reading comprehension exam may rely heavily on multiple choice questions. A teacher's knee-jerk criticism might be: "this format confuses the students; it mixes them up too much; even I find it confusing." But an achieving teacher's response might be: "teaching to the multiple choice test gives me a opportunity to introduce the topic of symbolic logic, and mathematical relations as well as to explore the interpersonal relationships of the stories we are reading. For example, an answer option might be 'D, A, and C but not B.' This option requires that my students understand what options A, B, and C, are and their relations to each other, which requires a real reading comprehension and some logical thought. I'm lucky that preparing my students for the reading comprehension test helps me teach both."

Frequent standardized testing allows educators to more accurately identify students who are having learning problems and what areas those problems are in. Once the deficits are identified, special programs can be employed to ameliorate if not overcome the deficit. These programs should be directed *at* the deficit, *on* the problem, *not around the problem*. A child with a reading problem should not be allowed to skip reading, have notes taken for him, and be excused from required reading. This only puts the child further behind (Davidson & Flora, 1999). Instead, a child with a reading problem should be required to read more, not less. Of course the successive approximations required for reinforcement should be more gradual, and reading behavior should be more frequently reinforced than may be necessary for children without the deficit. As a "dyslexic," I would not be writing this book if I had been allowed to avoid my spelling. Fortunately, my father attacked rather than avoided my deficit. (Before my weekly spelling tests, I may have been required to, and reinforced for, spelling a single word up to a hundred times [Flora, 1998].) Once learning problems are identified (and they can be identified with standardized testing), they should be attacked with repetitious positive reinforced responding. Learning problems should not be used as an excuse.

Of course, there are *very rare* cases where standardized testing may not work. A child with very bad vision problems could not be expected to pass a visual reading test. However, the child could be required to, and reinforced for, learning to read braille.

The more frequently standardized testing occurs, the more frequently teachers have opportunities to reinforce academic gains. Teachers can more accurately know each child's current academic abilities so that they know what the child is currently capable of and what will likely be a successful starting point to begin reinforcing successive approximations to further academic gains. Each successive standardized test will provide teachers with—hopefully reinforcing—feedback as to how successful their teaching behaviors are. Teaching to the test and standardized testing provide outstanding opportunities for learning and opportunities for positive reinforcement for both teachers and students.

11

REINFORCEMENT IN DRUG USE, ABUSE, AND TREATMENT

Hundreds of millions of people use and abuse both legal and illegal drugs. The most basic, useful, and honest, explanation for the use and abuse of behaviorally altering and "mind-altering" psychotropic drugs is that the use of drugs is reinforcing. "Drugs control behavior by acting as reinforcers, the same way that food and sex and water and heat can do that," says University of Vermont psychiatry professor Stephen T. Higgins (from D. W. Miller, 2000, p. A19). When drugs are taken to "calm the nerves," "forget about life's troubles," or "alleviate pain," to escape or avoid aversive stimulation or an aversive physiological state, then the drugs are being taken for negative reinforcement. When drugs are taken to "party," "get high," or "catch a buzz," for the pleasurable effects they bring, then the drugs are being taken for positive reinforcement.

When drug use is negatively reinforced then it is much more likely to become abusive or addictive (Franken, 1994). Excessive drug use is a product of the natural generalization process and occurs with both illegal and legal drug use. For example, a high school student may flunk an important exam or a business person may lose an important contract. The high school student's and businessperson's friends may then encourage them to come out for a drink, smoke some "pot," or take some other drug to forget about their failure and get rid of the "blues" (escape). If the drug use is successful, if they consequently forget about their failure and get rid of the blues, at least temporarily, then their drug use behavior has been negatively reinforced. By virtue of the reinforcement and generalization processes, the next time they are in a situation where they experience failure or feel blue, even if it is not caused by what occasioned the initial drug use, then they are likely to engage in drug use behavior. For example, the aversive feelings produced by getting turned down on a date may be responded to by drug use. Several instances for drug use may cumulate in being put on academic probation or in a job demotion, both aversive experiences. Unfortunately by this time the individual has learned that any aversive situation may, temporarily but immediately, be escaped by more drug use, and therefore, each unpleasant situation may be responded to with drug use. One may even begin to avoid aversive feelings altogether by engaging in drug use behavior prior to potentially unpleasant events. In essence the individual has learned, via the process of negative reinforcement, that "any time I feel bad or any time I expect to be in an unpleasant situation I can escape or avoid the unpleasantness by taking drugs."

The use and abuse of legal, prescribed drugs often follows a similar path. An individual may be involved in a car accident and be prescribed pain medication. If the medication is effective, if the pain is alleviated, lessened, or removed, then taking pain medication has been negatively reinforced. Due to the reinforcement process, the next time the person is in pain or discomfort, including "emotional pain," there is an increased likelihood that the person will take pain medication. If the individual cannot get legally prescribed pain medication, then he may begin to "self-medicate" with alcohol or illegal drugs.

CONTINGENCY TRAPS

The immediately reinforcing effects of drug use function as a contingency trap, making more use likely and life without drugs more difficult with each use. In a contingency trap, immediate reinforcement "traps" the behavior that produces immediate reinforcement, but may, in the long run result in punishment, or preclude larger delayed reinforcers. Impulsive responses, the choice for a smaller sooner reinforcer, occur in contingency traps and may prevent working toward larger later reinforcers—"self-control." Each time the high school student and businessperson use drugs to forget about their troubles they may indeed forget about their troubles (immediate negative reinforcement) and even have a good time (immediate positive reinforcement). But if they are intoxicated, using drugs, that means they are not working on the next exam or next contract, increasing the probability of another low grade or lost contract. That is, when they "come back to reality," when effects of the drugs wear off, they are likely to find that their troubles are worse, their situation is even more aversive than when they started taking drugs in the first place. Paradoxically and unfortunately, these increased troubles are increasingly likely to be escaped (and in turn compounded) by more drug use—a downward spiral contingency trap of negative reinforcement.

Contingency traps trap the behavior of legal drug use as well. For example, a college student may fear giving a class presentation. To deal with the "social anxiety," a doctor may prescribe anti-anxiety medication even though behavioral treatment of social phobia is more effective, has less relapse, and has no side effects (Ballenger, 1999). Consequently, instead of learning to confront and deal with potentially embarrassing public situations (as almost everyone must do), the student has learned to take drugs. The next time the student is to encounter a potentially anxiety-producing social situation, be it a class presentation or party with friends, the process of negative reinforcement makes drug use behavior increasingly likely.

The ultimately more effective and widely useful behavior treatment may require several sessions of role playing; systematic relaxation training; and gradual, guided anxiety-exposure exercises. But because the drug use behavior produces immediate effects without effort and the more effective behavioral treatment does not, drug use behavior becomes more likely. Drug use gets snared by the contingency trap of immediate negative reinforcement. Each potentially anxiety-producing situation is increasingly likely to occasion more drug use and ultimately, paradoxically, the anti-anxiety medication will compound the person's anxiety problems because as a result of the drug use, potentially anxiety-producing situations will elicit even more anxiety than originally would have occurred if no "medication" had ever been given in the first place.

Unfortunately, this situation describes a former student of mine (and likely millions of other people). For my former student and almost all college students (and professors as well) sometimes even just going to class produces anxiety (as it naturally should to some degree: "Have I read?" "Am I caught up?" "Am I prepared to answer potential questions from the professor [or students]?"). Because the student, a drama major, had learned, via negative reinforcement, to deal with performance anxiety by taking drugs, she began to take anti-anxiety medication to alleviate the anxiety associated with going to class and eventually to alleviate the anxiety associated with many social situations such as parties and family gatherings. When her doctor would not renew her prescription, she found a doctor who would give her a new prescription. When her legal medications ran out, to escape anxiety she "self-medicated," with marijuana and other illegal drugs. Because drug use was immediately reinforcing, produced immediate "escape" and relief, my student learned to be a drug abuser.

ENVIRONMENTAL INFLUENCE

When humans are in aversive environments their impulsive behavior increases. Responses that produce immediate reinforcement increase even if the immediate consequences do not remove or reduce the aversiveness (Flora et al., 1992). Therefore, people in aversive situations, abusive relationships or living in environmentally toxic environments, are at an increased risk for drug abuse because of the immediately reinforcing consequences that drug use produces. Taking drugs will produce escape *right NOW*, taking drugs will make the abused feel better *immediately*. But leaving an abusive relationship or moving from a toxic environment (assuming leaving is even possible) both require hard work and may result in immediate pain. While leaving a relationship or moving would result in greater long-term gain and safety, this reinforcement is long delayed and therefore exerts less of an effect on behavior.

PAIN

Similarly, when people are in physical pain their ability to show self-control, their ability to maximize long-term overall reinforcement decreases. When people are in pain, responses that produce immediate reinforcement increase even if the immediate consequences do not remove or reduce the pain (Flora & Wilkerson, 2001). People experiencing physical or emotional pain are at an increased risk for drug abuse because of the immediately reinforcing consequences that drug use produces. Thus, to quote the rock group Pink Floyd, people in pain may abuse drugs to "become comfortably numb," not because being numb is ultimately the most reinforcing state, but because the drug-induced numbness produces immediate, but temporary, escape from the pain. Drug use produces immediate reinforcement.

POSITIVE REINFORCEMENT OF DRUG USE AND ABUSE

Of course, people don't drink alcohol only at funerals. Since the beginning of recorded time people have drunk alcohol and taken other drugs to celebrate: at weddings, at victory celebrations, at graduation parties, and at New Year's Eve parties. A college student is just as likely to get drunk to celebrate earning an "A" as he is to forget about receiving an "F." A businessperson is just as likely to get drunk to celebrate winning a contract as he is to escape the pain associated with losing one. Almost anytime and anywhere people are gathered to have a good time, drug use is likely to occur. People take drugs because *taking drugs feels good*, and if you already feel good, taking drugs may make you feel even better. *Taking drugs produces immediate strong, positive reinforcement*. People take drugs to "get high," "feel good," and "party." When a drug user answers the question, "what are you doing?" with "partying," he may in fact be all alone. For many the phrase "partying," is synonymous with "using drugs." *All* drugs of abuse, including alcohol and nicotine, work physiologically by activating the reinforcement circuits in the brain.

LEVELS OF UNDERSTANDING

Millions of people "know" and "understand" how a manual transmission car works. Give them one on the East Coast and they can drive it to the West Coast. Put the car in neutral, put the key in and turn the ignition, put in the clutch, shift into first, let off the clutch while putting on the gas, and so on. The proof that they "know how it works" is in the fact that they can effectively "work it." Millions more "know" how an automatic transmission car "works." But relatively few people "know" how a car works at the mechanical level of the four cycles of the standard four-stroke internal combustion engine, much less how the power generated on the pistons (or even what a piston is) ultimately results in the tires spinning.

Similarly, in laying out evolution through natural selection, Charles Darwin never saw a gene or DNA, but he "knew" how evolution occurred. He understood, through thousands of observations, that the environment selects those characteristics that allow organisms to reach reproductive age and have offspring. Organisms possessing those characteristics will increase in population. Organisms "less fit," organisms lacking those characteristics, will die out. For hundreds of years (even before Darwin), this *functional understanding* of evolution has been, and still is used in artificial selection in selective breeding and cross-pollination. It is not necessary to have a map of the horse's genome to understand that breeding a fast horse with a slow horse is less likely to produce a race winner than breeding a fast horse with another fast horse. Although he did not know, or need to know, the genetic basis behind the dangers of inbreeding, Darwin understood that breeding with close relatives increased the potential of maladaptive recessive traits becoming manifest in any resulting offspring. As a consequence of this knowledge, Darwin fretted that the illnesses and sicknesses of his children was a product of his marrying and breeding with his first cousin (Desmond & Moore, 1991). At the level of the organism-environment interaction it is possible to understand evolution through natural selection without any reference to genetic analysis.

Likewise, at the level of the behavior-environment interaction it is possible to understand reinforcement without any reference to the physiological mechanisms of reinforcement. We know, through thousands of observations, that the environment selects those behaviors that produce reinforcing consequences. Reinforced behaviors increase in frequency. "Less fit" behaviors, behaviors that don't produce reinforcement, will "die out." It is not necessary to understand the physiological basis of reinforcement to know that providing tokens exchangeable for backup reinforcers for academic behaviors and time-out from positive reinforcement for fighting will increase academic behaviors and decrease fighting. One can understand and use reinforcement effectively without any knowledge of the physiology of reinforcement.

However, because drugs tend to immediately and strongly affect the brain's natural reinforcement circuits, a brief understanding of the physiological effects of reinforcement and drugs can go a long way toward understanding both drug abuse in particular and reinforcement in general. Understanding the biological basis of reinforcement and drugs can help us understand why a person "voluntarily" continues to abuse drugs when it is clearly apparent to all other observers that the person is killing himself.

THE PHYSIOLOGY OF REINFORCEMENT
AND ADDICTIVE DRUGS

A reinforcer is a consequence of behavior that increases the probability of repetition of the behavior that immediately preceded or occurred concurrently with the reinforcer. Reinforcement is the process of increasing behaviors with reinforcers. The reinforcement process can be natural or intrinsic as is the case when sexual orgasms increase the probability of the behaviors that preceded orgasm. Or the reinforcement process can be contrived as the case when a parent reinforces homework with praise and contingent video game access. Primary reinforcers include such events and stimuli as orgasm, eating carbohydrate and fat rich foods, warmth and physical touch, and various sensory stimulation (Baldwin & Baldwin, 2001). If humans and other primates did not find these events reinforcing, they would become extinct. Evolution must have provided a *physiological* mechanism for reinforcement. Evolution must have provided a mechanism that during and following sexual intercourse, and during and after eating energy dense foods, the body says in effect, "*keep doing this, and when finished, do it again.*" Without such a mechanism, sex and eating, if they occurred, would not recur. Without such a mechanism, extinction of the species would occur instead.

Of course the label for this "do it again" process is *reinforcement*. The physiological mechanism of reinforcement provided by evolution is the "reward pathway" in the brain. The activation of the "reward pathway" is the mechanism for the experience of pleasure. When reinforcement occurs dopaminergic neurons, neurons that release the neurotransmitter molecule *dopamine*, increase activity. More specifically reinforcement stimulates increases in the neurotransmitter dopamine in brain circuits from the midbrain through the hypothalamus to the prefrontal cortex (for physiology students, this account may be too superficial. However, it should be sufficient for a better understanding of drug abuse and reinforcement.)

When animals are operated on so that pressing a lever will directly stimulate the reinforcement circuits—self-electric stimulation of the brain ("self-ESB")—they will press the lever—self-ESB—nonstop for up to twenty-four hours, pass out, sleep for about eight hours, wake, and immediately begin to self-ESB again. If they are not removed from the experimental chamber they will continue this process, forsaking food and water, until they die. In short, direct stimulation of these brain circuits is the most reinforcing activity an animal can do.

Of course Homo sapiens (humans), and animals are not born with wires protruding from the reinforcement circuits in their brains that can be electrically stimulated to experience pleasure. However, certain behaviors and experiences activate the reinforcement circuit. And the more immediately and intensely the circuit is activated the more reinforcing the behavioral experience will be. If a behavior is not associated with an activation of the reinforcement circuit, the experience will not be pleasurable or reinforcing, and there will be no increased probability of the behavior recurring.

Not surprisingly, reinforcing behaviors activate the brain's reinforcement circuit. "Activating this circuit, also called the reward circuit, produces a feel-good sensation," summarizes *Newsweek* reporter Sharon Begley. "Eating cheesecake or tacos or any other food you love activates it. So does sex, winning a competition, acing a test, receiving praise and other pleasurable experiences" (Begley, 2001, p. 40). In short, positive reinforcement activates it. "The pleasure circuit communicates in the chemical language of dopamine," continues Begley. "This neurotransmitter zips from neuron to neuron in the circuit like a molecular happy face, affecting the firing of other neurons and producing feelings from mild happiness to euphoria" (p. 40).

A word of praise may produce mild happiness, and a night of sexual passion may produce a night of euphoria. Further increasing the dopamine activity further increases the feel-good sensations and the tendency to repeat the behaviors associated with the sensations—the reinforcement process. Being praised while eating cheesecake followed by a night of sexual activity should keep the circuit fairly activated. But the most direct and immediate way to increase the activity is to directly simulate the dopamine neurons with electric brain stimulation. Since most humans do not want wires implanted into their brains, the next most direct and quick way to stimulate the circuit is to take drugs that increase the concentration of dopamine in the circuit. Electrical stimulation takes a few milliseconds (1/1,000s of a second). Inhaling dopamine-increasing drugs takes a few seconds to effect the brain. Injecting the drugs into the bloodstream takes a few more seconds, and ingesting (swallowing) the drugs may take a few minutes. The greater the amount of drug used, the greater the (temporary) increase in dopamine activity. Acing a test, being praised, eating cheese-cake, and having sex activate the circuit, and having it all in one day will be a very good day indeed. But by a magnitude of several fold, smoking a few rocks of crack cocaine will more highly activate the dopamine-pleasure-reinforcement circuit than a night of praise, cheesecake, and sex ever will. When a drug addict claims that his drug of choice is "better than sex," at the biological level of reinforcement circuit activation, the addict is telling the truth.

All drugs of addiction, including but not limited to nicotine, alcohol, cocaine, amphetamines, and heroin, activate the reinforcement circuit. While all activate the circuit to varying degrees, the different effects of the different drugs are accounted for by the other neurotransmitters and brain circuits that the drugs may activate or depress. How strongly and quickly different drugs become addictive depends in part on how strongly and quickly the drugs activate the reinforcement circuit. Thus by short-cutting the usual process by which valuable behaviors important for individual and species survival activate the brain reinforcement circuit, drugs of addiction cheat the organism by directly exploiting the normally evolutionarily adaptive reinforcement system.

Although they activate the dopamine-pleasure-reinforcement circuit—an evolved *survival mechanism*—other than making the user feel good temporarily, drug use usually has no—*zero*—adaptive value. No survival value. Drug use provides no evolutionary benefit to the organism. Drug use is the ultimate contingency trap, providing immediate, and strong reinforcement but ultimately resulting in delayed punishment and costing long-term reinforcement.

COSTS OF DRUG USE

Even without considering drug-induced accidents, fighting, and other maladaptive behavior, drug use produces several aversive consequences at both the physiological level and level of behavior-environment interaction. Physiologically, the effects of drugs on the dopamine system are analogous to what happens to a country that receives an abundant, cheap, easily accessible, and usable foreign energy source. When the cheap energy is flowing into the country, all is good—Sunday drives, gas guzzlers, three-car garages, air conditioning set at 65 degrees, heat at 80 degrees, public transportation? Ha! But something also happens to the country's internal energy and transportation systems. Public transportation (buses, railways, and subways) is not developed; technologies for potential internal sources of energy (wind, solar, and hydro) are not pursued; and the existing internal energy system deteriorates—pipelines and slow but steady wells are shut off and rust. Why explore and pump oil internally when it can be had in much larger quantities and more cheaply from foreign countries? Consequently, as happened during the United States' energy crisis of the 1970s, when the flow of foreign oil is shut off, the "addicted" country experiences much pain. So much pain that the next time the external source of oil is threatened a country is willing to go to war to preserve the source of cheap oil, as was the case when the United States declared Kuwait of "vital national security interest" and went to war with Iraq in the 1990s to preserve the flow of oil to the United States.

Analogously, like cheap foreign energy, when the dopamine system is being activated by drugs, as far as the brain is concerned, all is good—euphoria. Go to class or work? Just do some more drugs. But something also happens to the dopamine-reinforcement system when it is artificially stimulated by drugs. To deal with the artificially activated dopamine levels, dopamine receptors shut down as the brain tries to cool the overheated system and, depending on the drug being abused, the dopamine stores may also become depleted. With less dopamine and fewer dopamine receptors, normally reinforcing activities become less reinforcing. Cheesecake, praise, and sex don't feel as good as they did before drug use began. In a vicious cycle to experience high levels of pleasure again, the drug user is likely to take more drugs that ultimately further reduce dopamine receptors and ironically reduce the individual's ability to experience pleasure—the ultimate contingency trap. Consequently, when access to the drug is shut off, the addicted experiences much pain. So much pain that the next time the access to the drug is threatened, even as drug use and everything else become less and less pleasurable, the addict may be willing to cheat, lie, steal, and kill to ensure that their drug is available to them.

While drugs such as cocaine and amphetamines that most directly and strongly stimulate the dopamine-reinforcement circuit are the most addictive, the deceitful contingency trap of drug addiction also precisely describes the progression of nicotine addiction. The data consistently and repeatedly show that smoking tobacco (a highly effective nicotine delivery system) does not reduce stress, but smoking *causes* stress. According to Andy C. Parrott of the University of East London, "the stress levels of adult smokers are . . . higher than those of nonsmokers, adolescent smokers report increasing levels of stress as they develop regular patterns of smoking" (Parrott, 1999, p. 817). "Far from acting as an aid for mood control," argues Parrott, "nicotine dependency seems to exacerbate stress." Adult smokers have "normal moods during smoking and worsening moods between cigarettes," writes Parrott. "The apparent relaxant effect of smoking only reflects the reversal of the tension and irritability that develop during nicotine depletion. Dependent smokers need nicotine to remain feeling normal" (p. 817).

Behaviorally there is no difference between office workers huddled outside buildings regardless of the weather getting their fix and heroin addicts huddled in alleys getting their fix. Only the specific drug of addiction is different. Like heroin addicts who smoke or inject heroin to get a "fix," cigarette smokers say they smoke to feel better. At the instant of smoking they may very well feel better. But the moment nicotine levels begin to decrease and the dopamine-reinforcement circuit calms, the addicted smokers begin to feel worse than if they had never started smoking in the first place. To feel better, they light up again. Thus, as the case with other drugs, the contingency trap of nicotine addiction produces a seductive illusion. At the moment when the addict may be in pain (from withdrawal or otherwise), or experiencing aversive stimulation, smoking will in fact make the addict feel better. But overall, in the long term the addict would feel better if she had never started smoking in the first place.

REINFORCEMENT AND BEGINNING DRUG USE

Even without any knowledge of the physiologically damaging effects of drug abuse, the behaviorally punishing, damaging effects of drug use can be seen by all: the drunkard who repeatedly misses work or school and is consequently fired or flunked; the smoker who cannot go up a flight of stairs without stopping to catch her breath. The car accidents, blackouts, apathy, neglect of personal hygiene, nausea, and vomiting just touch on the obvious, observable perils of drug use. Furthermore, although drugs activate the pleasure-reinforcement brain circuit, because of other physiological effects first-time users may experience—such as anxiety or depression, nausea, dizziness, chills, or sweating—initial drug use is often physiologically quite aversive. Yet, despite aversive initial experiences, millions of people repeat drug use until tolerance and addiction develop. Given the aversive and potentially life-ruining effects of drug use, the question as to why people begin to use drugs in the first place is complex. Modeling and reinforcement play a central role in beginning drug use.

While initial drug use may not be physically reinforcing, it is likely to be socially reinforced. Peers may provide both positive and negative reinforcement for drug use. A child may be picked on or teased, called a "baby," "chicken," or worse until he starts experimenting with drugs. (In the eighth grade a friend told me "Stephen, one day you might be cool enough to smoke pot.") By using drugs, a child escapes or avoids being picked on—social negative reinforcement of drug use. Once the child begins to use drugs he becomes "cool," "one of the gang," that is, he becomes accepted—social positive reinforcement of drug use.

Peers and parents also provide a model for both the physiological and socially reinforcing effects of drug use. Alcohol companies would not spend hundreds of millions of dollars on advertisements showing socially and physiologically pleasurable consequences of alcohol use if modeling did not increase alcohol consumption. When Junior sees Dad come home from work tired and irritated but lighten up and become happy after a few drinks, Dad has modeled drug use behavior. When a child repeatedly sees Mom stop all activities so she can go out for a smoke and hears her express how good smoking makes her feel, Mom has modeled drug use behavior. Even if the parent spends all day Saturday and Sunday moaning and groaning in bed; if a child saw the parent, or heard him dancing, singing, laughing, and doing drugs (including alcohol) Friday night, then the parent has modeled reinforcing drug use behavior. Adults may also reinforce initial drug use in children by offering them "just a sip" or "just a puff," and then provide physical affection and praise ("Look at big Tom! Don't get too crazy like your Uncle Bob!"). In all these cases the beginning user is being taught that drug use is pleasurable.

Adults also model the negative reinforcing, for example, escape-producing, properties of drug use. When a parent yells, "You are driving me crazy! Leave me alone until I finish my cigarette," then smokes a cigarette, and after smoking calmly approaches the child and says, "Now what do you want, Honey? Mommy just needed a smoke; I feel all better now," the parent is teaching the child that drug use is negatively reinforcing. Likewise when a parent drinks alcohol or takes other drugs to alleviate pain or to forget about a bad day at work, the negative reinforcement of drug use has been modeled.

As a result of this social reinforcement and modeling, a person who may not enjoy the physiological effects of initial drug use, may continue to experiment with drugs because continued use provides continued acceptance and status—social positive reinforcement—and avoids bullying and ostracism—social negative reinforcement of drug use. Because they see others apparently enjoying drugs and seemingly effectively using drugs to manage their moods and behaviors, the beginning users are likely to assume that they "just aren't doing it right." They just haven't learned to inhale, chug, or "handle their alcohol" correctly yet. Consequently, they continue drug use, increasing the probability that they will be caught by the dopamine-reinforcement circuit contingency trap of drug use.

The power of social reinforcement to shape drug use behavior, in particular cigarette smoking, can be readily seen on college campuses across the United States. I have observed the same pattern many times. The students claim they smoke "only" at bars and parties, times when social reinforcement and peer pressure are strong. But many college students go to several bars and parties each month. So the "only at parties and bars" smoker may actually be smoking quite frequently. The group that a student parties with is also likely to be the group the student studies with. One in the group may decide to take a coffee break and have a cigarette and encourage and pressure the "bar and party only" smoker to join in. Now the student has learned, via social reinforcement, to smoke at parties, bars, while drinking coffee, and studying. Eventually the student will be offered cigarettes before class. By this time, shaped by social reinforcement, the student has learned to smoke across a wide variety of situations. During these times the student has likely developed tolerance to the nausea-producing effects of smoking, and the dopamine-reinforcement brain circuit has started to depend on the nicotine for activation.

REINFORCEMENT AND CASUAL USE

Millions of people drink but do not become drunks or alcoholics. Many people also experiment with nicotine, heroin, cocaine, and other drugs but do not become addicts. As is the case with understanding addiction, understanding why many people can use drugs casually and not become addicted is also a complex issue. But, again reinforcement plays a fundamental role in understanding drug use behavior.

Whether one abuses, becomes addicted, or just experiments with or casually uses a drug depends on whether the use is primarily motivated by negative or positive reinforcement. In *Human Motivation* author Robert E. Franken argues that "there is considerable evidence that if people use drugs to avoid a noxious or aversive situation [negative reinforcement] they are more likely to become addicted than if they merely use drugs for entertainment purposes [positive reinforcement]" (Franken, 1994, p. 184). Franken describes this negative reinforcement process for heroin addiction. "Because heroin will effectively reduce a variety of discomforts, including hunger, fatigue, anxiety, and pain . . . the heroin addict may have fortuitously learned to use heroin to reduce such discomforts. For example, a person who used heroin at one point to eliminate withdrawal symptoms might learn, through continued use, that heroin is an effective way of coping with anxiety" (p. 187). It is easy to see that this process applies equally well for any number of drugs including alcohol or nicotine. To paraphrase Franken: Because alcohol or nicotine will effectively reduce a variety of discomforts, including hunger, fatigue, anxiety, and pain . . . the alcohol or nicotine addict may have fortuitously learned to use alcohol or nicotine to reduce such discomforts. For example, a person who used alcohol or nicotine at one point to eliminate withdrawal symptoms might learn, through continued use, that alcohol or nicotine use is an effective way of coping with anxiety. Through negative reinforcement addiction occurs.

Unfortunately, people who use drugs to reduce pain and in aversive situations are not likely to have many potential sources of positive reinforcement available to them (if they did have these sources available it is improbable that their situation would be aversive). Conversely, people who experiment with drugs or use them casually for entertainment purposes—for positive reinforcement—are likely to have other sources of reinforcement available to them. Thus for people who use drugs for positive reinforcement, drug use behavior must compete with already established reinforcing activities. Heroin users who returned from Vietnam to environments with few sources of reinforcement were more likely to continue heroin use (see part 1 in this book). Those who returned to environments rich in sources of reinforcement (e.g., a stable family, educational, and employment opportunities) were likely to stop use (e.g., Franken 1994; McKim, 2000).

PERSONAL EXPERIMENTATION

The reason why I never became a cigarette smoker was because smoking behavior competed with an already established reinforcing activity. As a child I was an avid bicycle motocross rider (a "BMX'er") and would spend hours riding on trails and tracks deep in the woods either with friends or by myself. One day when I was in the sixth grade a friend brought along some cigarettes for us to smoke. When we reached the top of a hill we would attempt to smoke. We had to stop, take the cigarettes and lighter out, pass them around, attempt to light the cigarettes, and try to inhale the nasty, dirty-tasting smoke without coughing. None of it was very reinforcing. It was aversive and took time away from what I already knew was reinforcing. If I just pushed off and pedaled hard, within seconds I would be bouncing over "whoop-de-dos," pulling "wheelies" and flying through the air on jumps. Physiologically, my body already "knew" this would give me an adrenaline rush and activate my pleasure circuits. Before the afternoon was over, while fumbling with the cigarettes I said "this is stupid," gave the cigarette back, and sped off down the hill. My cigarette experimentation was over.

In high school while I did some light experimentation, several of my friends began to smoke tobacco and/or marijuana, get drunk regularly, and do other drugs at any time including during the school day. Those who developed real life-altering problems and abused drugs the most almost invariably had problematic home lives with abusive parents or parents going through messy divorces and remarriages. These friends used drugs to escape—their drug use was a function of negative reinforcement. Other friends liked to get drunk and high but usually only on weekends and hardly ever during school hours. These friends developed fewer problems with drugs. They were using drugs for excitement and fun—their drug use was a function of positive reinforcement. For others, including myself, high school experimentation was much lighter. I knew drug use would interfere with my athletic performance, so it was almost automatically out. If I wasn't participating in a sport I was training and preparing for one which I enjoyed doing. Like many other kids who had reinforcing activities, be it band, drama, science clubs, other academic clubs, or athletics, I never established a drug habit because it would have to compete with already established sources of reinforcement.

When my school athletic career was over, my major reason not to experiment was gone—I lost a powerful alternative source of positive reinforcement—and I began to "party hard." Fortunately my experimentation was always for positive reinforcement—fun, excitement, and I really believed *to learn*; to "break on through to the other side," as the late Jim Morrison of the rock group The Doors advised.

Although I did not necessarily know the terms, by the time I entered college, through education and observation, I knew that consistent drug use almost always resulted in aversive consequences and lost positive reinforcers. But successful academic behavior produced many opportunities for positive reinforcement. Therefore I adopted two rules; always go to class no matter how late I was out the night before and "no partying starting two days before a test or exam." With a full course load there was almost always a test coming up, so by adopting these rules I managed to avoid the contingency trap of consistent drug abuse and my dopamine-reinforcement circuit was never allowed to become dependent on "foreign" sources of stimulation.

TRUTH IN ADVERTISING

Millions of dollars are spent each year on antidrug advertisement campaigns. But hundreds of millions of dollars are spent each year on pro-drug advertisement campaigns. Have a headache? Take a drug and you'll feel better. Can't sleep? Take a drug and you'll feel better. Can't wake up? Take a drug and you'll feel better. Trying to eat less? Take a drug. Trying to relax? Take a drug and you'll feel better. Is your kid a pain? Put him on drugs. Going to a party? Take a drug—alcohol—and you'll have more fun. Going to a ball game? Take a drug—alcohol—and you'll have more fun. And on and on. These advertisements are meant to teach people, including children, that using drugs produces negative reinforcement—relief from pain, anxiety, depression, or whatever aliment one could possibly have. Or they are meant to teach that drugs, primarily alcohol and nicotine, produce positive reinforcement, or, increase the reinforcement of already reinforcing activities, be it weddings or ball games,. "You've come a long way baby—have a cigarette." If you are drinking beer "it doesn't get any better than this." This advertisement campaign implies that if you are *not* drinking then it can get better by drinking alcohol.

Parents, peers, and siblings also advertise drug use. People, including children, observe that drug use is in fact reinforcing (if it was not in fact reinforcing; by definition of reinforcement people would not repeat drug use). People drink and they do have fun. They smoke nicotine and they do feel better. They smoke marijuana and they do get "high." The truth is, people "do drugs," legal and illegal, because *drugs work. Drug use is reinforcing.*

Furthermore, despite the fact that it has been long established (e.g., Ayllon et al., 1975) that behavioral approaches centered on positive reinforcement are just as effective, or more effective, than drug therapy for hyperactivity and attention deficit disorder (Walker, 1998), children as young as 3 1/2 years old are increasingly being prescribed psychiatric medications for hyperactivity and other problems even though some of the medications being given have not ever been tested on children for effectiveness or side effects (Zito et al., 2000)! The long-term effects of drugging the current generation of children are not known.

Yet it is clear the children are being taught something about drugs. Prescribing very young children psychiatric drugs teaches them at a very early age that to change the way one feels, one can take drugs. They are being taught that to change the way one behaves, one can take drugs. They are being taught that the easy quick way to change behavior or "states of mind" is to take drugs.

A likely reason why parents and other adults are so quick to put children on drugs, legally of course, is the same reason why many adults endorse corporal punishment (beatings). Like beating children, putting children on drugs, usually produces quick changes in the children's behavior, usually decreases in behavioral intensity. Adults may put children on drugs because it provides the adult with relief and decreases their aversive stimulation, not necessarily for the long-term benefit of the child. That is, putting children on drugs is a function of negative reinforcement for the adult!

It can be very tiring, stressful, and at times aversive to work with children who are highly active (another reason why effective teachers need to be paid more). Adults in charge of the safety, growth, and teaching of active children have three options, and combinations of the options, available to manage the children's behavior—(1) aversive techniques: punishment and threats; (2) pharmaceutical behavioral management: drugging the children; or (3) positive reinforcement-based approaches: systematic praise, token reinforcement systems, etc. Both punishment and drug based approaches generally take less effort and, for the teacher but not the children, provide more immediate relief and are consequently easily trapped by the *adult*'s immediate negative reinforcement contingency. However, while providing the adult with the most immediate consequences, the drug and punishment approaches are not the most effective approaches to behavior management or education. Approaches based on positive reinforcement are the most effective. But it is easier for a teacher to sit in front of a class of medically sedated children and harshly reprimand any child for an occasional behavioral outburst than it is to constantly reinforce appropriate behaviors and frequently praise the correct academic work of highly active children. Parents, teachers, and other caregivers should not do what is immediately easiest for them. They should do what is best for the children.

The messages and lessons provided by society about drug use are contradictory. Politicians speak of a "war on drugs." Police and school systems provide "antidrug" education and speak of "zero tolerance." Yet, athletes and entertainers regularly promote alcohol and tobacco use. At school children are told to "just say no," that drugs are bad and kill. But every day millions of children are required to take behavior and mood-altering drugs at the school nurse's office.

HONEST DRUG EDUCATION

If drug education were honest, perhaps it would be more effective. On one hand, current drug education usually only informs individuals about what is wrong with drug use. On the other hand, as soon as an individual experiments with drugs, as most people eventually do, something else is discovered—drug use is reinforcing. Drug use relieves pain and escapes aversive stimulation. Drug use activates the brain's pleasure circuits. Once this truth is experienced firsthand, the one-sided, antidrug education propaganda is undermined—"They said drugs would make me feel bad and kill me. But I feel alive and great! What a lie. They are full of bull!"

An honest drug education would tell people, "Yes, taking drugs, getting drunk, smoking tobacco, or whatever, *will* make you feel better, *will* make you high, *will* help you forget about your troubles—for a while. No doubt about it, drugs make you feel great. But as soon as the drugs start to wear off, you will feel worse than before. You will be lower than if you didn't get high in the first place. Once your drugs start to wear off, your troubles will return with vengeance and since you weren't working on them while you were on drugs, you will find that your troubles have gotten worse than before you started using drugs. Furthermore, because of what the drugs do to your body and behavior you will have even more problems. Trying to escape these new problems with more drug use may work for a very brief time but ultimately it will only make your troubles worse. Think about that before you do drugs." If drug education accurately told people that using drugs activated the reinforcement-circuit; that drug use is pleasurable, but that pleasure would likely be less and less with each drug episode; and that other naturally pleasurable activities—from sex, to eating, to riding a bike, to being praised—may never be as enjoyable as they were before drug use, then drug education might be more effective. Current drug education is simply dishonest that contributes to its ineffectiveness.

DECREASING DRUG USE

Most people who use and abuse, either briefly or extensively, both legal and illegal drugs, significantly decrease or quit use without any formal treatment (referred to as "maturing out"). These people reduce or quit drug use behavior because it conflicts with other sources of established, important reinforcement. For example, when drinking interferes with family life or employment, most individuals quit or reduce alcohol consumption. Whether or not they quit or reduce, or how much they reduce, depends on how directly drug use conflicts with other sources of reinforcement and the relative value of the alternate sources of reinforcement.

An individual in an unhappy marriage may keep right on drinking if the spouse gives the ultimatum, "quit drinking or I'm leaving." Conversely, an individual with a highly reinforcing marriage and family life is much more likely to immediately give up drinking or keep it to a minimum the very first time it interferes with family life. Likewise college seniors drink and get drunk less than juniors who get drunk less than sophomores.

Despite the fact that most college freshmen are below the legal drinking age, freshmen drink and get drunk most often. Some of them drop out or flunk out. But most college students drink less as they advance because their studies and other activities become more important and reinforcing than drinking. They "mature out." Drinking and other drug use also increasingly come into conflict with other reinforcing activities. Being drugged out at a freshman dorm party may have no aversive consequences, but being drugged out at a party at one's major professor's house is likely to prove more costly. Being hung over or high for a test in a freshman class outside of one's major will likely not be too damaging to one's academic career. But being hung over or high for an exam in a junior or senior class in one's major could adversely impact the rest of a student's life.

Increasing restrictions on smoking should result in decreases in smoking because each new restriction can put smoking in conflict with other reinforcing activities. Years ago people could smoke anywhere and anytime—in the office, in restaurants, in the school and nursery, and during pregnancy. Now smoking is not allowed in most places. In some places even smoking within certain distances to the entrances to buildings is illegal. When the value of nonsmoking activities sufficiently outweighs the immediate reinforcement from smoking, smoking should decrease or stop.

Some individuals, social drinkers, social smokers ("chippers"), and even users of "hard drugs" continue to use drugs intermittently for years without becoming trapped or "addicted." These individuals seem to be able to limit their use in ways and to times when use does not interfere with other established reinforcing activities. Their use must also be infrequent enough to keep their dopamine reinforcement circuits from becoming dependent upon drug use for the experience of pleasure. Of course, this is a dangerous game to play. Many casual users do eventually become addicted. Many do lose other sources of reinforcement (significant others, friends, and jobs) as a result of drug use. Fortunately, others do give up drug use to avoid losing important nondrug sources of reinforcement or to gain additional nondrug reinforcers. For example, many casual users quit using most drugs if they must pass a drug test for possible employment (these people can still abuse many drugs, e.g., alcohol and nicotine, which they may not be tested for).

Whether or not nondrug activities will ever be as pleasurable and reinforcing as they would have been if drug use never took place depends on how much drug use has altered the user's physiology. That depends on the amount, frequency, and length of time drug use occurred. The more drug use has occurred the greater the physiological damage and the more likely that some of the damage is permanent. Some former smokers reach the point of many who have never smoked where even secondhand smoke makes them nauseous. It is likely that their nervous system has completely recovered from previous smoking. Other former smokers, who may not have smoked for years, still crave a cigarette first thing in the morning and after every meal. These former smokers likely have some permanent changes, damage to their nervous system as a result of past smoking. For these unfortunate people, a good meal will *never* be completely satisfying without a cigarette afterward.

TREATMENT

While most people who experiment with drug use "mature out" without any treatment, or as is the case for many alcohol and nicotine users, many simply continue drug use until they die a drug-shortened life, others are required or strongly encouraged—by the court system, guardians, employers, or loved ones—to enter formal drug treatment programs. Still others, usually those who have "hit bottom," enter treatment on their own.

The most widely known and popular treatments are Alcoholics Anonymous (AA), its cousin Narcotics Anonymous (NA), and many copycat "12 step" programs. Because AA is anonymous, it keeps no records or statistics and members are known to other members by their first names only. As a result of this anonymity it is difficult to judge the effectiveness of AA and related programs. *Chronicle of Higher Education* reporter D. W. Miller reached the same conclusion, "12-step programs for drug abusers, such as Narcotics Anonymous, can point to little scientific evidence of their effectiveness, in part because their tradition of anonymity makes outcomes difficult to evaluate" (D. W. Miller, 2000, p. A20). However, the evidence that does exist suggests that the AA approach is *not* very effective (Gelman, 1991; Peele 1989). (Likely in part because it contains a large religious component, criticizing AA in the United States often produces the same responses as does criticizing any part of mainstream Christian dogma—it is off-limits or dismissed out-of-hand. As a consequence, AA continues to be promoted despite the lack of evidence for its effectiveness and despite evidence of effectiveness of other approaches. The interested reader is referred to Gelman, 1991; Maralott et al., 1993; Miller, 2000; Peele 1989). Advocates of AA claim that AA *never* fails if one follows the program (e.g., Gelman, 1991). If an AA member drinks, it is said that the individual failed to stay sober, but AA did not fail. Logically, this is blaming the victim. It is the same as if I say I have a fail proof program to win every race—"run faster than everyone else in the race." If you fail to win every race it is not the program's fault. You failed to follow the program. You did not run faster than everyone else.

The vast majority of people with alcohol or narcotic problems effectively deal with them—quit or reduce use to nonproblematic levels—

without any formal treatment or programs, and the vast majority of the remaining population of users can be effectively treated with a brief, primarily educational program. These brief but effective programs educate users to the physiological, behavioral, educational, occupational, and social consequences of drug abuse. Actually only a small minority of drug abusers require specialized treatment (Maralott et al., 1993). The most effective programs for the remaining few individuals who do require treatment are based on contingent reinforcement for productive nondrug behaviors. (*In vivo cue exposure* treatment is also a very important component of effective treatment. Like reinforcement-based approaches [see chapter 1 of this book] the roots of cue exposure treatment are in basic research with animals. Cue exposure compliments reinforcement-based programs [Drummond et al., 1995].)

To the extent that AA is effective, its effectiveness is likely from the unacknowledged fact that AA replaces drug reinforcement with social reinforcement. In almost every U.S. city there are several AA meetings each day. At the meetings members introduce themselves, are warmly greeted, cheered, and given warm affection for announcing how long it has been since they've had a drink. Members have "sponsors" who they can call twenty-four hours a day for support and encouragement. Attending AA meetings escapes loneliness and the reason many people drink or take other drugs is to escape loneliness.

Indeed, in the chapter "The Lonely Addict" in *The Science of Self-Control,* Distinguished Professor of Psychology at SUNY, Stony Brook, Howard Rachlin argues that addiction is caused by a low rate of social reinforcement, by loneliness:

> Relative addiction theory says that social support, the benefit obtained from social activity, is crucial for both prevention and cure of addiction. Groups such as Alcoholics Anonymous and Gamblers Anonymous that stress social support generally believe it to be ancillary to the operation of some more fundamental process (physiological, cognitive, behavioral, or spiritual). Relative addiction theory, on the other hand, places social support or its lack at the center of the addiction process. It says that addicts are addicts *because* they lack social support—*because* they are lonely . . . lack of social support leads down the path to addiction just as directly as does the first drink, the first cigarette, the first line of cocaine. (Rachlin, 2000, p. 82, emphasis in original)

A Harvard-trained behaviorist, Rachlin builds the argument that lack of social reinforcement is responsible for addiction with data generated from the laboratory behavior of rats and pigeons ("rat psychology" again, see chapter 1 in this book).

> Of course it is impossible to perform precisely controlled experiments on this question [effects of social deprivation on drug addiction] with human subjects, but it *is* possible to do so with nonhumans. Indeed, several experiments have found that socially isolated rats consume significantly more addictive substances than socially active rats do. (Rachlin, 2000, p. 98, emphasis in original)

In the inductive scientific tradition, once the relative reinforcement addiction process was established in the laboratory it is shown to function in human situations outside the laboratory:

> Social interaction is substitutable for other addictive activities such as consumption of alcohol and other drugs [and vice versa]. . . . More direct evidence comes from a study by [Rudy] Vuchinich and [Jalie] Tucker (1996) of relapses of alcoholics who had participated in a treatment program. Relapse was significantly more frequent among those with low social support. A comprehensive review of alcohol treatment techniques (W. R. Miller et al., 1995) found training in social skills to be *much more effective* than any of the more frequently used long-term techniques (involving drugs, aversion therapy, twelve-step methods, and the like). (Rachlin, 2000, p. 101, emphasis added)

Although by far not the most effective treatment overall, with AA escaping loneliness is just a phone call to a sponsor or a drive to the next meeting away. AA meetings provide an alternative source of reinforcement (social positive reinforcement) and an alternative way to escape loneliness and life's problems (negative reinforcement).

Members of AA are taught to believe that they are "in recovery" for life and are encouraged to attend meetings for life. When they attend meetings they receive social reinforcement for attending. If they miss a meeting, their sponsor may try to track them down and take them to the next meeting. Thus, there may be socially aversive consequences of not attending AA meetings. In fact, AA has been criticized for substituting one type of dependency, alcohol, for another, AA itself. According to sociologist Jean Kirkpatrick, founder of Women for Sobriety, a woman may already be "dependent on alcohol, on her husband, on everything but herself. [In AA] she develops new dependencies, on a sponsor, on a higher power, on going to meetings for the rest of her life" (from Gelman, 1991, p. 63). Indeed, just like drug dependency, dependency on AA can also result in the loss of other potential reinforcers. If one spends *the rest of one's life* "in recovery" going to several AA meetings each week, then only attending AA meetings and abstinence have been reinforced. Conversely, instead of just attending AA meetings, if employment skills, hobbies, child care, physical fitness and nutritional eating, and other reinforcer-producing behaviors had been systematically developed, then more sources of reinforcement would become available and a return to drug use would be less probable.

Nevertheless, the untold, uncountable, lifelong members of AA who claim that AA has helped them to live drug free at the very least argues that social support can be more reinforcing overall than drug use. This observation reemphasizes the argument that the most useful way to understand drug use is to recognize that drugs act as reinforcers.

In reinforcement approaches to drug treatment, it is first acknowledged that drugs do, in fact, act as reinforcers. This honest, frank acknowledgment in itself sets behavioral approaches apart from many of the ineffective pseudoscientific approaches. A second important acknowledgment is that drugs produce *immediate reinforcement*. Attaching punishers to drug use—prison time, job loss, and fines—may reduce the long-term value of drug use. However, since the punishment is delayed, but drug use is immediately reinforcing, increasing the penalties and threats of penalties for drug use will not and has not reduced drug use. Because drug use provides both immediate positive reinforcement and immediate negative reinforcement (escape), drugs remain a very effective contingency trap and laws against drug use remain ineffectual against it.

Because drugs are such powerful reinforcers and attaching (delayed) punishment for drug use does not reduce drug use, an alternative to reducing drug use is to make other, more, reinforcers available for behaviors *other* than drug use. AA, NA, and similar programs provide social reinforcement for behavior other than drug use (e.g., attending meetings), but this social reinforcement is a tangential, nonsystematic, largely unrecognized, and uncredited part of the programs (e.g., none of the "12 steps" in any way refers to social reinforcement for nondrug, nondrinking behaviors). On the other hand, reinforcement-based behavioral approaches directly reinforce nondrug behaviors, and with reinforcement contingencies work toward developing behavioral skills (e.g., job training) that produce nondrug reinforcement.

University of Connecticut researchers, Nancy M. Petry and her colleagues (Petry et al., 2000) found contingency management far superior to standard treatment for alcohol-dependent veterans. In the contingency management treatment, by submitting negative Breathalyzer samples and completing treatment goals, veterans earned opportunities to win prizes as reinforcers. After the eight-week program 69% of the contingency management veterans were still abstinent but only 39% of the veterans in the standard outpatient treatment remained abstinent. When sobriety is reinforcing, sobriety increases. When people are drunk, it is difficult to teach them productive skills. But if they can be reinforced for being sober, then during the time they are sober they may also be taught important behaviors (e.g., job skills and social skills) that also produce reinforcement. Once these behaviors are learned and producing reinforcement, then direct reinforcement for sobriety can be faded without a return to drug use. Indeed, University of New Mexico researchers William R. Miller, Robert J. Meyers, and Susanne Hiller-Sturmhofel (1999) evaluated studies published between 1973 and 1999 and found the Community Reinforcement Approach to be more effective than traditional treatments. The Community Reinforcement Approach rearranges an addict's life so that abstinence is more reinforcing than drug use by providing positive reinforcement for practicing coping skills, goal setting, and analyzing drug patterns. It also involves significant others in providing social reinforcement for productive nondrug behaviors. When an individual learns to obtain reinforcers from his community for productive socially appropriate behaviors, drug use decreases.

The effect of reinforcement for one behavior is relative to the reinforcement available for other behaviors. If drug use is occurring, then relative to other possible behaviors, drug use must be the most reinforcing behavior at that moment. But by increasing the value, by increasing the reinforcement, for other behaviors, the relative reinforcing value of drug use will decrease and consequently drug use will decrease. Johns Hopkins University researchers Kenneth Silverman, Mary Ann Chutuape, George E. Bigelow, and Maxine L. Stitzer applied this knowledge to decrease cocaine abuse by treatment-resistant methadone patients (Silverman et al., 1999). Methadone provides a physiological substitute for heroin and is the standard pharmaceutical treatment for heroin addicts. Unfortunately, many heroin addicts are also addicted to cocaine, and methadone does not affect cocaine craving. The patients had previously failed to provide cocaine-free urine samples even though they could earn vouchers worth over one hundred dollars per week. This means that for these addicts using cocaine was more reinforcing than the vouchers received for cocaine-free urine samples. But when the money value of the vouchers was increased threefold, more than half of the patients achieved cocaine abstinence. On one hand, this result reveals the brutal reality that for many addicts, cocaine use is highly reinforcing. But, on the other hand, for many even "hard-core" addicts, the results show that if nondrug use can be made sufficiently more reinforcing, then the *relative value* of cocaine as a reinforcer will decrease and use will decrease or stop.

Cynics may argue: "I don't get paid for not using drugs. Why should we pay junkies for not using drugs?" To some extent this objection is a matter of political and social philosophy; to a larger extent this type of objection against the use of reinforcement has been discredited (see part 1 in this book). If nothing is done to curb drug abuse then it will continue—which is costly for society and for the individual abusers. The two remaining approaches are either to punish drug use, imprison users, and continue the war on drugs—which really functions as systematic minority oppression (Helmer, 1975)—or to provide treatment, education, and reinforcement for productive nondrug behaviors. The punishment, zero tolerance, "just say no" approach, which has been in effect for over thirty years—former president Richard Nixon ran on a "war on drugs" platform—is based on ignorance and simply doesn't work. Not only is the punishment, war on drugs approach not effective, it is by far the most costly approach. According to the director of the RAND Corporation's research center on drug policy, "In order to decrease the consumption of cocaine by 1 percent from current levels we would have to spend $783 million more on source-country controls, $366 million more for interdiction, $246 million more for domestic enforcement [the punishment, war on drugs approach], or $34 million more for treatment [the reinforcement approach]" (from D. W. Miller, 2000, P. A22). Even the cheapest war on drug approach costs over seven times as much as the treatment approach.

The fact is, however, that people who do not use drugs *are* paid and otherwise reinforced for not using drugs. People who have a secure, well-paying job, and reinforcing family and social life are highly reinforced for not using drugs. The proof is that if they started to abuse drugs they would most likely lose their jobs, or at least lose raises and promotions, and if they did not lose them entirely, their family and social lives would become less reinforcing. In a very real sense they are paid and reinforced for not using drugs. When people who had been abusing drugs start to abuse drugs less or quit use altogether, their family and social lives are likely to become more reinforcing and they are more likely to gain jobs, raises and promotions (assuming jobs are available in their environment, e.g., assuming low local unemployment rates).

Unfortunately, for a variety of reasons, including but not limited to abuse, neglect, poverty, and chronic illness or pain, some people are in environments that do not provide much reinforcement for nondrug behaviors, or they do not have the behavioral skills necessary to obtain possible reinforcers. Why work hard in school when it only gets you beat up for "acting White," and your parents don't give a damn one way or another as long as you don't annoy them. Nondrug reinforcement for these people will be little and long in coming, if reinforcement comes at all. But taking drugs will provide escape and feel good *immediately*. It is no wonder there is chronic drug abuse in such situations. (Indeed, it is a wonder why there is not *more* drug use in such situations.) Unfortunately this drug abuse is a contingency *trap* that only makes the user's situation worse and worse, costing society more and more. In such cases the cheapest approach for society, and the most effective and beneficial approach for the abusers are proactive treatments based on positive reinforcement for productive, socially appropriate nondrug behaviors.

A review of the research related to the efficacy of contingency management, reinforcement programs on treating alcohol and other drug problems during the years 1969 to 1998 (twenty-nine years of research!) by Stephen J. Higgins and Nancy M. Petry of the University of Vermont found that the interventions effectively reinforced—increased—alcohol abstinence, medication compliance, and treatment attendance (Higgins & Petry, 1999). Similarly, a meta-analytic statistical evaluation of the outcomes of thirty studies on the effectiveness of contingency management reinforcement programs for methadone patients, heroin addicts, found that the reinforcement programs did in fact significantly reduce drug use (Griffith et al., 2000). While the programs are not free, they are effective. Furthermore, even the most expensive contingency management reinforcement program for drug abuse is much cheaper than the expense to society, families, and the criminal justice system of having individuals with substance abuse problems being treated as criminals and pushed through the courts to an eventual extended stay in taxpayer-funded prison.

Even the most ideal drug treatment program will have individuals who relapse and return to drug abuse. Depending on each person's unique situation and behavior-reinforcement history, some will stop drug use forever; others will repeatedly relapse and recover; and an unfortunate few will relapse and die a drug-related death. In the behavioral stream of life there will be inevitable setbacks and achievements. How smoothly and richly one's behavioral stream flows depends on the reinforcers available to a person and what behaviors produce those reinforcers. Drugs are like eddies or whirlpools that can trap the behavioral flow. Whether one can avoid, or if not, escape these eddies and whirlpools depends on the currents provided by reinforcement for other behaviors. If the environment, families, and society provide no reinforcers, too few or too weak reinforcers for nondrug behaviors, then it should come as no surprise when the contingency trap of drug abuse captures behavior.

12

REINFORCEMENT AND CRIME, MISCONDUCT, AND CORRECTION

Quite simply for the same reason that addicts abuse drugs, some individuals repeatedly commit crimes because criminal behavior is reinforcing. Criminal behavior is reinforcing in several ways. Peter B. Wood of Mississippi State University, Walter R. Gove and James A. Wilson of Vanderbilt University in Tennessee, and John K. Cochran of the University of South Florida, provide an evidence-based argument that criminal behaviors produce reinforcers from three interrelated categories: "Exogenous Rewards," including "money, social status, and other instrumental rewards"; "Psychological Rewards" including "source of identity and self-worth," and "recognition of the attainment of exogenous rewards"; and "Physiological Rewards" that are "pleasurable sensation experienced through stimulation of [an] endogenous neurophysiological reward system" (Wood et al., 1997, p. 347).

The material reinforcers, or "Exogenous Rewards," are the most obvious source of reinforcement for many crimes. Not surprisingly, burglars report that their main reason for burglary was money (Bennett & Wright, 1984). If one person successfully robs another person, then robbing will be reinforced by the victim's money. If one child gets away with taking another child's lunch money, then stealing money will be reinforced by getting the victim's money. People high in social status within their peer group generally have access to more reinforcers (e.g., money, cars, and sexual opportunities), relative to individuals lower in social status. Within the mafia, street gangs, or even within more loosely, or unorganized groups of people who engage in criminal activities, successfully completing crimes will elevate one's social status within the group and consequently increase one's access to other reinforcers.

181

The "Psychological Rewards" of criminal behaviors are related to the receipt of exogenous rewards and other reinforcers. Criminals are highly likely to come from unstable and aversive family environments, have often been physically or psychologically abused, received limited education, poor work history, and low income (e.g.,Wood et al., 1997, p. 343). In short, criminals are likely to have a history scant in positive reinforcement and have developed few appropriate behaviors that can produce reinforcers. As a result the possible loss of reinforcers that law-abiding people attain is not a costly one for criminals. Because they have little materially and behaviorally, criminals have little, or nothing to lose by committing crimes. Consequently, criminal behaviors provide, in addition to material wealth, something that normal society does not provide the criminal: perceived self-determination, perceived self-actualization, and feelings of control and omnipotence (Lyng, 1990; Wood et al., 1997). Feelings of control and perceived self-determination are associated with the receipt of reinforcers. When a law-abiding, middle-class adolescent earns all As on his report card he is likely to receive praise, affection, and recognition: "I knew your hard word would pay off, Honey. Give me a hug and keep up the good work." This will increase the adolescent's perceived self-determination. Similarly the aspiring, or already "hardened," adolescent criminal will receive praise, affection, and recognition for successful criminal behavior: "You da man! Give me some skin! Nobody better mess with the main man!" This attention increases the criminal's perceived self-determination. The "Psychological Rewards" of criminal behavior simply reflect the fact that for criminals, criminal behavior is reinforcing. Criminal behavior is a function of reinforcement.

The "Physiological Rewards" of criminal behavior that gives "pleasurable sensation experienced through stimulation of endogenous neurophysiological reward system" (Wood et al., 1997, p. 347) is the same mechanism that reinforces drug abuse (see chapter 11 in this book for more detail). And like drug abuse, crime functions as a contingency trap in that committing crimes immediately and intensely activates the reinforcement circuits in the criminal's brain. Most hardened criminals are also hard-core drug abusers. The immediately and intensely reinforcing aspects of the criminal act coupled with the unpredictability of success can make a criminal as "addicted" to crime as some gamblers are "addicted" to gambling.

Understanding that criminal behavior immediately and intensely activates the physiological dopamine reinforcement system helps to understand why "punishing criminals" is so ineffective and rehabilitation is so difficult. ("Punishing criminals" is in quotes because technically people can't be punished; behavior is punished.) The physiological reinforcement system is activated immediately during the criminal act. Any punishment for crime is delayed. Scores of studies show that delayed consequences are less effective than immediate ones. The more any consequence is delayed the less effective it is. Punishment is likely to be effective only if a child is "caught in the act" and is punished immediately. If the crime is eventually discovered, even if it is the same day, the punishment is likely to be less effective. For older individuals, even those caught in the act, punishment is even more delayed. They are likely to first be taken to the principal's office, or taken to the police station where they are likely to be released until their trial and may not receive any "punishment" for their crime for several years, and possibly for many more crimes, after the fact.

Furthermore, compared to law-abiding citizens, criminals are generally less responsive to both reinforcers and stimulation that others find aversive. Criminals have habituated, developed tolerance, and are desensitized to pain relative to noncriminals. Therefore criminals find "punishment" less "punishing" than noncriminals would. Like the long term drug addict who has lost many dopamine receptors, criminals are not physiologically as responsive as noncriminals in general. While a noncriminal may find an ice cream treat sufficiently pleasurable, a criminal may have to get added excitement of stealing the ice cream to experience the same pleasurable stimulation as the ice cream alone provides the noncriminal (Blum et al., 2000).

Adding or increasing the threat of punishment for a crime will paradoxically add to the pleasure experienced while committing the crime. Portals of the "perfect crime" always have a high element of risk and severe punishment associated with getting caught. If there was not much risk or threat of punishment, the crime would not be considered to be much of a crime—hardly worth committing—much less "perfect." The mere existence of the phrase "the perfect crime" suggests that crime can be highly reinforcing. "Perfect" things are reinforcing. "Imperfect" behaviors are often punished. The greater the risk and the greater the threatened punishment—the greater the thrill, the greater the excitement, and the greater the reinforcement for criminal behavior. As they become "addicted" to crime—dependent on crime for reinforcement—criminals often take ever-increasing risks to experience the same level of excitement for crime just as drug abusers must take ever-increasing doses to experience the same level of pleasure. An inmate convicted of child molestation, sodomy, and rape by instrument reported:

> When I was breaking into houses with the intent to molest children, beforehand I would masturbate and fantasize about what I would do in the house, and that would give me *a rush just thinking about what could go wrong, how I might be caught* . . . that

played a big part in pumping me up—ejaculation was one of the biggest reinforcers to what I was doing. . . . Once I did break into the houses the rush was incredible. . . . And *once I got away with it, I went to more dangerous things, more daring. Each time I did something a little more bold, a little more daring*, until I was right out in front of everybody. Robbery, or burglary, or shoplifting—it wasn't the same rush, but when I added a sexual component with it the rush was heightened. I preferred that rush over anything else. (from Wood et al., 1997, p. 358, emphasis added)

Of course it is not possible to monitor criminals' brain dopamine circuits while they are committing crimes, but almost all criminals report pleasurable sensations while committing crimes and these sensations become more pleasurable as the crimes become more violent. Wood and his co-workers claim that "the data suggest that property and violent crimes are reinforced by a neurophysiological high and a personal sense of accomplishment, but these endogenous reinforcements are particularly relevant to violent personal crimes" (Wood et al., 1997, p. 351).

In contrast to the pleasure criminals report, Wood and his co-workers found that most college students report that they would feel *worried, afraid,* and *tense* if they were to commit a crime. These are words associated with the threat of punishment, not reinforcement. *"But inmates and students who know crimes very well do not differ significantly in the* [reinforcing] *sensations they would feel when committing crime"* (Wood et al., 1997, p. 356, emphasis added). That is, like convicts, college students who have committed crimes find criminal behavior to be just as reinforcing as the convicted criminals find criminal behavior. This finding raises the question why, other than the obvious, trivial answer "they got caught," do some people who commit crimes end up in prison and others end up in college? Evidenced by the fact that they are in college, another obvious answer is that individuals with other reinforcing options are likely to find crime, although reinforcing, not as reinforcing overall, not as valuable, as other behavioral options. And since they do have other options such as college, getting caught is more costly for them than it is for the option-less. A more revealing question is, What are the reinforcement histories and environments that produce persistent criminal behaviors?

EARLY CRIMINAL LEARNING, DISOBEDIENCE, AND "CONDUCT DISORDER"

Disobedient, noncompliant children, antisocial children, children with high rates of "misconduct," and children given the psychiatric label of conduct disorder, are at very high risk of criminal behavior relative to other children, even "hyperactive" children who do not have conduct problems. For example, similar to his other findings of over thirty years of research on hyperactivity, conduct problems, and criminality, in a multiyear study of males, James H. Satterfield of the Oregon Health Sciences University and his co-worker Anne A. Schell found that "Childhood conduct problems predicted later criminality, and serious antisocial behavior in adolescence predicted adult criminality. . . . The risk for becoming an adult offender is associated with conduct problems in childhood and serious antisocial behavior (repeat offending) in adolescence. [But] hyperactive children who do not have conduct problems are not at increased risk for later criminality" (Satterfield & Schell, 1997, p. 1726). Early reinforcement contingencies for aggression, coercion, misconduct, and disobedience, coupled with little to no reinforcement for socially appropriate behaviors occasion the development of these precriminal and criminal behavior patterns. Coercive family patterns shape and reinforce and *unwittingly teach* children to be aggressive, coercive, and noncompliant. Pioneering research in family reinforcement dynamics led by Gerald R. Patterson of the University of Oregon Social Learning Research Center (e.g., Patterson, 1982) and in parent behavioral training led by Rex Forehand of the University of Georgia (e.g., Wierson & Forehand, 1994) have found that children's noncompliance, aggression, and coercive behaviors are a result of both positive reinforcement traps and negative reinforcement traps existing in family dynamics.

In a negative reinforcement trap a child given a request, order, or command is noncompliant, disobedient. The child may kick, scream, yell, or hit. If parents "break down," remove, or reduce the request, then the parents have negatively reinforced the child's noncompliance. In future occurrences the parents may try "tough love" and attempt to be more firm. However, because noncompliance has been reinforced in the past, the child's response to the increased firmness will be to increase the intensity and duration of the disobedient behavior. Most parents find it impossible to remain consistently firm and in order to "get some peace" will occasionally give in. The *parent's behavior* of "giving in" is also negatively reinforced because giving in results in the child's ceasing, but only temporarily, the disobedient behavior. Unfortunately and unwittingly by establishing this interpersonal negative reinforcement dynamic, the parents are teaching the child to be noncompliant. Through negative reinforcement, the child is learning that "As long as I'm disobedient enough, loud enough, and aggressive enough—long enough, I will get my way."

The rate of any behavior, whether it is a compliant behavior or an aggressive, noncompliant behavior, is a direct function of its relative rate of reinforcement. If aggression produces reinforcers relatively more frequently than nonaggressive behaviors, then aggression is most likely. James Snyder of Wichita State University and Patterson confirmed the relationship between aggression and reinforcement for aggression in a study of twenty single mothers with sons between the ages of four and five. Some of the parent-child relationships had high rates of aggression, by both parent and child, and some had low rates of aggression. In aggressive families both mother and son frequently provided the other with aversive stimuli (yelling, disapproval, and commands). When the son became aggressive, the mother typically terminated the aversive stimulation she was providing, and consequently the son was more aggressive during later observations. The son's aggression was negatively reinforced. Likewise, when the mother became aggressive the son typically terminated the aversive stimulation he was providing, and the mother consequently became more aggressive during later observations. Like the son's, the mother's aggression was negatively reinforced. Snyder and Patterson concluded that

> The behavior of mothers and sons in both aggressive and nonaggressive dyads was clearly tuned to its [reinforcement-producing] utility in dealing with conflict. However, what was being taught about dealing with conflict in those dyads was quite different. Mothers and sons in aggressive dyads were more likely than those in nonaggressive dyads to reinforce each other's aggressive means of dealing with conflict. The primary strategy in dealing with conflict in these dyads was to out-coerce the other person. Paradoxically, the functional value of this strategy increases the frequency and duration of mother son conflicts. (Snyder & Patterson, 1995, p. 388)

CRUISIN' FOR A BRUSIN'

Noncompliant, deviant behavior patterns may also be learned, trapped, early in life by positive reinforcement as well as by negative reinforcement. The positive reinforcement that traps noncompliance is usually parental attention, even when the attention is meant to decrease, to punish, the noncompliance. Especially in families where the parent(s) are very busy, stressed, or tired, peace and quiet is at a premium. In such families (which may be the majority of families) when the children are "playing quietly" parents may be tempted to ignore the children and get some rest or housework done. But to mature optimally, to achieve and educationally advance or excel, children *need* high rates of parental attention, conversation, and affection (e.g., Gottman et al., 1997; Hart & Risley, 1995).

If children do not get this needed attention for behaving appropri- ately—drawing, painting, singing, talking, sharing, counting, building, writing, cooperating, or helping mother—they *will* get it by behaving inappropriately—yelling, screaming, snatching, fighting, by being non- compliant and disobedient. When a child is usually ignored and attended to only when being beaten, because love and violence co-occur, love and violence will be viewed as the same thing. This was the case for Candy, an on-again off-again drug dealer, drug addict:

> My husband was like my father: I was a child-abused daughter, and I became a child-abused wife. . . . I thought it was love. I not gonna lie. I loved'ed [sic] to get beat 'cause I was used to it as a baby to thirteen, and then my husband was doing it from thirteen to thirty-two. So I thought life was that: Getting beat up. I used to look for fights for him to beat my ass. You see when you're a child-abused daughter from the age of eight months to thirteen then you find an abused husband. You think that the way a man shows you love is by beating you because, I says, "my father loves me, that's why he's beating me." (from Bourgois, 1996, pp. 220–221)

Candy's husband beat her so much that she eventually shot him. But not before she had five miscarriages as a result of being beaten. Unfortu- nately, as is the case with many abused people, after she shot her husband, Candy took up with another man whom she encouraged to beat her. During the beatings she became sexually aroused. After her husband recovered from his gunshot wound, she eventually returned to him (Bour- gois, 1996). While not all cases are as tragic as Candy's, it is well estab- lished that the more children are spanked, the more likely they are to end up in abusive relationships as adults (e.g., Straus, 1994). Even if the atten- tion includes yelling, spanking, beating, or other violence, parental atten- tion is as important to children as food and water. Disobedience, noncompliance by children, readily evokes parental attention. If parents most often provide reinforcing attention for noncompliance, rather than give attention for compliance, then even if the attention includes beatings, the parents are, unwittingly perhaps, *training, teaching, their children to be noncompliant.*

Parents may also trap misconduct with material positive reinforce- ment when they "break down" and give the children what they want. When a child yells, screams, or cries until a parent gives the child a coveted treat or toy—for example, in a store checkout line, "OK, OK, you can have the candy bar; just shut up!"—the parent has reinforced misconduct with an immediate material reinforcer. The next time the child wants a candy bar, toy, or other treat, the child is more likely to scream and yell, to engage in misconduct until the parent gives in and gives the child the treat, again reinforcing misconduct—trapping misconduct.

Regarding positive and negative reinforcement traps, the phrase "the squeaky wheel gets the grease" is translated as "the misconduct gets the reinforcers." But ideally, the best way to prevent squeaks is to keep the wheel well greased. The best way to eliminate misconduct is to richly provide reinforcement for appropriate conduct before misconduct can become established—to provide at least five approvals for every disapproval (Flora, 2000). "Greasing the squeaky wheel"—unwittingly providing reinforcement for noncompliance and misconduct—may result in temporary cessation of the unwanted behavior, but ultimately children are being taught that noncompliance and misconduct are reinforced. As reinforced behavior, noncompliance and misconduct will increase in frequency, putting the children at increased risk of future deviant and criminal behavior.

SIBLING REINFORCEMENT OF AGGRESSION

Within families, in addition to parents, siblings are rich sources of stimulation and reinforcement for children. Coercive reinforcement dynamics among siblings also contribute to deviant, noncompliant behavior patterns. When a sibling is providing aversive stimulation to a child, for example, being a "copycat" or teasing, and the teased child responds with aggression that terminates the sibling's aversive teasing, then aggression has been negatively reinforced. When one sibling is playing with a preferred toy and a child engages in aggression or other misconduct to gain possession of the toy, then aggression has been positively reinforced by the receipt of the toy. Indeed, a study by Patterson, Thomas Dishion, and Lew Bank of the OSLC of 91 families found that family coercive interactions served as "basic training for fighting" (Patterson et al., 1984, p. 264) and there was a large "role of siblings in generating coercive chains that lead to physical fighting" (p. 264). Likewise, in a study of 57 families and boys who had been referred for treatment of conduct problems, James Snyder and Lynn Schrepferman of Wichita State University in Kansas and Carolyn St. Peter of Arizona State University found that parents and siblings reliably (but probably unknowingly) reinforced the boys' aggressive behaviors. The researchers concluded that; "Children's performance of aggressive behavior is tuned to and shaped by the social-environmental [reinforcement] contingencies engendered by that behavior during interaction with siblings and parents" (Snyder et al., 1997, p. 206). This family training in aggression results in later problems: The researchers found that "negative reinforcement and boy's startup and reciprocate [aggression], whether derived from interaction with siblings or parents, were reliable predictors . . . of the boys' antisocial behavior 2 years later" (p. 207). In fact, by the two-year follow-up 45% of the boys had been arrested at least once, 35% had been removed from their homes and almost half had four or more official school discipline problems.

Fighting by children is aversive to parents, and parents are likely to respond to fighting with aggression themselves. In fact mothers of aggressive boys are seven times more likely to hit their sons than mothers of nonaggressive boys (Patterson, 1982). Hitting children for fighting may end *that* fight, but by modeling aggression, parents also train children to be violent. The lesson the parent is teaching the child is, "don't fight when there are bigger people around or you will be hit. But the biggest person can successfully be violent to get what they want." Indeed, Patterson, Dishion, and Bank argue that "aggressive child behaviors are maintained by mixed schedules of *positive* and *negative* reinforcement plus frequent punishment. An experienced aggressive child has had, then, a great deal of experience with aversive stimuli. Such events, in fact, constitute the warp and woof for much of his coercive behavior" (Patterson et al., 1984, p. 256, emphasis in original).

ADOLESCENT DELINQUENCY TRAINING

While families remain a powerful source of reinforcement throughout people's lives, as children mature, their environments expand as do potential sources of reinforcement. In adolescence one's peers become powerful sources of reinforcement. For children with deviant tendencies initially shaped by family reinforcement dynamics, peer attention is likely to continue the unplanned training in delinquency. Because children from coercive families have not been reinforced or trained to take turns, share, cooperate, and help but have been "trained to fight" and to "out-coerce," these children are rejected by normal peers. Rejected by these peers, children with antisocial tendencies form friendships with other antisocial boys. This occurs as a result of a shopping process according to Franciois Poulin and Michael Boivin of the Universite Laval in Canada. Shopping:

> refers to the tendency to seek social settings providing the maximum level of social reinforcement for the minimum social

energy. This activity takes place randomly during peer interactions, until two children "hit it off" on the basis of common interests. For antisocial boys, these common interests could be disruption of the classroom or ganging up on other children, as they were commonly observed in proactively aggressive boys. (Poulin & Boivin, 2000, p. 238)

Poulin and Boivin found that "a majority of them [aggressive boys] are involved in peer affiliations that may perpetuate or even promote aggression. These relationships . . . support and reinforce aggression-related behavior, . . . provide training ground for antisocial acts, . . . and ensure the strategic alliances through which aggressive children might gain access to resources [reinforcers] by coercive means" (Poulin & Boivin, 2000, p. 233). Poulin and Boivin found that proactively aggressive boys formed stable and lasting friendships with other proactively aggressive boys and suggested that mutual reinforcement of aggression contributed to the maintenance of the friendship as well as aggressive behaviors. A coercive family provides the initial aggressive experiences and reinforces the aggressive behavior pattern (e.g., Patterson et al., 1992) which then generalizes to the peer system. "According to Kenneth Dodge (1991)," argue Poulin and Boivin, "experiences involving frequent exposure to aggressive tactics and their positive consequences, as well as endorsements of these tactics by the social environment, will positively reinforce the use of proactive aggressive behaviors over time" (Poulin & Boivin, 2000, p. 238).

Peers continue the training in deviancy started by coercive family dynamics, by reinforcing deviant behaviors. In a study asking adolescents to solve problems, Dishion and Kathleen M. Spracklen (1996) of the OSLC found that rule-breaking talk—"gross activities (e.g., mooning the camera), drug use, stealing, vandalism, victimization of women or minorities, obscene gestures, getting into trouble at school, and behavior that was inappropriate to the task" (Dishion & Spracken, 1996, p. 7)—was a direct function of social reinforcement—"positive affective reactions . . . actual laughter . . . thumbs-up, discernible smiles" (p. 7)—for rule-breaking. That is, the more peer reinforcement for discussing criminal and inappropriate behaviors, the more rule-breaking talk occurred and less appropriate problem solving occurred. Antisocial, criminal behavior is shaped and learned, by dynamic family and peer positive and negative reinforcement processes.

Just as early training in, and reinforcement for, industriousness and effortful achievement sets the behavioral course for success and creative achievement (e.g., chapter 8 in this book), early training and reinforcement for antisocial, coercive behaviors set the course for later criminal behavior. Deborah M. Capaldi, Patti Chamberlain, and Patterson of the OSLC succinctly summarized this process:

Family members inadvertently reinforce the child's coercive behavior and conduct problems. . . . Noncompliant and aggressive behavior are learned at home, then generalize to other settings, such as school. . . . Deviant peer association [then] contributes directly to the development of conduct problems through peer reinforcement of behavior problems. (Capaldi et al., 1997, p. 345)

This reinforcement process is not without consequence. The OSLC researchers found that with ineffective (coercive) discipline, antisocial behavior "was found to predict a . . . serious juvenile arrest record (two or more arrests) and failure to enter higher education" (Capaldi et al., 1997, p. 343).

"NIP IT IN THE BUD."
REDUCING MISCONDUCT AND ANTISOCIAL BEHAVIOR

Because family members "inadvertently" reinforce coercive behavior and aggressive behavior is "learned at home," the most promising way to reduce antisocial, aggressive, and criminal behavior is to start at home, early in the at-risk child's life—to teach parents how to *advertently, purposefully*, reinforce *non*coercive, socially appropriate behavior; to teach parents effective noncoercive discipline including encouragement, time-out from positive reinforcement and response cost (privilege loss) (e.g., Capaldi et al., 1997). To this end both Forehand and Patterson have developed highly similar Parent Behavioral Training (PBT) programs to teach parents effective positive reinforcement-based parenting skills and practices (see Bank et al., 1987; Wierson & Forehand, 1994 for reviews and summaries).

Parents of antisocial children do not adequately monitor the whereabouts of their children or appropriateness of their behavior (e.g., Patterson et al., 1984). When they do pay attention to their children, "mothers of problem children are more likely to provide attention and positive consequences [reinforcement traps] for troublesome child behavior than for positive child behavior" (Capaldi et al., 1997, pp. 345–346). Therefore, because the parents do not attend to appropriate behavior but provide reinforcing attention for inappropriate behaviors, the first step in PBT is to teach parents (with role playing, practice, homework exercises, etc.) to monitor appropriate, prosocial behaviors—compliance, "minding," doing homework, completing chores, and so forth. This initial attending, monitoring, and tracking of appropriate behaviors constitutes a major change of parenting practices in antisocial families and in and of itself may serve as initial reinforcement of appropriate prosocial behaviors. "Many parents express surprise as their children increase appropriate behavior just in response to attention" report Michelle Wierson and Rex Forehand (Wierson & Forehand, 1994, p. 147).

"The second treatment component involves teaching parents *reinforcement* strategies," continue Wierson and Forehand. "Parents are taught to use verbal praise statements contingent upon compliance and other appropriate behaviors" (Wierson & Forehand, 1994, p. 147, emphasis in original). Once parents are sufficiently attending and praising appropriate prosocial behaviors other reinforcers may also be systematically implemented in a token economy or point system (e.g., Bank et al., 1987). Points earned for established appropriate behaviors are later exchangeable for predetermined privileges, toys, or treats.

Finally *nonaversive, mild* punishment procedures are taught, specifically *ignoring, time-out from positive reinforcement ("time-out")* and *response cost.* Both time-out and response cost involve the loss of positive reinforcers contingent upon inappropriate behaviors. Prior to training, parents of noncompliant children typically reinforce inappropriate behaviors (unknowingly with attention in coercive reinforcement traps). Consequently there is a very low rate of appropriate behaviors; therefore, it is *vital* to teach parents positive reinforcement for compliance and prosocial behaviors and have those behaviors shaped to a substantial rate of occurrence *before* the introduction of any punishment procedures.

Especially for parents of young children, once they have been shown how effective attention is at increasing and reinforcing appropriate behaviors, it is not difficult to convince them that ignoring minor inappropriate behaviors (whining and temper tantrums) will effectively decrease their rate. For the educated, this observation may seem so obvious that it hardly merits mention. However, prior to training, in coercive families the likely parental response to whining or tantrums would be to beat or yell at the child. In the long run the attention given during the beating and yelling would reinforce the whining and tantrums, increasing their occurrence. Conversely, ignoring—withholding reinforcing attention contingent on inappropriate behavior—results in differential attention, reinforcement, for appropriate behavior only. This will increase the rate of appropriate behaviors.

Ignoring is essentially one form of time-out from positive reinforcement. It is time-out from attention contingent on inappropriate behavior. The other side of this coin is time *in* for positive reinforcement—attention—as long as appropriate behavior is occurring. Older children may need occasional time-outs that are more systematic than simply ignoring. The child is removed from the reinforcing situation for a brief period of time. Again, as long as appropriate behavior is occurring there is time *in* for positive reinforcement. For even older children response cost may be the most effective punishment. In response cost, positive reinforcers are lost contingent upon inappropriate behaviors. The inappropriate response *costs* a positive reinforcer. TV time, movie, or driving privileges may be lost for engaging in deviant behaviors.

Neither response cost or time-out involve beating, yelling, or applying aversive stimulation to a child in any way. Instead they establish additional contingencies for *positive reinforcement*. Positive reinforcers are simply lost (response cost) or made temporarily unavailable (time-out) contingent on unacceptable behaviors. As long as there is no inappropriate behavior there is time *in* for positive reinforcement. Furthermore, time-out and response cost are two of the major punishment contingencies widespread in society, so teaching children to accept time-out and response cost teaches an important lesson in accepting consequences from authority. Traffic tickets and fines of all sorts are response cost—the loss of money—contingent upon legally defined inappropriate behaviors. Jail and prison time are meant, in part, to serve as time-out contingent on illegal behavior. "Sin taxes," taxes on cigarettes and alcohol are meant to decrease consumption, and in fact do decrease consumption. "Sin taxes" function as response cost.

DOES PARENT BEHAVIORAL TRAINING WORK?

Yes. Weirson and Forehand report that "the parent behavioral training program is effective in reducing child noncompliance. . . . Treated children are at least as compliant as community control subjects (i.e., children who have not been referred to any clinic), despite having had higher levels of non-compliance before treatment." Follow-ups at 4 1/2 years, 10 years, and 14 years—into adulthood—show that "behavior change is maintained successfully" (Weirson & Forehand, 1994, p. 148). Likewise, for two years following family training at the OSLC, 28 teenagers who had at least three prior recorded law violations spent 2,247 *fewer* days combined in institutional confinement than did 27 control youths assigned to community treatment (Bank et al., 1987). When Myra B. Middleton and Gwendolyn Cartledge of Ohio State University (1995) provided reinforcement-based social skill-training and parent training for five aggressive 8-year-old African American males, aggressive acts were reduced from 125 during pretreatment to 21 during intervention (a 79% decrease) and zero during a follow-up observation. Parent behavioral training works because the systematic use of positive reinforcement works.

Like Parent Behavioral Training, "Home Point Systems," teach parents how to systematically reinforce appropriate behaviors and are very effective at increasing those behaviors and decreasing unacceptable behaviors (e.g., Christophersen et al., 1972). Home Point Systems are token economies that deliver positive reinforcers, points or tokens for appropriate behaviors such as emptying the trash, bathing, or cleaning, and have response cost fines for unacceptable behaviors such as teasing or whining. As in other token economies, the points earned are exchangeable for backup reinforcers such as TV time, treats, and movies. This relationship between appropriate behaviors and privileges, and unacceptable behaviors and privileges loss may occur more or less "naturally" in noncoercive families—"If you pick up your trash and get into the bath, you can see the movie with your friends tomorrow," a parent may say. "But if you don't stop whining, the only place you'll be tomorrow is in your room." However, in coercive families there is little, if any, relationship between appropriate behaviors and privileges, and a coercive behavior by either parent or child often results in additional inappropriate behaviors by both parent and child. Home Point Systems make the relationships between appropriate behaviors and privileges, and unacceptable behaviors and privilege loss *systematic*. When parents learn to systematically reinforce appropriate behaviors, prosocial behaviors increase while antisocial, inappropriate behaviors decrease concurrently. This process makes it less likely that the children will develop deviant or criminal behavior patterns. Home Point Systems work because systematic positive reinforcement works.

OLDER CHILDREN, OUTSIDE OF THE HOME

The longer children are involved in coercive family dynamics and the more peer reinforcement children have received for misconduct and delinquent behavior, the more difficult treating misconduct, noncompliance, deviance, precriminal, and criminal behaviors becomes. However, "more difficult" is not the same as "impossible." As is the case within the home, the most effective and most acceptable (to staff, parents, and participants) approaches are based on the systematic use of positive reinforcement. For residential treatment (group homes), institutionalized programs (detention centers and prisons), and community-based interventions, positive reinforcement-based approaches generally, and the Teaching-Family model specifically, offer the best hope for problem children (e.g., Bedlington et al., 1988; Hicks & Munger, 1990).

The Teaching-Family model (described in chapter 3) provides points exchangeable for privileges for prosocial, appropriate, achievement-oriented behaviors and response cost, point loss for antisocial, inappropriate behaviors typically (but not always) in residential settings. John G. Youngbauer of the University of Kansas studied police and court data and found that compared to other group home programs, individuals from programs using the Teaching-Family model were less likely to be arrested despite the fact that "tougher and less socially skilled" youths are typically assigned to Teaching-Family programs (Youngbauer, 1998). Cross-cultural, international research shows that the Teaching-Family model produces decreases in delinquent behavior and increases in social competence yet costs about one-fourth of the cost of institutional placement (Slot et al., 1992). Emotionally disturbed youths who participate in these model programs improve their grades while decreasing their court contacts, criminal offenses and, future residential placements (e.g., Hicks & Munger, 1990)

Not only is the reinforcement-based Teaching-Family model the most effective approach to rehabilitating juveniles with delinquency records, it is also the "kindest and gentlest" approach to helping juveniles. Indeed, University of South Florida researcher Martha M. Bedlington and University of Kansas researchers Curtis J. Braukmann, Kathryn A. Ramp, and Montrose M. Wolf found that compared to other programs, Teaching-Family programs scored higher on measures of "structure and control," "positive interpersonal relationships," "pleasantness," "family-likeness," and "had higher scores on measures indicating support for prosocial behavior" (Bedlington et al., 1988, pp. 360–361). The researchers concluded that

> Contrary to the commonly held criticism of behavioral programs as cold, mechanical, or rigid. . . . Teaching-Family youth gave higher satisfaction ratings concerning the fairness, pleasantness, concern, and effectiveness of their programs—ratings that are correlated negatively and significantly with delinquency (Kirigin et al., 1982). . . . Behavioral procedures such as teaching and the use of a flexible positive token economy allow the consistent delivery of necessary discipline in a nonpunitive manner, thereby permitting a greater percentage of staff attention to be positive, constructive, and relationship-enhancing. (Bedlington et al., 1988, pp. 361–362)

PRISON

Serious youth crime is a continuing concern and threat to society. The trend of treating younger and younger offenders as adults is likely to backfire. Incarcerating children with older criminals does nothing but provide the children a "higher education" in crime. In prison there are no trained Teaching-Family "parents" to provide reinforcement for prosocial, achievement oriented behaviors and serve as appropriate law-abiding role models. Instead there are "correction" officers and criminals who continue the delinquents' training in coercive interpersonal manipulation; there are criminal role models who reinforce and provide additional "schooling" in antisocial, criminal behavior. (In prison and street slang one person severely beating another is referred to as "schooling" the victim; "I schooled that punk.") As basic behavioral research on aggression (Baron, 1977) and centuries old conflicts across the globe demonstrate, approaches based on vengeance and retaliation only invite more aggression and coercion. However, approaches based on "unconditional" positive regard, "self-esteem building," or other unproven humanistic approaches are also likely to fail. Youths already skilled in coercion and manipulation easily exploit such systems without attaining any real rehabilitation.

Systematic, *proven* approaches to reduce antisocial, delinquent, criminal behaviors of youthful offenders exist. What all these programs—Parent Behavioral Training and Home Point Systems for younger children, and Teaching-Family programs and their variations for older youths—have in common is systematic, contingent, positive reinforcement for prosocial, appropriate behaviors. Opposed to so-called correctional programs (prisons and detention centers) that are actually harsh training grounds for criminal behavior, behavioral programs based on positive reinforcement succeed in the *correction* of criminal behaviors. Behavioral programs based on positive reinforcement do not "coddle" the offenders. Instead, as is inherent in the very definition of *contingency*, programs based on positive reinforcement *contingent* upon appropriate behavior *demand* appropriate behavior for the receipt of positive reinforcers. Likewise, the contingency of *response cost* demands that inappropriate behaviors do not occur or positive reinforcers are lost. These reinforcement contingencies are the same contingencies that exist for all of society. Programs based on positive reinforcement make these contingencies clear, consistent, and systematic so that they can be *learned* by youths whose previous reinforcement history and training has been for coercion based on negative reinforcement.

Unfortunately, some individuals' behaviors (e.g., robbery, rape, and murder) have proven so harmful to society that these individuals must be removed from society at large and put into institutions until their behavior is no longer a threat to society. But prison life itself is a society with many complex interpersonal relationships and behavioral interactions. If there is any truth or ambition for those that control prisons with titles like "The Department of *Corrections*," then there should be programs in place to *correct* criminal behavior. The most fair, effective, and constructive approach to both correct criminal behavior and to manage prison society are behavioral approaches based on positive reinforcement. In a review of meta-analyses on the effectiveness of interventions for criminal behavior, Ted Palmer of the California Youth Authority found that "behavioral approaches were most often effective" (Palmer, 1991, p. 335). In a nation-wide survey of sex offender rehabilitation programs in state prisons, Allen D. Sapp of Central Missouri State University and Michael S. Vaughn of Sam Houston State University found that "behavioral therapy was most often desired by treatment providers. . . . Adult sex offender treatment program directors, given the opportunity and resources, would considerably increase the number of behavior modification techniques" (Sapp & Vaughn, 1991, p. 66).

If positive reinforcement is made contingent upon appropriate behavior, appropriate behaviors increase even with so-called *incorrigibles, untouchables,* and the *worst of the worst.* Janet E. Ellis of the University of North Texas instituted a reinforcement program for maximum security prisoners in "administrative segregation"—the prisoner's prison within the prison. Ellis's program was very basic: "Our program consisted of providing privileges and other rewards for useful and appropriate behavior such as cleaning their cells, interacting with guards and other people politely. . . . [Inmates] learned the kinds of skills people need in order to live together, and they learned that behaving well pays off" (Ellis, 1999, p. 1). The results were striking. "Aggressive and other anti-social behavior decreased, and good behavior increased. Guards liked working in the program and resisted being transferred from the wing. Our unit was the first such unit to be allowed off monitoring by the federal judge" (p. 1). Unfortunately the program was cut. While clearly *corrective,* it was not seen as punitive.

The evidence is clear that positive reinforcement *can* be used effectively to reduce coercion, misconduct, noncompliance, and crime. Even people who have a history of reinforcement for criminal behavior can learn that legal, appropriate behaviors ultimately produce the greatest long-term reinforcement returns and can change their behavior patterns into those of law-abiding citizens. For this to occur, society must change its focus from hard-line demands of retribution and vengeance to prevention and reha-bilitation. But such a change is not popular. Consequently, as suggested by Ellis, the likely result will be more crime: "Humane prison programs . . . are not popular with taxpayers, many of whom consider them forms of coddling and a waste of money. But street crime and high taxes are not popular either, and if we do not change the way we treat prisoners, we are going to continue to have more of both" (Ellis, 1999, p. 2).

13

REINFORCEMENT IN THE CAUSE, COURSE, AND CORRECTION OF DEPRESSION, CHRONIC PAIN, AND ILLNESS

Pain and illness are often correctly seen as physiological, not psychological, problems. Especially by the drug companies, depression is increasingly viewed (promoted) as a physiological, biological problem. Despite these views, there is overwhelming evidence that reinforcement plays a critical role in many, if not all, cases of depression, chronic pain, and illness. Of course, no one, or next to no one, wakes up and consciously decides, "I think I'll be depressed or chronically ill because that's how I can get the most reinforcement." (Deliberate faking of illness for gain is "malingering." Deliberate faking of illness for unidentified reasons, but likely for social reinforcement, is known as a factitious disorder.) Yet, while not the only factor, millions of people *do* suffer from pain or depression as a result of reinforcement for pain behavior or depressive behavior.

Just as great creative achievement is produced by years of training and thousands of reinforced approximations (chapters 7 & 9 in this book), and just as becoming a drug abuser or criminal is not a conscious decision but the result of years of, usually inadvertent, reinforcement of misconduct and antisocial behavior (chapters 12 & 13 in this book), the development of depression and chronic illness is also in no small part the result of years of reinforcement for behaving depressed and ill *relative* to reinforcement for behaving optimistically and well.

DEPRESSION'S DEVELOPMENT

If it were known *exactly* how depression developed, then it should be easier to prevent and there would be no need for this chapter. While it is not known exactly how depression occurs in all cases, there is very strong evidence that reinforcement processes play a central role. In the case of *learned helplessness* (introduced in chapter 10 in this book), depression results from consistent nonreinforcement of behavior. Individuals suffering from learned helplessness find that behaviors that are usually reinforcing for others are not reinforced for them or are thwarted. When behavior has no effect on one's experiences, learned helplessness, hopelessness, and depression are likely to occur.

Like so much in psychology and in science generally, understanding of learned helplessness began with basic research with animals. Usually when dogs are placed in a "shuttle box"— a cage with a wire floor and two halves separated by a small hurdle with a light signal that indicates that in ten seconds a mild electric shock will occur in whichever side the dog is in—dogs quickly learn to shuttle back and forth, avoiding the shock as soon as the light goes on. At first, the dog will not know that the light signals impending shock and may receive a shock; however, it will quickly cross to the other side, thus escaping the shock. In the standard procedure, after a few trials, as soon as the signal occurs, via negative reinforcement, the dog will cross, easily avoiding shock altogether. As doctoral student Martin E. P. Seligman (e.g., Seligman, 1975, 1990) at the University of Pennsylvania discovered, most dogs could *not* learn to escape or avoid the shock if they were first strapped into hammocks and given shocks that were *inescapable*. That is, if the dogs first received inescapable, uncontrollable shocks they learned to be helpless—hopeless. Their behavior became depressed. While dogs that did not receive inescapable shock easily learned to avoid shock in the shuttle box, the dogs that first received inescapable shock appeared helpless, depressed. They just sat in the box and needlessly endured the shock.

Learned helplessness findings were first replicated with humans by Donald S. Hiroto at Oregon State University (Hiroto, 1974; Hiroto & Seligman, 1975). In Hiroto's first experiment, humans could turn off an aversive noise simply by moving their finger from one side of a small box to another—a human "shuttle box." But like the dogs first exposed to inescapable shock, humans first exposed to inescapable noise usually did not learn the simple finger task. Prior exposure to inescapable noise taught the humans to be helpless in another task.

The effects of learned helplessness appear to be quite general. In Hiroto's second study, compared to humans not exposed to inescapable noise, humans first exposed to inescapable noise performed much worse, or not at all, on an academic task, unscrambling anagrams. In a similar experiment, compared to humans not previously given unsolvable anagrams, humans first given unsolvable anagrams performed much worse, or not at all, on the shuttle box noise termination task. Thus, regardless of the specific nature of the uncontrollable aversive event, previous experience with uncontrollable aversive events may produce learned helplessness and depressed behavior. In fact, Seligman found that the shuttle box performance of nonclinically depressed subjects given experience with uncontrollable aversive noise was virtually as poor as that of clinically depressed subjects not given uncontrollable aversive noise in the laboratory (D. C. Klein & Seligman, 1976).

Outside of the laboratory, a sense of hopelessness is critical in the development of depression (e.g., Barlow & Durand, 1999, p. 205). People feel hopeless when they experience uncontrollable life events. Reviews of studies on depression find that stressful life events are highly linked to the development of depression (Kessler, 1997). Due to illness or injury, youths who must limit their activities, and thus limit their potential sources of reinforcement are at great risk for depression (Lewinsohn et al., 1997). For example, John M. Chaney and his co-workers at Oklahoma State University and at the University of Oklahoma found that adolescents and young adults with long-standing asthma "demonstrated significantly greater problem-solving deficits following response-noncontingent feedback [a laboratory-learned helplessness manipulation], compared to [a] healthy cohort group" (Chaney et al., 1999, p. 259). Additionally, the long-standing asthma sufferers were also more likely to make internal attributions (e.g., self-blame) following response-noncontingent failure. That is, the asthma sufferers tended to blame themselves even if their behavior had nothing to do with their experimentally manipulated failure. The researchers concluded that "individuals with long-standing asthma may be at increased risk for depression and for learned helplessness deficits" (p. 259). Many people, children in particular, find running and playing outside, often with animals, fun and reinforcing. But when people with long-standing asthma had attempted to play outside with animals, they may have repeatedly experienced asthma attacks that would function as punishment, not reinforcement, for attempting to play outside with animals. After years of such experiences, the asthma sufferers may learn to be helpless, hopeless, and depressed when seeing healthy others romping outside with their pets. When behavior, and thus reinforcement, is limited, or behavior does not produce reinforcing consequences, hopelessness and learned helplessness—depression—is likely.

A person is at increased risk of depression if as an infant the person's cries were usually ignored, and as a child drawings and play never produced praise and affection, schoolwork was ignored, and attempts at interpersonal socialization were not reinforced. Why behave when behaviors are useless? Why behave when behaviors are not reinforced? Why try to play outside when it will only result in difficulty breathing followed by an extended stay in bed? The person has *learned* to be helpless—taught to be depressed by a lack of reinforcement. Hopelessness results from uncontrollable, aversive, nonreinforcing life events. Childhood experiences of marital conflict, divorce, or death are all linked to emotional problems including depression (e.g., J. B. Kelly, 1998). Because behaviors that typically produce reinforcing consequences—cries, play, schoolwork, and interpersonal interactions—are seldom reinforced for people suffering from learned helplessness, behavior becomes *depressed*, pressed down. As their behavior becomes depressed, fewer normal, achievement-oriented, proactive, prosocial, *non*depressed behaviors occur and a self-perpetuating downward spiral into despair is likely.

As argued in the pioneering work of Peter A. Lewinsohn (e.g., 1974), depression results from the absence of, or a low rate of, positive reinforcement. This low rate of positive reinforcement comes from (1) little availability of reinforcement in the individual's environment, (2) few possibly reinforcing events as a result of personal characteristics, and (3) little instrumental activity by the individual. The resulting depression feeds on the individual's personal characteristics and further decreases activity, perpetuating the lack of positive reinforcement and depression.

Environments that cannot provide much positive reinforcement for productive behaviors cannot support, or reinforce productive behaviors; thus, depression is more probable. There was more behavioral depression during the economic depression of the 1930s than there was during the "roaring" 1920s. When unemployment increases, admissions to mental hospitals increase and even in good times admissions are higher among the lower socioeconomic classes (S. Schwartz, 2000, p. 19). One is at increased risk of depression following a death in the family or a wage cut (Shrout et al., 1989). Like unemployment, death and wage cuts are largely uncontrollable events that reduce sources of positive reinforcement from the environment.

Fair or not, it is a reality that beginning in infancy, physical characteristics such as obesity and physical attractiveness, characteristics initially totally beyond an individual's control, determine how frequently people receive reinforcing attention and affection. Physically attractive infants receive more care and attention from caregivers relative to unattractive infants. Physically attractive children are better liked and receive more attention from their teachers and peers than do less attractive children. Tall thin people are more likely to be promoted and judged effective than short or obese people. Behavioral characteristics also determine how frequently people receive reinforcing attention and affection. For example, infants with high initial "positive emotionality," and low "constraint" (behavioral tendencies that seem to have a strong genetic component, e.g., Tellegen et al., 1988), are more likely to be played with and talked to, that is, more likely to have their behaviors reinforced, than are infants high in "negative emotionality" and "constraint." A constrained, aversely emotional infant is likely to receive relatively little interpersonal interaction and as a child and teenager this constraint may develop into shyness resulting in fewer friendships and interpersonal relationships that further stunts the development of possible behaviors that can produce reinforcement. A low rate of behavior can only receive a low rate of reinforcement. In a circular process, a low rate of reinforcement produces an even lower rate of behavior. An inactive person who has few reinforcing personal characteristics and is in an environment that cannot, or does not provide much positive reinforcement, will not receive much positive reinforcement. This situation is, in a word, *depressing* and individuals in such situations are likely to be *depressed.*

REINFORCEMENT OF DEPRESSIVE BEHAVIORS

While owing to an overall lack of reinforcement, a depressed individual's behavior will be *depressed, pressed down,* occurring at a low rate, there are behaviors associated with depression such as crying and self-deprecative talk. Just as coercive and deviant behaviors may be inadvertently reinforced by the family of antisocial youths (chapter 13 in this book), depressive behaviors may be inadvertently reinforced by the depressed person's family, shaping and reinforcing the depression. Indeed, Lisa Sheeber and her co-workers at the Oregon Research Institute argue that

> There is evidence indicating that depressive behavior may be functional in its capacity to elicit desirable social consequences. In particular, . . . women's depressive behavior is negatively reinforced by reduced aggressiveness on the part of their spouses and children. Additionally, a positive reinforcement mechanism may also be operative in that depressive behavior has been found to elicit help and support. (Sheeber et al., 1998, p. 418)

Sheeber and her co-workers studied the family interactions of 86 families of depressed adolescents and 408 families of nondepressed adolescents to determine "whether parents may inadvertently teach their children to behave in a depressed manner through a process of negative and/or positive reinforcement" (Sheeber et al., 1998, p. 418). They found that in fact *parents do teach their children to behave in a depressed manner through a process of negative and positive reinforcement.* Specifically the researchers' results showed that

> Mothers were more likely to emit problem-solving and faciltative behaviors in response to adolescent depressive behavior in families of the depressed adolescents than in families of the non-depressed adolescents. This suggests that positive reinforcement may be a mechanism by which depressive behavior is learned in the family environment. Adolescent depressive behavior was also more likely to suppress paternal aggressive behavior in families of depressed adolescents. This suppressive effect is consistent with a negative reinforcement model and suggests that depressive behavior may provide a brief respite by decreasing family members' aggressive behaviors. (Sheeber et al., 1998, p. 423)

In short, in depressive families, but not in nondepressive families, mothers facilitate or positively reinforce acting depressed, and in depressive families, but not in nondepressive families, parents decrease aggression in response to depressive behaviors and thus negatively reinforce acting depressed. Although likely not a conscious process, the adolescent learns that "if I act depressed, cry, and degrade myself, Mom will help me (positive reinforcement) and Dad will get off my back (negative reinforcement)." Through this process of positive and negative reinforcement *parents train their children to be depressed.*

WHY DO PEOPLE CRY?

There are many hypotheses as to why people cry. Tears are falsely presumed to remove toxins. Tears are falsely presumed to restore homeostasis, physiological balance, and quiescence. It is falsely presumed that a "good cry" makes people feel better and one must cry to "get the hurt out before the healing can begin." In fact, people cry and learn to cry because it produces reinforcement from the social environment.

In a comprehensive study of "the psychophysiology of crying," James J. Gross and Robert W. Levenson of the University of California, Berkeley, and Barbara Fredrickson of Duke University found that crying *increased* sadness and pain, and *increased* somatic and autonomic nervous system activity. Crying *increases*, not decreases, aversive feelings (Gross et al., 1994). But, people do feel better after a cry. However, they would feel better sooner if they did not cry in the first place. Whether one cries or not, emotions dissipate over time. Crying just prolongs feeling bad. Since physiologically and emotionally, crying is detrimental, the researchers argue that crying must serve a social function. Specifically crying evolved because it usually results in social reinforcement from those in proximity to the crier. The researchers concluded that, because crying is aversive to both the crier and those observing the crying, "through the principle of negative reinforcement, crying may motivate proximate others to do something to end the tears, thus serving to increase the cohesion of social groups" (p. 467). In turn, although aversive in and of itself, because crying produced reinforcing consequences, crying is increasingly probable. Of course, one may cry frequently but not be depressed, and crying is just one of the behaviors associated with depression. Nevertheless, that crying can come under operant control of the reinforcing social environment argues that depression, or at least the behavior of depressed individuals, is a function of reinforcement just like the behavior of the nondepressed.

PAIN

In addition to depression, crying is a behavior associated with pain. As paradoxical as it may seem, pain, especially chronic pain, is more of a psychological phenomenon, controlled and maintained by reinforcement, than it is a physical phenomenon. Of course, tissue damage, cuts, and broken bones are harmful and usually force the individual who suffers an injury to change many of their behaviors. But *unquestionably* pain behaviors and to a large extent the subjective experience of pain is a function of psychological, reinforcement processes *not* tissue damage or neuronal firing indicating pain. For example, 65 percent of war veterans wounded in combat report feeling *no pain* (Melzack & Wall, 1982). Likewise, athletes who sustain injuries including broken bones during competition often continue to compete and do not even notice their injury until after the competition is over. Some people, however, sustain very minor injuries or illnesses that most would not even notice, but these people become bedridden or disabled for extended lengths of time.

In their book on abnormal psychology, clinical psychologists David H. Barlow of Boston University and V. Mark Durand of the State University of New York, Albany, point out: "Chronic pain . . . may begin with an acute episode but *does not decrease* over time, even when the injury has healed or [medically] effective treatments have been administered" (Barlow & Durand, 1999, p. 282, emphasis in original). This chronic pain affects sixty-five million Americans argue Barlow and Durand, and furthermore, "researchers now agree that the cause of chronic pain and the resulting enormous drain on our health care system *are substantially psychological and social*" (p. 282, emphasis in original).

More specifically, the psychological and social causes of pain are frequently reinforcement of pain behavior. In combat, screaming, yelling, and displaying other pain behaviors is not likely to produce much reinforcement, especially if the injury is not immediately life threatening. But screaming and yelling during combat could get one shot, and betray one's position resulting in the deaths of others as well. Displaying pain behaviors during athletic competition is likely to get one removed from the competition, precluding one from all the reinforcers associated with competition, not the least of which is victory. One can't win if one is not in the game. But, crying, screaming, moaning, or yelling in pain in the hospital or at home in front of loved ones is much more likely to be reinforced.

As Paul Bebbington and Ivan Delemos of the University College, London Medical School suggested in their editorial research review titled "Pain in the Family," pain may be more a function of family dynamics than it is a function of body, biological, physical dynamics. Bebbington and Delemos argue that "communication of pain functions partly to elicit caring responses (and may even have a . . . role in deflecting anger). . . . [Furthermore,] positive reinforcement may sometimes occur in circumstances where there is some gain for family members in maintaining the patient in the sick role" (Bebbington & Delemos, 1996, p. 452). Even when there is not obvious gain for family members, "reinforcement effects are . . . apparent in ordinary family interaction." Indeed, the research shows that "spouse reinforcement of overt expressions of pain leads to an *increase in* the reported *severity* of pain, and to a *decrease in activity* levels" (p. 453, emphasis added). (Decreased activity is associated with increased depression.) The conclusion is inescapable: "it is clear from this literature that the reinforcement of chronic pain has an important role in maintaining it" (p. 453). Like other behavioral phenomenon: Pain *is* as pain *does* and pain does as pain is *reinforced*. For example, Karen M. Gil and her co-workers in a study of fifty-one chronic pain patients in the Duke University Pain Program found that pain patients' level of satisfaction varied as a function of social support. Chronic pain patients who were satisfied received positive reinforcement—social support—when they engaged in pain behavior (Gil et al., 1987).

The concept of "secondary gain," beginning with Sigmund Freud, is used in clinical psychology to refer to increased attention and sympathy from significant others —social positive reinforcement—and avoidance of difficult situations, such as a family reunion with disliked in-laws or work—negative reinforcement—that may occur as a function of mental or physical illness or pain. Illness-produced reduction in patient anxiety (which would be negative reinforcement) was considered to be the "primary gain" for maintaining the illness. However the evidence is clear that so-called secondary gain *produces* the mislabeled primary gain. If increased attention and sympathy from loved ones and escape or avoidance of unpleasant situations or tasks does not reduce "anxiety," what will? Indeed, a review of 166 studies referring to "secondary gain" by David A. Fishbain and his co-workers (1995) at the University of Miami Comprehensive Pain & Rehabilitation Center found that spouses reinforce chronic pain patients' pain behavior and that disability benefits reinforced disability perception.

In fact, both pain behavior and healthy behavior are tightly coupled to their relative rates of reinforcement for pain and healthy behaviors respectively. Ephrem Fernandez of Southern Methodist University and J. J. McDowell of Emory University studied the behaviors of chronic pain sufferers between the ages of 26 and 68 and their spouses over a two-week observation period (Fernandez & McDowell, 1995). The researchers found that spousal reinforcement of pain behavior accounted for 86% of pain behaviors and spousal reinforcement of healthy behaviors accounted for 76% of healthy behaviors. An earlier study by Herta Flor, Robert D. Kerns and Dennis C. Turk (1987) of the University of Pittsburgh School of Medicine Center for Pain Evaluation & Treatment found that duration of the pain problem and both *perceived pain* and activity levels of 32 chronic pain patients between the ages of 27 and 69 years was significantly related to spouse reinforcement of overt expressions of pain. When expressions of pain are reinforced, *pain* as a class of behavior (perceptions, activity level, disability, and expressions related to pain) increases.

REINFORCEMENT AND DEPENDENCY IN THE ELDERLY

Unfortunately for elderly persons, the reinforcement of pain and depression related-behaviors is so ubiquitous, occurring with the elderly in institutions as well as in families, that Margret M. Baltes of the Free University of Berlin, and Hans-Werner Wahl of the University of Heidelberg in Germany, have termed the relationship between social reinforcement and dependency the *dependence-support script* (e.g., Baltes & Wahl, 1992). A *script* refers to a standard, widespread, pattern of interaction (e.g., teenagers engaging in a "dating script"). In the dependence-support script, any dependent behaviors (requests for help in dressing, weakness, illness, pain, or depressive behaviors) produce support, caring behaviors (positive reinforcement) from the caregivers, staff, or spouse. As a result of the dependence-support script, dependent behaviors increase. Compounding the problematic dependence-support script is the equally robust *independence-ignore* script where *independent behaviors*, wellness behaviors, are ignored—

extinguished—by the caregivers, staff, or spouse. Consequently, just as dependence behaviors are being reinforced and increasing, independent behaviors are being extinguished, decreasing. Baltes and Wahl's extensive research repeatedly finds that "the social world of older people can be characterized as one in which their dependent behaviors are immediately attended to, while independent behaviors are widely ignored" (Baltes & Wahl, 1996, p. 217). Because dependence is reinforced and independence is extinguished, or not reinforced, in the dependence-support script, positive social reinforcement contingencies may maintain dependency, illness, pain, and depression.

Of course, like all other biological systems, as the human body ages it "breaks down" more frequently, heals more slowly, becomes less efficient, less functional, more prone to illness and damage. This unavoidable biological fact necessitates some level of increasing dependence by older people. However, as Baltes argues in "The Etiology and Maintenance of Dependency in the Elderly":

> Some people have become dependent at 50 while others are still fully independent at 80. Some are dependent when required to cope with their financial situations, others with loneliness, and still others with daily self-care. How early or how late we become unable to cope with this or that aspect of our life seems to depend largely on differences in biological make-up as well as on differences in social and physical life events. (Baltes & Wahl, 1988, p. 302)

One's biological makeup is generally fixed. But the social and physical life events are not fixed and Baltes's data consistently support the finding that "dependency is the product of specific reinforcing contingencies, that apparently stem from a gross underestimation of still existing competencies" (Baltes, 1988, p. 314). Furthermore, dependency is not a pleasant state of affairs; it is depressing. Baltes writes that "dependency in the gerontological literature is generally defined as helplessness or powerlessness" (p. 301). Even though, by necessity humans become more dependent as they age, the support or reinforcement of dependent behavior is excessive. It fosters further dependency than would be required by decreased biological functioning alone. According to the findings by Baltes and Wahl, in institutions and at home the social environments of the elderly are "overresponsive, thereby fostering dependent behaviors at the cost of independent behaviors" (Baltes & Wahl, 1996, p. 223).

In their research studies designed to "analyze the impact of social environmental consequences on dependent behaviors of older people,"

Baltes and Wahl found that "it was dependent rather than independent behavior on the part of older people that 'produced' social responses [social reinforcement]. Dependent behaviors, *more than any other behaviors* in the behavioral repertoire of older people, resulted in immediate and positive reactions from the social environment" (Baltes & Wahl, 1996, p. 221, emphasis added). Conversely, independent behaviors, "when they occur, did not initiate social responses. Instead, they were in most cases simply ignored" (p. 221). Punishment—"active behavioral discouragement of further independent behaviors" (p. 221)—was more frequent than a reinforcing consequence for any independent behavior that was not simply ignored. Thus, for the elderly, although associated with "helplessness," and "powerlessness," *dependent behaviors are functional.* More than any other behaviors, dependent behaviors produce positive social reinforcement. However, Baltes and Wahl point out, "this does not imply that dependent behavior as a whole is desirable. The consequences of dependent behavior also include potential negative consequences, such as a trajectory toward less competence and less autonomy" (1992, p. 417).

REINFORCEMENT TRAINING FOR SICKNESS AND PAIN: CHILDHOOD

While the dependent-support script is the most dominant pattern of social interaction for the elderly, fortunately for children, including institutionalized children, "the dominant schedule is not one of attention following dependent self-care behaviors, but rather attention following constructively engaged behaviors of the children" (Baltes et al., 1987, p. 390). However, just as children may be trained to be depressed by inadvertent parental reinforcement (e.g., Sheeber et al., 1998), people who suffer from chronic health problems have a learning history of family reinforcement for sickness behavior and modeling of sickness behavior.

In a study of 242 undergraduates at the State University of New York, Stony Brook, Sussie Eshun found that students' reinforcement history for pain predicted pain expression (1997). Similarly, a study of 180 undergraduates by Robert A. Moss of Greenville General Hospital Pain Therapy Center, South Carolina, found that the best predictors of current work or school avoidance was a previous history of work stoppage and school absence as a child and a father's history of work avoidance (e.g., modeling). Moss also found that a history of reinforcement for illness behavior as a child and a child's mother's attention for illness behavior predicted current perceived positive reinforcement for illness behavior (Moss, 1986).

Getting to the heart of the matter with their report's title, William E. Whitehead of the University of North Carolina Division of Digestive Diseases and his co-workers at institutions across the country straightforwardly state: "Modeling and Reinforcement of the Sick Role During Childhood Predicts Adult Illness Behavior" (Whitehead et al., 1994). Previous research from Whitehead's laboratory found that

> Health care utilization and the frequency of somatic symptoms were found to be correlated with ... reports that the subject's parents encouraged sick role behavior or modeled sick role behavior during the subject's childhood. ... Women who exhibited illness behavior by answering questions that their colds were more serious than those of most other people, that they went to a doctor for treatment of a cold, and that they had more disability days and went to doctors more often were also more likely to report that their parents had given them toys, gifts, or treat foods, such as ice cream, when they had a cold or influenza as a child. (Whitehead et al., 1994, p. 541)

Whitehead and his co-workers found "the effects of childhood social learning appeared to be relatively specific in that subjects were most likely to report the symptoms and to take disability days for the symptoms that their parents reinforced and modeled" (Whitehead et al., 1994, p. 548). In general then, reinforcement of sick behaviors during childhood predicts (e.g., at least partially causes), sick role behavior during adulthood. But specifically, just as early reinforcement of vocal behavior determines which language a person will first speak (see chapter 1 & appendix 1 in this book), early reinforcement of specific symptoms determines, at least in part, what symptoms a person will have as an adult:

> The principal findings were as follows. First, childhood reinforcement of menstrual illness behavior significantly predicted adult menstrual symptoms and disability days, and childhood reinforcement of cold illness behavior significantly predicted adult cold symptoms and disability days. These effects were independent of stress and neuroticism. Second, childhood reinforcement scales were useful to predict which functional disorders (dysmenorrhea or irritable bowel syndrome) these subjects had even after we controlled for stress and neuroticism. (Whitehead et al., 1994, p. 541)

Similarly, in a study of medical care-seeking for menstrual symptoms, Melanie L. Thompson and Mary L. Gick of Carleton University, Canada, found that adolescents who sought medical intervention for menstrual difficulties "reported more symptoms that had been problematic since menarche." Care seekers also acknowledged having had more "reinforcement for adolescent menstrual illness behaviors" than did girls who did not seek care for menstrual problems. They also saw "their symptoms as more serious and more difficult to ignore. The perceived seriousness and severity of symptoms were both correlated with reinforcement for adolescent menstrual symptoms" (Thompson & Gick, 2000, p. 137).

The findings of Thompson and Gick (2000), Whitehead and his colleagues (1994), and others (e.g., S. M. Schwartz et al., 1994; Turkat & Noskin, 1983) suggest that *perceived* seriousness and severity of illness is *not* a function of biological, physiological health. *One's perceived seriousness and severity of illness is a function of, caused by, one's history of reinforcement for illness.*

PREVENTION OF PAIN AND SICK-ROLE BEHAVIORS, DEPRESSION, AND DEPENDENCY

In reinforcement-produced pain, illness, and depression just as in physically caused pain, illness, and depression (due to viruses, bacteria, injury, hormone, or neurotransmitter imbalances), an ounce of prevention is worth a pound of cure. The way to prevent reinforcement-produced pain, illness, depression, and dependency is contained in the studies on reinforcement-produced pain, illness, depression, and dependency.

Pain and Illness

Parents and caregivers naturally and correctly attend to and give affection to children who are injured or sick. However, to prevent the development of chronic pain and sick-role behaviors relatively *more* attention and affection should be given to children when they are well and actively engaged. More encouragement and praise should be given for *getting better*, than affection given while sick or injured. For example, generally a child should not be given ice cream or other treats at the height of a bout of the flu. Instead a parent may be encouraging. "I feel bad that you don't feel well. But when you start to feel better and get stronger again we'll go get a sundae. How's that, Honey?" Patterns of interaction like this show concern and sympathy for the child but also teach the child that wellness is the expected and reinforced state of health.

To prevent sick-role behaviors, parents should make sure sickness is not negatively reinforced. A child should not be allowed to use illness or injury as a means to escape or avoid schoolwork or chores. Instead, the child should be told that they will have to make up all the work (within reasonable limits) as soon as they are well enough. By making it clear to children that if they are too sick or injured to attend school or work, that means they are too sick to—and will not be allowed to—play outside later, visit friends, participate in, or attend sporting or social events on days they miss school or work, parents teach children that being sick has serious social consequences and that being well is ultimately a more reinforcing and productive state.

Depression

Behavioral characteristics of depression include lethargy and inactivity or low levels of activity. Behavior is *depressed* from normal or optimal levels. Therefore, to the extent that active, productive behavioral engagement can be shaped, depression may be prevented. If creative achievement (chapters 7 & 9 in this book) is being encouraged, prompted, shaped and reinforced, creative and achievement-oriented behaviors will be occurring, not inactivity or behaviors characteristic of depression. If a child's environment is structured for educational excellence and educational achievement is nurtured (chapter 10 in this book), then active educational engagement will occur. Children who are *actively engaged* in educational, athletic, prosocial, creative, or other appropriate behaviors are not depressed. Their behavior is not pressed down.

However, given the chaotic nature of the world with constant human-made disasters (e.g., war, murders, and adultery) and natural disasters (e.g., floods and storms), most people will inevitably experience several aversive uncontrollable, unpredictable events. Experience with such events is said to produce learned helplessness—depression. Yet while most people experience aversive events, most people do not develop depression.

Learned helplessness can be prevented if one is "immunized" or develops "learned optimism" (e.g., Seligman, 1990) prior to experiencing aversive uncontrollable, unpredictable events if one is first given experience with *controllable, predictable* events. This early learning history teaches individuals that their behavior can produce meaningful consequences, and their behavior can reduce the aversiveness of events they experience. As Martin Seligman discovered early in his initial work with dogs, such experience "immunizes" one against, or prevents, learned helplessness: "Learning that responding matters actually prevents helplessness. We even found that dogs taught this mastery as puppies were immunized to learned helplessness all their lives. The implications of that, for human beings, were thrilling" (Seligman, 1990, p. 28).

The thrilling implication for humans was that if children were taught that responding matters, that their behavior is functional in producing meaningful consequences, then people too could be "immunized" against learned helplessness. To immunize against depression children need to be given experiences with successful outcomes as a result of their efforts and skill (Seligman, 1975). The successes do not need to be great in order to develop a sense of mastery and optimism. Just as creative achievement is shaped by reinforced approximations so is a sense of control and optimism. For example, a child may be given the choice of what book to read or fruit to eat. If the choices are enjoyable, then while that in and of itself will not produce lifelong optimism or industriousness, it will be part of a lifelong reinforcement history that contributes to the development of optimism and perceived control. If the choices are not enjoyable, the child should be allowed to chose again. The next choices are likely to be different and more enjoyable. This pattern of behavior and consequences will also contribute to a life long history of behavior contingent successes, contributing to optimism and preventing learned helplessness when later uncontrollable events are inevitably experienced.

Dependency

The natural law of entropy, the tendency of all systems, including biological systems to become less efficient with time, makes increasing dependency of the elderly unavoidable. However, the work of Baltes and Wahl clearly shows that the rate at which the elderly become dependent and the extent to which they are dependent is as much, if not more, due to reinforcement for dependent behaviors than to decreasing biological efficiency.

Yet, "given that the process of aging is characterized by a general weakening of biological reserve capacities," argue Baltes and Wahl, "one may even look at dependent behaviors of older people as a prerequisite for successfully aging" (Baltes & Wahl, 1996, p. 228). To prevent unnecessary, generalized dependency, dependent behaviors should be *selectively* reinforced contingent upon actual, *unalterable* biological deficiencies. For example, if someone loses his sight due to glaucoma or cataracts, he will become dependent upon others for transportation and some food preparation. However, becoming blind does not make one an invalid. A blind elderly person should still be strongly encouraged to, and reinforced for, maintaining an exercise program, preparing what food is possible, and since he cannot read printed words he should be encouraged to, and reinforced for learning to read and write in braille. Such selective dependency and reinforced independency helps elderly people maintain rich and full lives.

Encouraged, reinforced independency can increase the richness of one's life. In his sixties my father suffered a shattered elbow, and wrist and internal bruising as a result of a fall from a ladder. He was unable to walk for two weeks, had surgery, and lost much of the movement in his elbow and wrist. Instead of reinforcing dependence: "don't try to do that with your bad arm; let me get it," he was encouraged and reinforced for increasing the strength and range of motion in his elbow. Because he has a lifelong history or reinforcement for persistence, effort, and industriousness—which really may be the best way to prevent excessive dependence in the elderly—he did not need much encouragement and the improvements in his motion and strength served as intrinsic reinforcements for his rehabilitation efforts. While his range of motion will never be more than 80 percent of his original, as a result of his rehabilitation program, now at sixty-seven my father does twenty push-ups a day and lifts weights several times a week alongside many people more than forty years his junior. Thus, although dependence could have easily been fostered as a result of his injury, because independence was reinforced instead, my father developed a new hobby, weight training, which has improved his health and increased the richness of his life.

TREATING CHRONIC PAIN, ILLNESS, DEPRESSION, AND DEPENDENCY

Given the current state of the world, even though the knowledge exists to, if not eliminate, then greatly ameliorate the amount of chronic pain, illness, depression, and dependency, reductions are not likely anytime in the near future. All told, the number of people suffering from chronic pain or depression is in the hundreds of millions (that's one hundred million people several times over). Just as faulty, unplanned reinforcement contingencies are responsible for much of this suffering, planned, effective reinforcement programs can reduce much of this suffering.

Chronic Pain and Illness

If the experience of pain and illness is to a great extent a product of reinforcement for pain and sick-role behaviors, and this evidence strongly suggests it is, then reducing or eliminating the reinforcement for pain and sick-role behaviors while simultaneously increasing the reinforcement for behaviors associated with wellness and a healthy lifestyle should eliminate or greatly reduce experienced and reported pain and suffering. Not surprisingly that is exactly what happens. When pain behaviors no longer produce reinforcement, pain decreases or is eliminated.

For example, a classic study (Kallman et al., 1975) reports of a forty-two-year-old, retired, wheelchair-bound man with years of medical treatment including previous back surgery who was admitted to a medical center for pain. His simple treatment consisted of a female assistant visiting his room three times a day for ten minutes and asking him to stand and walk as far as possible. She provided social reinforcers for each successive improvement. "I'm proud of you." At first there was little noticeable improvement, but as is often the case with reinforcement of successive approximations to a desired instrumental response (see chapter 1 & appendix 1 in this book), soon there were dramatic results. He was walking normally and discharged after eighteen days. However, because his family reinforced his pain behaviors he was back in the hospital within a month. When consequently they were given training to ignore his pain complaints and reinforce his physical activity, his pain went away with no further problems.

Similarly, when a twenty-six-year-old female who had been suffering from daily debilitating migraine headaches no longer received social reinforcement for her pain behaviors (they were ignored) and simultaneously had her well behaviors such as exercising and domestic chores reinforced (praised), her headaches were eliminated (Aubuchon et al., 1985). The headaches that she had been "suffering" from since the age of thirteen had allowed her to stay home from school and produced parental and professional attention—social reinforcement, "secondary gain." Other treatments including medication, acupuncture, chiropractic, psychotherapy, and even electroconvulsive shock were previously tried and all were unsuccessful. Instead, given the fact that a simple reinforcement program of ignoring pain behavior and praising wellness cured her headaches, it is quite possible that the previous "treatments," actually served to reinforce her pains.

EMPIRICALLY SUPPORTED TREATMENTS

In a special issue of the *Journal of Pediatric Psychology* on empirically (e.g., outcome-evidenced) supported treatments in pediatric psychology for Recurrent Abdominal Pain, RAP (Janicke & Finney, 1999); Procedure Related Pain (Powers, 1999); and Disease-Related Pain (Walco et al., 1999), "cognitive-behavioral" treatments were consistently rated more effective than all other treatments for pain. Cognitive-behavioral intervention strategies include operant reinforcement procedures as a *fundamental element* of effective treatment programs (e.g., Janicke & Finney, 1999, p. 119).

Virginia Polytechnic Institute and State University researchers David M. Janicke and Jack W. Finney's review included a summary of "the earliest investigations of treatments for RAP [that] examined the efficacy of fundamental operant [reinforcement] procedures through two controlled case studies" (Janicke & Finney, 1999, p. 118). In the first study (Miller & Kratochwill, 1979), the treatment for a ten-year-old girl with severe stomach pains was time-out from positive reinforcement consisting of the loss of social activities and adult attention following pain complaints. Complaints decreased from two per day to one per month. Similar improvements occurred at school when the procedure was implemented there. In the other study, a ten-year-old boy with severe stomach pains was given tokens for nonpain behaviors and attention was withdrawn following pain complaints. This treatment produced a decrease in pain attacks and pain ratings and an increase in school attendance (Sank & Biglan, 1974). According to Janicke and Finney "these preliminary investigations were of great significance as they served as a foundation for the establishment of alternative treatments, which include operant [reinforcement] procedures as one fundamental element of a treatment program" (Janicke & Finney, 1999, p. 119). Fundamental elements of effective cognitive-behavioral treatments include "differential reinforcement of competing [nonpain] activities" and training parents to "prompt and reinforce appropriate coping behaviors" (p. 121).

University of Cincinnati College of Medicine researcher Scott W. Powers' (1999) review of empirically supported treatments for procedure-related pain also consistently found cognitive-behavioral treatments to be the most effective treatment. One reviewed study (Jay et al., 1987) found cognitive-behavioral treatment to be more effective at reducing pain than Valium. As is the case with effective treatments of Recurrent Abdominal Pain, fundamental elements of cognitive-behavioral treatments include many reinforcement-based procedures including reinforcers (praise, trophies, prizes, video game time, etc.) for breathing skills and lying still, reinforcement for coping skills, cooperation, and reinforcement for participation in child and parent training (Powers, 1999). In sum, when reinforcement procedures are utilized in conjunction with medically necessary distressful procedures, experienced pain can be greatly reduced.

It would be a mistake to believe that reinforcement procedures can only reduce the pain of children. Glenn Geiger's research team at the University of South Florida examined the effects of feedback and contingent reinforcement for the exercise behavior of thirteen adults with chronic lower back pain. They found that no-reinforcement and noncontingent reinforcement (reinforcement regardless of performance, or lack of performance) produced no effect. But reinforcement contingent on the rate of walking and feedback on progress produced systematic increases in walking rate and decreases in reported pain (Geiger et al., 1992). The conclusion is inescapable: when pain behaviors are reinforced, pain increases. Thus the most effective way to treat pain is to decrease the reinforcement for pain behaviors and increase the reinforcement for behavior that is incompatible with sick-role behaviors—wellness and healthy behaviors.

Treating Depression

Since depression is, in part at least, *behavior that is depressed*, behavior that is flattened, lower than general, behavior that is in a recession or slump, an effective treatment should be to *inflate behavior*, pump up, expand, or in other words increase the rate of behavior. In fact, increasing behavior generally and exercise specifically *is* effective treatment for depression.

In many cases exercise may be the *most effective treatment for depression*. In a review of fourteen studies that examined the effects of exercise on mild to moderate depression, Gregg A. Tkachuk and Garry L. Martin of the University of Manitoba, Canada, found that depressed individuals who exercise—walked, ran, or strength trained—20 to 60 minutes a week, 3 times a week were significantly less depressed five weeks later. As long as the exercise was maintained so were the improvements. The effects of exercise in treating depression are comparable or better than individual psychotherapy, group psychotherapy, and cognitive therapy. Furthermore, exercise was found to be an important part of effective behavioral treatments in reducing pain of chronic pain patients (Tkachuk & Martin, 1999). Exercise forces the reinforcement of wellness not sick-role behavior. "Not only is exercise a viable treatment option for mild to moderate depression," argues Tkachuk, "it is four to five times more cost-effective than traditional forms of psychotherapy." One reason why exercise is effective according to Tkachuk is that it provides opportunities for increased social reinforcement. "It gets people out in an environment where they receive positive reinforcement from others" (Tkachuk, 1999, p. 24).

It would be a mistake to conclude that exercise is only effective for mild to moderate depression, but couldn't possibly be effective for older adults suffering with major depressive disorder. Actually, exercise effectively treats major depressive disorders of older adults and over the long term is more effective than medication. At the Duke University Medical Center an extensive multi-investigator study of 156 adults (50+ years) with major depressive disorders compared the effects of aerobic exercise, sertraline (a Selective Serotonin Reuptake Inhibitor, [SSRI], like Prozac), or a combination of exercise and sertraline. Four months after treatment all three groups showed significant improvements. However, subjects in the exercise group had lower relapse rates than subjects in the medication group and exercising on one's own further reduced the probability of future depression (Babyak et al., 2000).

The Duke and Manitoba exercise findings conclusively support the behavioral interpretation of depression. *Depression is de-pressed, pressed down behavior.* To alleviate depression, behavior needs to be uplifted, increased. Exercise may be the most direct way to increase the rate of behavior. When behavior is no longer de-pressed, when one is observably behaviorally active, the subjective "internal" feelings of depression are also alleviated.

The form of the increased activity does not seem to matter. As long as activity levels are increased—by walking, running, or weight lifting, for example—depression is decreased (Tkachuk & Martin, 1999). The beneficial effects of exercise result even from esoteric forms of exercise. Nebojsa Toskovic of Auburn University found that a single session of Tae Kwon Do martial arts exercise produced significant decreases in mood profile measures of tension, depression, anger, fatigue, and confusion and significant increases in vigor and global mood (Toskovic, 2000). Lorna M. Hayward, Annemarie C. Sullivan and Joseph R. Libonati of Northeastern University found that group exercise reduced depression in obese women even though the exercise was not vigorous enough to result in weight loss (Hayward et al., 2000). Exercise programs not only alleviate depression but may prevent depression. A team of University of Missouri researchers found that a twelve-week exercise program not only improved fitness but produced psychological benefits that lasted over a year (Dilorenzo et al., 1999).

Although true, simply telling someone suffering from major depressive disorder, "just exercise and you'll feel better," is likely to be no more effective than simply saying, "don't worry; be happy." Someone suffering from major depression is likely to feel too depressed to *start* exercising. Once again, the principle of shaping by reinforcing successive approximations is critical. Small increases in activity are encouraged and reinforced that provide the foundation for further improvements. For example, Aaron Beck (1976) had a severely depressed hospitalized patient who had refused to get out of bed for one year (talk about behavioral inactivation!) and antidepressant drugs had been ineffective. Beck's treatment consisted of encouraging the patient to get out of bed and walk just ten yards that was reinforced with approval. Next the patient was encouraged to walk twenty yards. Within forty-five minutes the patient was walking about the ward where he received other reinforcers such as candy from the vending machine. In a month, the patient was discharged. Reinforcing successive approximations did in a month what drugs could not do in a year.

All effective psychological treatments for depression include *behavioral activation,* such as reinforced practice of social skills, or behavioral rehearsal as a critical component (e.g., Gossette & O'Brien, 1992). Therapists typically schedule "activities to *reactivate* depressed patients who have given up on most activities, helping them put some fun [reinforcement] back into their lives. Along similar lines," argue clinical psychology authors Barlow and Durand, "other investigators have shown that exercise and/or increased activities alone can improve self-concept and lift depression" (Barlow & Durand, 1999, p. 214, emphasis in original).

While exercise may be the most direct way to increase activity levels, even the best athlete can exercise effectively only for a few hours a day. And most people only devote only a portion of that time to exercise. Ultimately to treat and prevent depression, activity, including nonvigorous activities, such as reading or cooking, need to be shaped and maintained in contexts outside of formal treatment and exercise contexts. Here, reinforcement from the social environment, and especially reinforcement from family members, becomes critical. To this end clinical psychologist Myrna Weissman developed interpersonal psychotherapy that teaches depressed clients how to resolve interpersonal conflicts and to learn to form new relationships. When one learns to resolve interpersonal conflicts and form new relationships, the potential for social reinforcement is greatly increased. Interpersonal psychotherapy benefits approximately 50% to 70% of clients compared to 30% improvement in control or placebo conditions (Barlow & Durand, 1999, p. 215).

Getting active and receiving social reinforcement alleviate depression. In London, Guy's, King's, and St. Thomas' schools of medicine researcher Tirrill Harris assigned chronically depressed women to a volunteer "befriender" who was instructed to be a confidant and meet the depressed women regularly over coffee or tea or for outings for one year. Seventy-two percent of the women receiving a befriender experienced a remission in their depression while only 45% of the women in the wait-list control group experienced remission (Harris et al., 1999). These results are comparable to the effects seen with antidepressant medications. For individuals suffering from depression, no drug is more reinforcing than friendship.

Treating Depression and Dependency in the Elderly

Activity by, and social reinforcement for, the elderly are just as important in preventing and treating depression as activity and social reinforcement are for other populations. Lack of activity and social contacts cause much of the depression seen in the elderly. As the *independence-ignore script* suggests, when the elderly are independently active they are ignored by others even if they are living at home in a family environment instead of in an institution (e.g., Baltes & Wahl, 1996). Being ignored by others for any reason is usually depressing. Consequently many elderly become increasingly dependent thus furthering depression. According to the National Institute of Mental Health, nineteen million Americans suffer from depression and 39 percent are older than forty-five. Exercise and socialization can greatly reduce these numbers. In the Duke University study (discussed in this chapter) that found exercise to be more effective in the long term than medication in treating depression the participants were all middle aged or elderly.

Exercise is important for many elderly persons because it gets them out among others who provide reinforcing socialization. "Socialization is the most important thing in [treating] depression," according to Carol Winter, a Hollywood, Florida, senior center health support coordinator. "Just being out of their homes and coming to different activities helps them." One senior citizen who used exercise class to overcome depression after the death of her husband said "It helped me out a lot. Now I don't have time to be depressed. I'm busy, busy, busy, all the time" (from Liang, 2000, F2). When behavior is not *depressed*, elderly do not suffer depression. B. F. Skinner, remained intellectually active throughout his life—finishing his last article (Skinner, 1990) only a few days before his death at eighty-seven. In his book *Enjoy Old Age* Skinner devoted an entire chapter to "Keeping Busy"(Skinner & Vaughan, 1983). If the retired do not keep busy, they will become depressed. In the chapter "Feeling Better" Skinner also argues that *doing* something will ultimately be more effective than *taking* something—drugs:

> Americans take billions of pills every year to feel better about their lives even when their lives remain wretched. For the same reason, and without a doctor's help, they turn to alcohol, marijuana, cocaine and heroin. You are, of course free to do so, but changing what you feel rather than how you feel is a better policy. Just as aspirin may cure a headache without curing the condition responsible for it, so drugs that make you feel better can keep you from attacking the condition [inactivity and decreased social reinforcement] that makes you feel bad. You can feel better by improving what you feel. Depression is a good example. It is said to be the most prevalent mental-health disorder for people over sixty-five. . . you may also feel depressed, as we have seen, simply because you can no longer do many of the things you have enjoyed. Perhaps you liked talking to people but now there is no one to talk to. Perhaps you have enjoyed the countryside but are now cooped up in

the city. Finding someone to talk to or some way of getting to the countryside will be better than remaining alone in the city taking Valium. (Skinner & Vaughn, 1983, p. 118)

Unfortunately, it is an unalterable fact of life that as people age functioning declines from previous levels. Consequently, to continue to function at all, some level of decreased activity and increasing dependence is absolutely necessary. The trick is to maintain as much independence as possible. In *Enjoy Old Age* Skinner described how large amounts of independence can be retained by keeping active and by careful design of the physical environment. For example; when reading becomes difficult, eyeglasses can be worn and/or large print books read (*Enjoy Old Age* was published in large print). Special lighting and seating can also be designed to accommodate decreasing visual functioning. Even with well-designed physical environments, older persons will eventually become socially dependent in some areas of life—from cooking or driving to dressing, bathing, and, for some, even toileting. Baltes argues that successful aging necessarily involves *selective dependence* in order to keep independent in enjoyable areas.

> Due to increasing biological vulnerability with old age, the elderly are forced to make decisions as to which activities to give up in order to keep up good performance in other activities. Thus, in order to remain active and independent in certain domains, the elderly give up independence or autonomy in other domains. In short, the elderly become selectively independent. . . . Old people in particular have to cope with a great number of life events which come at a time when they also experience an increase in biological vulnerability. In other words, when resources available to deal effectively with those diverse events decrease. Thus, [by becoming selectively dependent] the elderly can maintain or even increase their performance in some domains, but no longer maintain a *general* level of high productivity. (Baltes, 1988, pp. 314–315, emphasis in original)

Baltes continues that unfortunately, "Instead of supporting dependency only where and when wanted, and fostering independence and optimization where and when wanted, institutions most often tend towards 'overcare.' Dependence is supported and fostered more frequently than the elderly need or want" (Baltes, 1988, p. 315).

This overresponsive environment leads to dependence and depression in the elderly. Fortunately, caregivers can be taught to increase support for independence and to provide support for dependence only when actually needed. When Baltes and Wahl (e.g., 1996) taught caregivers to use positive reinforcement based behavior modification programs to reinforce independence in the elderly, independence increased and dependency decreased. Baltes and Wahl's findings show that

> Following training, helpers were able to exhibit systematically more independence-supportive behaviors contingent on independent behaviors of older adults [helpers reinforced independence], as well as in response to their dependent behaviors [helpers prompted independence]. As a consequence of this increase in the independence-supportive behaviors among the staff, independent behaviors among older residents also increased. . . . The resulting environment should be one that continues to be responsive to dependency when it is appropriate (e.g., in the face of severe chronic illness) but becomes more differentiated in stimulating [prompting and encouraging] and fostering [reinforcing] independence as much and as long as possible. (Baltes & Wahl, 1996, p. 227)

These results show that the best way to treat dependence is not to offer increasing support for dependence, as is usually the case, but to encourage and reinforce independence. Baltes and Wahl's findings also show what has now been shown hundreds of times in this book. Regardless of the specific behaviors involved—be it behaviors related to crime, drug abuse, pain, dependency, or depression; or behaviors related to creativity, achievement, educational excellence, wellness, or independent functioning—if a behavior produces reinforcing consequences, the behavior's rate of occurrence will increase.

Reinforcement can continue to be misrepresented. Myths involving reinforcement can continue to be propagated. People can continue to be taught that reinforcement's effects on human behavior are always maladaptive, and that those who would knowingly systematically apply reinforcement contingencies to alter human behavior are always maladjusted or worse. People can continue to be taught that systematic reinforcement is best left out of human affairs as much as possible. But such an approach is an active embrace of ignorance—sticking one's head in the sand. It is just as much a fact that reinforcement contingencies are always affecting human behavior as it is a fact that the earth revolves around the sun.

As long as the effects of reinforcement on human behavior are ignored and not applied, reinforcement contingencies will continue to affect human behavior in a catch-as-catch-can manner, capriciously controlling human behavior. Such compassionless inaction will result only in increased depression; dependency; crime; underachievement; drug abuse; and aversive, punishing living conditions. In contrast, to the extent that programs based on contingent positive reinforcement can be systematically applied for appropriate, prosocial, healthy, creative, and achievement-oriented behaviors, the twenty-first century may very well come to be viewed as the dawn of the age of behavioral enlightenment.

REFERENCES

Abra, J. (1993). Competition: Creativity's vilified motive. *Genetic, Social, and General Psychology Monographs, 119(3)*, 291–342.

Alberto, P. A., & Troutman, A. C. (1999). *Applied behavior analysis for teachers, 5th ed.* Upper Saddle River, NJ: Merrill.

Amabile, T. M. (1983). *The social psychology of creativity.* New York: Springer-Verlag.

Amabile, T. M. (1988). A model of creativity and innovation in organizations. In B. M. Shaw & L. L. Cummings (Eds.), *Research in organizational behavior, vol. 10.* Greenwich, CN: JAI Press.

Amabile, T. M. (1996). *Creativity in context: Update to the social psychology of creativity.* Boulder, CO: Westview Press.

Amabile, T. M., & Cheek, J. M. (1988). Microscopic and macroscopic creativity. *Journal of Social and Biological Structures, 11*, 57–60.

Aubuchon, P. G., Haber, J. D., & Adams, H. E. (1985). Can migraine headaches be modified by operant pain techniques? *Journal of Behavior Therapy and Experimental Psychiatry, 16*, 261–263.

Ayllon, T., & Azrin, N. (1968). *The token economy.* New York: Appleton-Century-Crofts.

Ayllon, T., & Kelly, K. (1972). Effects of reinforcement on standardized test performance. *Journal of Applied Behavior Analysis, 5*, 447–484.

Ayllon, T., Layman, D., & Kandel, H. J. (1975). A behavioral-educational alternative to drug control of hyperactive children. *Journal of Applied Behavior Analysis, 8*, 137–146.

Ayllon, T., & Roberts, M. D. (1974). Eliminating discipline problems by strengthening academic performance. *Journal of Applied Behavior Analysis, 7*, 71–76.

Azrin, N. H., & Holz, W. C. (1966). Punishment. In W. K. Honig (Ed.), *Operant behavior: Areas of research and application* (pp. 380–447). Englewood Cliffs, NJ: Prentice-Hall.

Babyak, M., Blumenthal, J. A., Herman, S., Khatri, P., Doraiswamy, M., Moore, K., Craighead, W. E., Baldewicz, T. T., & Krishnan, K. R. (2000). Exercise treatment for major depression: Maintenance of therapeutic benefit at 10 months. *Psychosomatic Medicine, 62(5)*, 633–638.

Baldwin, J. D. & Baldwin, J. I. (2001). *Behavior principles in everyday life.* Upper Saddle River, NJ: Prentice-Hall.

Ballenger, J. C. (1999). Current treatments of the anxiety disorders in adults. *Biological Psychiatry, 46*, 1579–1594.

Baltes, M. M. (1988). The etiology and maintenance of dependency in the elderly: Three phases of operant research. *Behavior Therapy, 19*, 301–319.

Baltes, M. M., Kindermann, T., Reisenzein, R., & Schmid, U. (1987). Further observational data on the behavioral and social world of institutions for the aged. *Psychology and Aging, 2*, 390–403.

Baltes, M. M., & Wahl, H. W. (1992). The dependency-support script in institutions: Generalization to community settings. *Psychology and Aging, 7*, 409–418.

Baltes, M. M., & Wahl, H. W. (1996). Patterns of communication in old age: The dependence-support and independence-ignore script. *Health Communication, 8*, 217–231.

Bandura, A. (1986). *Social foundations of thought and action: A social cognitive theory.* Englewood Cliffs, NJ: Prentice-Hall.

Bandura, A. (1997). *Self-efficacy: The exercise of control.* New York: Freeman.

Bandura, A., & Kupers, C. J. (1964). The transmission of patterns of self-reinforcement through modeling. *Journal of Abnormal and Social Psychology, 69*, 1–9.

Bandura, A., Ross, D., & Ross, S. A. (1963). Vicarious reinforcement and imitative learning. *Journal of Abnormal and Social Psychology, 67*, 601–607.

Bank, L., Patterson, G. R., & Reid, J. B. (1987). Delinquency prevention through training parents in family management. *Behavior Analyst, 10*, 75–82.

Barlow, D. H., & Durand, V. M. (1999). *Abnormal behavior, 2nd ed.* Pacific Grove, CA: Brooks/Cole.

Baron, R. A. (1977). *Human aggression.* New York: Plemun.

Baum, W. M. (1994). *Understanding behaviorism.* New York: Harper Collins.

Beaman, R., & Wheldall, K. (2000). Teachers' use of approval and disapproval in the classroom. *Educational Psychology, 20*, 431–446.

Bebbington, P., & Delemos, I. (1996). Pain in the family. *Journal of Psychosomatic Research, 40*, 451–456.

Beck, A. T. (1976). *Cognitive therapy and emotional disorders.* New York: International University Press.

Bedlington, M. M., Braukmann, C. J., Ramp, K. A., & Wolf, M. M. (1988). A comparison of treatment environments in community-based group homes for adolescent offenders. *Criminal Justice and Behavior, 15*, 349–363.

Begley, S. (2001, February 12). How it all starts inside your brain. *Newsweek,* 40–42.

Bennett T., & Wright R. (1984). The relationship between alcohol use and burglary. *British Journal of Addiction, 79*, 431–437.

Bereiter, C., & Kurland, M. (1981). A constructive look at follow-through results. *Interchange, 12* (http://www.uoregon.edu/~adiep/ft/bereiter. htm).

Berg, W. K., Peck, S., Wacker, D. P., Harding, J., McComas, J., Richman, D., & Brown, K. (2000). The effects of presession exposure to attention in the results of assessments of attention as a reinforcer. *Journal of Applied Behavior Analysis, 33*, 463–477.

Berlau, J. (1998, April 12). Direct instruction's comeback. *Investor's Business Daily.*

Blum, K., Braverman, E. R., Holder, J. M., Lubar, J. F., Monastra, V. J., Miller, D., Lubar, J. O., Chen, T. J. H., & Comings, D. E. (2000). Reward deficiency syndrome: A biogenetic model for the diagnosis and treatment of impulsive, addictive, and compulsive behaviors. *Journal of Psychoactive Drugs, 32*, 1–68.

Bostow, D. E., Kritch, K. M., & Tompkins, B. F. (1995). Computers and pedagogy: Replacing telling with interactive computer-programmed instruction. *Behavior Research Methods, 27*, 297–300.

Bourgois, P. (1996). *In search of respect.* New York: Cambridge University Press.

Brands H. W. (1997). *T.R.: The last romantic.* New York: Basic.

Breyer, N. L., & Allen, G. J. (1975). Effects of implementing a token economy on teacher attending behavior. *Journal of Applied Behavior Analysis, 8*, 373–380.

Brigham, T. A., Graubard, P. S., & Stans, A. (1972). Analysis of the effects of sequential reinforcement contingencies on aspects of composition. *Journal of Applied Behavior Analysis, 5*, 421–429.

Brinkley, D. (1998, November). In the Kerouac Archive: Introduction. *Atlantic Monthly,* 50–51.

Buchalter, G. (2001, July 29). This isn't a cartoon: I get hurt. *Parade Magazine,* 4–7.

Campbell, C.A. (1957). *On selfhood and godhood.* London: George Allen & Unwin.

Cameron, J., Banko, K. M., & Pierce, W. D. (2001). Pervasive negative effects of rewards on intrinsic motivation: The myth continues. *Behavior Analyst, 24,* 1–44.

Cameron, J., & Pierce W. D. (1994). Reinforcement, reward and intrinsic motivation: A meta-analysis. *Review of Educational Research, 64,* 363–423.

Cameron, J., & Pierce W. D. (1996). The debate about rewards and intrinsic motivation: Protests and accusations do not alter the results. *Review of Educational Research, 66,* 39–51.

Capaldi, D. M., Chamberlain, P., & Patterson, G. R. (1997). Ineffective discipline and conduct problems in males: Association, late adolescent outcomes, and prevention. *Aggression and Violent Behavior,* 343–353.

Carson, B. (2001, March). Paging Dr. Carson. *Readers Digest,* 33–36.

Carter, S. C. (2000). *No excuses: Lessons from 21 high-performing, high-poverty schools.* Washington, DC: Heritage Foundation.

Chadwick, B. A., & Day, R. C. (1971). Systematic reinforcement: Academic performance of underachieving students. *Journal of Applied Behavior Analysis, 4,* 311–319.

Chance, P. (2000). Where are the robots? (*www.behavior.org/columns/chance2.cfm*).

Chaney, J. M., Mullins, L. L., Uretsky, D. L., Pace, T. M., Werden, D., & Hartman, V. L. (1999). An experimental examination of learned helplessness in older adolescents and young adults with long-standing asthma. *Journal of Pediatric Psychology, 24,* 259–270.

Cheney, L. (1999, May 12). Effective education squelched. *Wall Street Journal.*

Chernow, R. (1998). *Titan: The life of John D. Rockefeller, Sr.* New York: Vintage Books.

Christophersen, E. R., Arnold, C. M., Hill, D. W., & Quilitch, H. R. (1972). The home point system: Token reinforcement procedures for application by parents of children with behavior problems. *Journal of Applied Behavior Analysis, 5,* 485–497.

Condry, J. (1977). Enemies of exploration: Self-initiated versus other-initiated learning. *Journal of Personality and Social Psychology, 35,* 459–477.

Daniels, A. C. (1994). *Bringing out the best in people.* New York: McGraw-Hill.

Daniels, A. C. (2000). What in the world do we do with them? Dealing with generation "X." *PM E-Zine,1, Article 2* (www.pmezine.com/print/article8.asp).

Davidson K., & Flora, S. R. (1999). Using computer-interactive tutorial with contingent reinforcement to increase reading ability 3 grade levels in 2 months. Association for Behavior Analysis. Chicago.

Davis, H., & Perusse, R. (1988). Human-based social interaction can reward a rat's behavior. *Animal Learning & Behavior, 16,* 89–92.

DeCasper, A. J., & Carstens, A. A. (1981). Contingencies of stimulation: Effects on learning and emotion in neonates. *Infant Behavior & Development, 4,* 19–35.

Deci, E. L. (1971). Effects of externally mediated rewards on intrinsic motivation. *Journal of Personality and Social Psychology, 18,* 105–115.

Deci, E. L. (1995). *Why we do what we do: The dynamics of personal autonomy.* New York: Putnam.

Deci, E. L., Koestner, R., & Ryan, R.M. (1999). A meta-analytic review of experiments examining the effects of extrinsic rewards on intrinsic motivation. *Psychological Bulletin, 125,* 627–668.

Deci, E. L., & Ryan, R. M. (1985). *Intrinsic motivation and self-determination in human behavior.* New York: Plenum.

Deci, E. L., & Ryan, R. M. (1987). The support of autonomy and the control of behavior. *Journal of Personality and Social Psychology, 53,* 1024–1037.

Desmond, A., & Moore J. (1991). *Darwin.* New York: Warner.

"Despite test scores, critics blast teaching method" *Vindicator (Associated Press),* 31 May 1998.

Devers, R., Bradley-Johnson, S., & Merle, J. C. (1994). The effect of token reinforcement on WISC—R performance for fifth- through ninth-grade American Indians. *Psychological Record, 44,* 441–449.

Dickinson, A. M. (1989). The detrimental effects of extrinsic reinforcement on "intrinsic motivation." *Behavior Analyst, 12,* 1–15.

Dilorenzo, T. M., Bargman, E. P., Stucky-Ropp, R., Brassington, G. S., Frensch, P. A., & LaFontaine, T. (1999). Long-term effects of aerobic exercise on psychological outcomes. *Preventive Medicine, 28,* 75–85.

Dishion, T. J., & Spracklen, K. M. (1996, May). A matching law account of deviancy training within adolescent boys' friendships: An emphasis on duration. *Association for Behavior Analysis.* San Francisco.

Dodge, K. A. (1991). The structure and function of reactive and proactive aggression. In D. J. Pepler & K. H. Rubin (Eds.), *The development and treatment of childhood aggression* (pp. 201–218). Hillsdale, NJ: Erlbaum.

Drummond, D. C., Tiffany, S. T., Glautier, S., & Remington, B. (Eds.), (1995). *Addictive behavior: Cue exposure theory and practice.* New York: Wiley.

Durand, V. M., & Carr, E. (1991). Functional communication training to reduce challenging behavior: Maintenance and application in new settings. *Journal of Applied Behavior Analysis, 24*, 251–264.

Edlund, C. V. (1972). The effect on the behavior of children, as reflected in the IQ scores, when reinforced after each correct response. *Journal of Applied Behavior Analysis, 5*, 317–319.

Eisenberger, R. (1989). *Blue Monday: The loss of the work ethic in America.* New York: Paragon.

Eisenberger, R. (1992). Learned industriousness. *Psychological Review, 99*, 248–267.

Eisenberger, R., & Adornetto, M. (1986). Generalized self-control of delay and effort. *Journal of Personality and Social Psychology, 51*, 1020–1031.

Eisenberger, R., & Armeli, S. (1997). Can salient reward increase creative performance without reducing intrinsic creative interest? *Journal of Personality and Social Psychology, 72*, 652–663.

Eisenberger, R., & Cameron, J. (1996). The detrimental effects of reward: Myth or reality? *American Psychologist, 51*, 1153–1166.

Eisenberger, R. Haskins, F., & Gambleton, P. (1999). Promised reward and creativity: Effects of prior experience. *Journal of Experimental Social Psychology, 35*, 308–325.

Eisenberger, R., & Masterson, F. A. (1983). Required high effort increases subsequent persistence and reduces cheating. *Journal of Personality and Social Psychology, 44*, 593–599.

Eisenberger, R., Mitchell, M., McDermitt, M., & Masterson, F. A. (1984). Accuracy versus speed in the generalized effort of learning-disabled children. *Journal of the Experimental Analysis of Behavior, 42*, 19–36.

Eisenberger, R., Pierce, W. D., & Cameron, J. (1999). Effects of reward on intrinsic motivation: Negative, neutral, and positive. *Psychological Bulletin, 125*, 677–691.

Eisenberger, R., & Rhoades, L. (2001). Incremental effects of reward on creativity. *Journal of Personality and Social Psychology, 81*, 728–741.

Eisenberger, R. , Rhoades, L., & Cameron, J. (1999). Does pay for performance increase or decrease perceived self-determination and intrinsic motivation? *Journal of Personality and Social Psychology, 77*, 1026–1040.

Eisenberger, R., & Selbst, M. (1994). Does reward increase or decrease creativity? *Journal of Personality and Social Psychology, 66*, 1116–1127.

Eisenberger, R., & Shank, D. M. (1985). Personal work ethic and effort training affect cheating. *Journal of Personality and Social Psychology, 49*, 520–528.

Ellis, J. E. (1999). Behavior science goes to prison. *Beyond the data.* Concord, MA: Cambridge Center for Behavioral Studies (www.behavior.org/columns/ellis1.cfm).

Endler, N. S. (1965). The effects of verbal reinforcement on conformity and deviant behavior. *Journal of Social Psychology, 66,* 147–154.

Eshun, S. (1997). The relationship between past experiences and current pain responses. *Dissertation Abstracts International: Section B: The Sciences & Engineering, 57,* 11–B.

Etzel, B. C., & Gewirtz, J. L. (1967). Experimental modification of Care-taker-maintained high-rate operant crying in a 6– and a 20–week-old infant (*Infans tyrannotearus*): Extinction of crying with reinforcement of eye contact and smiling. *Journal of Experimental Child Psychology, 5,* 303–317.

Evans, M. J., Duvel, A., Funk, M. L., Lehman, B., & Neuringer, A. (1994). Social reinforcement of operant behavior in rats: A methodological note. *Journal of the Experimental Analysis of Behavior, 62,* 149–156.

Fernandez, E., & McDowell, J. J. (1995). Response-reinforcement relationships in chronic pain syndrome: Applicability of Herrnstein's law. *Behavior Research & Therapy, 33,* 855–863.

Fishbain, D. A., Rosomoff, H. L., Cutler, R. B., & Rosomoff, R. S. (1995). Secondary gain concept: A review of the scientific evidence. *Clinical Journal of Pain, 11,* 6–21.

Fletcher-Flinn, C. M., & Gravatt, B. (1995). The efficacy of computer assisted instruction (CAI): A meta-analysis. *Journal of Educational Computing Research, 12,* 219–242.

Flor, H., Kerns, R. D., Turk, D. C. (1987). The role of spouse reinforcement, perceived pain, and activity levels of chronic pain patients. *Journal of Psychosomatic Research, 31,* 251–259.

Flora, S. R. (1990). Undermining intrinsic interest from the standpoint of a behaviorist. *Psychological Record, 40,* 323–346.

Flora, S. R. (1998, September 16). Effort, correct repetition are keys to learning. *Vindicator.*

Flora, S. R. (2000). Praise's magic ratio: Five to one gets the job done. *Behavior Analyst Today, 1,* 64–69.

Flora, S. R., & Flora D. B. (1999). Effects of extrinsic reinforcement for reading during childhood on reported reading habits of college students. *Psychological Record, 49,* 3–14.

Flora, S. R., & Logan, R. E. (1996). Using computerized study guides to increase performance on general psychology examinations: An experimental analysis. *Psychological Reports, 79,* 235–241.

Flora, S. R., & Popanak, S. (2001, May). *Pay now: Payoff now and later: Childhood pay for grades produces differentially higher college G.P.A.s.* Association for Behavior Analysis. New Orleans.

Flora, S. R., Schieferecke, T. R., & Bremenkamp, H. G. (1992). Effects of aversive noise on human self-control for positive reinforcement. *Psychological Record, 42,* 505–517.

Flora, S. R. & Wilkerson, L. R. (2001, May). *Effects of cold pressor pain on human self-control for positive reinforcement*. Association for Behavior Analysis. New Orleans.

Fox, D. K., Hopkins, B. L., & Anger, W. K. (1987). The long-term effects of a token economy on safety performance in open-pit mining. *Journal of Applied Behavior Analysis, 20*, 215–224.

Franken, R. E. (1994). *Human Motivation, 3rd ed*. Pacific Grove, CA: Brooks/Cole.

Galentine, J. K. (1996). Reading before preschool: Reading behaviors of toddlers. *Infant-Toddler Intervention, 6*, 255–282.

Geiger, G., Todd, D. D., Clark, H. B., Miller, R. P., & Aori, S. H. (1992). The effects of feedback and contingent reinforcement on the exercise behavior of chronic pain patients. *Pain, 49*, 179–185.

Gelman, D. (1991, July 8). Clean, and sober—And agnostic. *Newsweek*, 62–63.

Gewiritz, J. L., & Bear, D. M. (1958). Deprivation and satiation of social reinforcers as drive conditions. *Journal of Abnormal and Social Psychology, 57*, 165–172.

Gil, K. M., Keefe, F. J., Crission, J. E., & Van Dalfsen, P. J. (1987). Social support and pain behavior. *Pain, 29*, 209–217.

Goetz, E. M., & Baer, D. M. (1973). Social control of form diversity and the emergence of new forms in children's block building. *Journal of Applied Behavior Analysis, 6*, 209–217.

Goldstein, I., & McGinnies, E. (1964). Compliance and attitude change under conditions of differential social reinforcement. *Journal of Abnormal and Social Psychology, 68*, 567–570.

Gossette, R. L., & O'Brien, R. M. (1992). The efficacy of rational-emotive therapy in adults: Clinical fact or psychometric artifact? *Journal of Behavior Therapy and Experimental Psychiatry, 23*, 9–24.

Gottman, J. M. (1994). *Why marriages succeed or fail*. New York: Simon & Schuster.

Gottman, J. M., Coan, J., & Swanson, C. (1998). Predicting marital happiness and stability from newlywed interactions. *Journal of Marriage and the Family, 60*, 2–22.

Gottman, J. H., Katz, L. F., & Hooven, C. (1997). *Meta-emotion*. Mahwah, NJ: Lawrance Erlbaum.

Green, L., & Kagel, J. H. (Eds.) (1987). *Advances in behavioral economics, Vol 1*. Norwood, NJ: Ablex Publishing Corporation.

Greene, L., Kamps, D., Wyble, J., & Ellis, C. (1999). Home-based consolation for parents of young children with behavioral problems. *Child & Family Behavior Therapy, 21*, 19–45.

Greenspoon, J. (1955). The reinforcing effects of two spoken sounds on the frequency of two responses. *American Journal of Psychology, 68,* 409–416.

Griffith, J. D., Rowan-Szal, G. A., Roark, R. R., & Simpson, D. D. (2000). Contingency management in outpatient methadone treatment: A meta-analysis. *Drug & Alcohol Dependence, 58,* 55–66.

Gross, J. J., Fredrickson, B. L., & Levenson, R. W. (1994). The psychophysiology of crying. *Psychophysiology, 31,* 460–468.

Hall, C. W., Hall, T. L., & Kasperek, J. G. (1995). Psychology of computer use: XXXIII. Interactive instruction with college-level science courses. *Psychological Reports, 76,* 963–970.

Hancock, D. R. (2000). Impact of verbal praise on college students' time spent on homework. *Journal of Educational Research, 93,* 384–389.

Hancock, L. (1994, December 19). A Sylvan invasion. *Newsweek,* 52–53.

Harris, T., Brown, G. W., Robinson, R. (1999). Befriending as an intervention for chronic depression among women in an inner city: 1: Randomised controlled trial. *British Journal of Psychiatry, 174,* 219–224.

Hart, B., & Risley, T. R. (1995) *Meaningful differences.* Baltimore, MD: Paul H Brookes.

Hayward, L. M., Sullivan, A. C., & Libonati, J. R. (2000). Group exercise reduces depression in obese women without weight loss. *Perceptual & Motor Skills, 90,* 204–208.

Heckhausen, H. (1967). *The anatomy of achievement motivation.* New York: Academic.

Hechtman, B. (2000, September). *The Bribery Curriculum: Since when did corrupting our kids become part of their education? Women's Day,* 80.

Helmer, J. (1975). *Drugs and minority oppression.* New York: Seabury.

Hennessy, B. A., & Amabile, T. M. (1988). The conditions of creativity. In R. J. Sternberg (Ed.), *The nature of Creativity* (pp. 11–38). Cambridge, MA: Cambridge University Press.

Hicks, T., & Munger, R. (1990). A school day treatment program using an adaptation of the teaching-family model. *Education and Treatment of Children, 13,* 63–83.

Higgins, S. T., & Petry, N. M. (1999). Contingency management: Incentives for sobriety. *Alcohol Research & Health, 23,* 122–127.

Hiroto, D. S. (1974). Locus of control and learned helplessness. *Journal of Experimental Psychology, 102,* 187–193.

Hiroto, D. S., & Seligman, M. E. P. (1975). Generality of learned helplessness in man. *Journal of Personality and Social Psychology, 31,* 311–327.

Hobbes, T. (1651, republished 1997). *Leviathan.* New York: Norton.

Holman, J. R. (1997, November). Are you using the right rewards? *Better Homes and Gardens*, 112–114.

Howe, M. J. A. (1990). *Encouraging the development of exceptional skills and talents*. Leicester, England: British Psychological Society.

Howe, M. J. A., Davidson, J. W., & Sloboda, J. A. (1998). Innate talents: Reality or myth? *Behavioral and Brain Sciences, 21,* 399–342.

Hursh, S. R. (1991). Behavioral economics of drug self-administration and drug abuse policy. *Journal of the Experimental Analysis of Behavior, 56,* 377–93.

Hursh, S. R. (1993). Behavioral economics of drug self-administration: An introduction. *Drug and Alcohol Dependence, 33,* 165–172.

Hursh, S. R., & Bauman, R. A. (1987). The behavioral analysis of demand. In L. Green & J. H. Kagel (Eds.) *Advances on behavioral economics* (pp. 117–165). Norwood, NJ: Ablex.

Institute of human science and services of the University of Rhode Island (1986). *Pizza Hut Inc.'s The BOOK IT national reading incentive program. Final evaluation report.*

Janicke, D. M., & Finney, J. W. (1999). Emperically supported treatments in pediatric psychology: Recurrent abdominal pain. *Journal of Pediatric Psychology, 24,* 115–127.

Jay, S. M., Elliott, C. H., Katz, E., & Siegel, S. E. (1987). Cognitive-behavioral and pharmacologic interventions for children's distress during painful medical procedures. *Journal of Consulting and Clinical Psychology, 55,* 860–865.

Johnson, K. R., & Layng, T. V. J. (1992). Breaking the structuralist barrier: Literacy and numeracy with fluency. *American* Psychologist, *47,* 1475–1490.

Julien, R. M. (2001). *A primer of drug action, 9th ed.* New York: Worth.

Kagel, J. H., Battalio, R. C., & Green, L. (1995). *Economic choice theory.* New York: Cambridge University Press.

Kallman, W. M., Hersen, M., & O'Toole, D. H. (1975). The use of social reinforcement in a case of conversion reaction. *Behavior Therapy, 6,* 411–413.

Karraker, R. J. (1971). Token reinforcement systems in regular public school classrooms. In C. E. Pitts (Ed.), *Operant conditioning in the classroom.* New York: Crowell.

Kazdin, A. E. (1985). The token economy. In R. Turner & L. M. Asher (Eds.), *Evaluating behavior therapy outcome.* New York: Springer.

Kazdin, A. E. (1994). Methodology, design, and evaluation in psychotherapy research. In A. E. Bergin & S. L. Garfield (Eds.), *Handbook of psychotherapy and behavior change, 4th ed.* New York: Wiley.

Kazdin, A. E., & Bootzin, R. R. (1972). The token economy: An evaluative review. *Journal of Applied Behavior Analysis, 5,* 343–372.

Kelly, J. B. (1998). Marital conflict, divorce and children's adjustment. *Child and Adolescent Psychiatric Clinics of North America, 7,* 259–271.

Kelly, D. (1995, July 17). Making reading pay: Gingrich-backed incentive program grows by volumes. *USA Today,* D1–D2.

Kessler, R. C. (1997). The effect of stressful life events on depression. *Annual Review of Psychology, 48,* 191–214.

Kestner, J., & Flora, S. R. (1998). *Are they using what we teach?* Association for Behavior Analysis. Orlando.

King, S. (2000). *On Writing: A memoir of the craft.* New York: Scribner.

Kirigin, K. A., Braukmann, C. J., Atwater, J., & Wolf, M. M. (1982). An evaluation of achievement Place (Teaching-Family) group homes for juvenile offenders. *Journal of Applied Behavior Analysis, 15,* 1–16.

Klein, D. C., & Seligman, M. E. P. (1976). Reversal of performance deficits and perceptual deficits in learned helplessness and depression. *Journal of Abnormal Psychology, 85,* 11–26.

Klein, S. B. (1982). *Motivation: Biosocial approaches.* New York: McGraw-Hill.

Knight, M. F., & McKenzie, H. S. (1974). Elimination of bedtime thumb-sucking in home settings through contingent reading. *Journal of Applied Behavior Analysis, 7,* 33–38.

Kohn, A. (1993). *Punished by rewards: The trouble with gold stars, incentive plans, A's, praise, and other bribes.* New York: Houghton Mifflin.

Kolb, D. (1965). Achievement motivation training for underachieving high school boys. *Journal of Personality and Social Psychology, 2,* 783–792.

Lea, S. E. G. (1987). Animal experiments in economic psychology. In L. Green & J. H. Kagel (Eds.) *Advances on Behavioral Economics* (pp. 95–116). Norwood, NJ: Ablex.

Leahey, T. H. (1991). *A history of modern psychology.* Englewood Cliffs, NJ: Prentice-Hall.

Lejuez, C. W., Schaal, D. W., & O'Donnell, J. (1998). Behavioral pharmacology and the treatment of substance abuse. In J. J. Plaud & G. H. Eifert (Eds.), *From behavior theory to behavior therapy.* Needham Heights, MA: Allyn & Bacon.

Lemann, N. (1998, November). "Ready, Read!" *Atlantic Monthly, 282,* 92–104.

Lepper, M. R., Greene, D., & Nisbett, R. E. (1973). Undermining children's intrinsic interest with extrinsic reward: A test of the 'overjustification' hypothesis. *Journal of Personality and Social Psychology, 28,* 129–137.

Lepper, M. R., Henderlong, J., & Gingras, I. (1999). Understanding the effects of extrinsic rewards on intrinsic motivation—Uses and abuses of meta-analysis: Comment on Deci, Koestner, and Ryan (1999). *Psychological Bulletin, 125,* 669–676.

Levinson, H. (1973). *The great jackass fallacy.* Boston: Harvard Graduate School of Business Administration.

Lewinsohn, P. M. (1974). A behavioral approach to depression. In R. J. Friedman & M. M. Katz (Eds.), *The psychology of depression: Contemporary theory and research* (pp. 157–185). Washington, D.C.: Winston-Wiley.

Lewinsohn, P. M., Gotlib, I. H., & Seeley, J. R. (1997). Depression-related psychosocial variables: Are they specific to depression in adolescents? *Journal of Abnormal Psychology, 106,* 365–376.

Liang, L. (2000, October 15). Exercise helps in treating seniors. *Vindicator, F2* (Sun-sentinel, South Florida).

Lipsitt, L. P., Kaye, H., & Bosack, T. N. (1966). Enhancement of neonatal sucking through reinforcement. *Journal of Experimental Child Psychology, 4,* 163–168.

Lloyd, M. E., & Zylla, T. M. (1988). Effect of incentives delivered for correctly answered items on the measured IQs of children of low and high IQ. *Psychological Reports, 63,* 555–561.

Locke, E. A., & Latham, G. P. (1990). Work motivation and satisfaction: Light at the end of the tunnel. *Psychological Science, 1,* 240–246.

Logan, R. E., & Flora, S. R. (1997). Efficacy of computerized study guides on chemically dependent clients' test performance. *Alcoholism Treatment Quarterly, 15,* 79–87.

Lovaas, O. I. (1987). Behavioral treatment and normal educational and intellectual functioning in young autistic children. *Journal of Consulting and Clinical Psychology, 55,* 3–9.

Lyng, S. (1990). Edgework: A social psychological analysis of voluntary risk taking. *American Journal of Sociology, 95,* 851–886.

Madsen, C. H. Jr., & Madsen, C. R. (1974). *Teaching discipline: Behavior principles towards a positive approach.* Boston: Allyn & Bacon.

Maralott, G. A., Larimer, M. E., Baer, J. S., & Quigley, L. A. (1993). Harm reduction for alcohol problems: Moving beyond the controlled drinking controversy. *Behavior Therapy, 24,* 461–504.

Martin, G., & Pear, J. (1999). *Behavior modification 6th ed.* Upper Saddle River, NJ: Prentice-Hall.

Maurice, C. (1993). *Let me hear your voice.* New York: Fawcett Columbine.

Mazur, J. E. (1998). *Learning and behavior, 4th ed.* Upper Saddle River, NJ: Prentice-Hall.

McClelland, D. C. (1961). *The achieving society.* Princeton, NJ: Van Nostrand.

McClelland, D.C. (1985). *Human motivation.* Glenview, IL: Scott, Foresman.

McClelland, D. C., & Winter, D. G. (1969). *Motivating economic achievement.* New York: Free Press.

McIntosh, D., & Rawson, H. (1988). Effects of a structured behavior modification treatment program on locus of control in behaviorally disordered children. *Journal of Genetic Psychology, 149*, 45–51.

McKim, W. A. (2000). *Drugs and behavior, 4th ed.* Upper Saddle River, NJ: Prentice-Hall.

McNinch, G. W., Steely, M., & Davidson, T. J. (1995). *Evaluating the Earning by Learning program: Changing attitudes in reading.* Paper presented at the annual meeting of the Georgia Council of the International Reading Association, Atlanta.

Melzack, R., & Wall, P. D. (1982). *The challenge of pain.* New York: Basic.

Merrett, F. (1998). Helping readers who have fallen behind. *Support for Learning, 13*, 59–64.

Meyer, K. A. (1999). Functional analysis and treatment of problem behavior exhibited by elementary school children. *Journal of Applied Behavior Analysis, 32*, 229–232.

Middleton, M. B., & Cartledge, G. (1995). The effects of social skills instruction and parental involvement on the aggressive behaviors of African American males. *Behavior Modification, 19*, 192–210.

Miller, A. J., & Kratochwill, T. R. (1979). Reduction in frequent stomachache complaints by time out. *Behavior Therapy, 10*, 211–218.

Miller, D. W. (2000, April 21). In the nation's battle against drug abuse, scholars have more insight than influence. *Chronicle of Higher Education*, A19–A21.

Miller, L. K. (1997). *Principles of everyday behavior analysis, 3rd ed.* Pacific Grove, CA: Brooks Cole.

Miller, N. E., & Dollard, J. (1941). *Social learning and imitation.* New Haven, CN: Yale University Press.

Miller, W. R., Brown, J. M., Simpson, T. L., Handmaker, N. S., Bien, T. H., Luckie, L. F., Montgomery, H. A., Hester, R. K., & Tonigan, J. S. (1995). What works? A methodological analysis of the alcohol treatment outcome literature. In R. K. Hester and W. R. Miller (Eds.), *Handbook of alcoholism treatment approaches, 2nd ed.* Boston: Allyn & Bacon.

Miller, W. R., Meyers, R. J., & Hiller-Sturmhofel, S. (1999). The community-reinforcement approach. *Alcohol Research & Health, 23*, 116–120.

Mills B., & Flagler, B. (2000, August 22). Pay for grades? Parents debate. Parent to Parent (United Feature Syndicate). *News and Observer*, E2. Raleigh, NC.

Monaghan, P. (1999, February 26). Lessons from the 'marriage lab.' *Chronicle of Higher Education*, A9.

Montaigne, M. (1958). *Essays* (J. M. Cohen, Trans.). Baltimore: Penguin. (Original work published 1580). Reprinted in *Journal of the Experimental Analysis of Behaviors, 57,* p. 176.

Moss, R. A. (1986). The role of learning history in current sick-role behavior and assertion. *Behavior Research & Therapy, 24,* 681–683.

Mueller, C. M., & Dweck, C. S. (1998). Praise for intelligence can undermine children's motivation and performance. *Journal of Personality & Social Psychology, 75,* 33–52.

National Public Radio (2000, November 14). Interview with Charlie Parker.

Nelson, B. (1994). *1001 Ways to reward employees.* New York: Workman.

Newman, B. (2000). On inventing your own disorder. *Skeptical Inquirer, 24,* 56–57.

O'Leary, K. D. (1991). This week's citation classic: Class behavior. *Current Contents, 40,* 5.

Ormrod. J. E. (1998). *Educational psychology, 2nd ed.* Upper Saddle River, NJ. Prentice-Hall.

Overskeid, G., & Svartdal, F. (1996). Effect of reward on subjective autonomy and interest when initial interest is low. *Psychological Record, 46,* 319–331.

Palmer, T. (1991). The effectiveness of intervention: Recent trends and current issues. *Crime & Delinquency, 37(3),* 330–346.

Parrott, A. C. (1999). Does cigarette smoking *cause* stress? *American Psychologist, 54,* 817–820.

Patterson, G. R. (1982). *Coercive family processes.* Eugene, OR: Castillia.

Patterson, G. R., Dishion, T. J., & Bank, L. (1984). Family interaction: A process model of deviancy training. *Aggressive Behavior, 10,* 253–267.

Patterson, G. R., Reid, J. B., & Dishion, T. J. (1992). *Antisocial boys.* Eugene, OR: Castalia.

Peele, S. (1989). *Diseasing of America.* San Francisco: Jossey-Bass.

Petry, N. M., Martin, B., Cooney, J. L., & Kranzler, H. R. (2000). Give them prizes and they will come: Contingency management for treatment of alcohol dependence. *Journal of Consulting & Clinical Psychology, 68,* 250–257.

Pietras, C. J., & Hackenberg, T. D. (2000) Timeout postponement without increased reinforcement frequency. *Journal of the Experimental Analysis of Behavior, 74,* 147–164.

Plamer, T. (1991). The effectiveness of intervention recent trends and current issues. *Crime & Delinquency, 37,* 33–346.

Plaud, J. J., & Holm, J. E. (1998). Sexual dysfunctions. In J. J. Plaud, & G. H. Eifert (Eds.), *From behavior theory to behavior therapy* (pp. 136–151). Boston: Allyn.

Poulin, F., & Boivin, M. (2000). The role of proactive and reactive aggression in the formation and development of boys' friendships. *Developmental Psychology*, 233–240.

Powers, S. W. (1999). Empirically supported treatments in pediatric psychology: procedure-related pain. *Journal of Pediatric Psychology*, 24, 131–145.

Rachlin, H. (2000). *The science of self-control.* Cambridge: Harvard University Press.

Ramely, C. T., & Finkelstein, N. W. (1978). Contingent stimulation and infant competence. *Journal of Pediatric Psychology*, 3, 89–96.

Rawson, H. E. (1973a). Academic remediation and behavior modification in a summer school camp. *Elementary School Journal*, 74, 34–43.

Rawson, H. E. (1973b). Residential short-term camping for children with behavior problems: A behavior modification approach. *Child Welfare*, 52, 511–520.

Rawson, H. E. (1992). Effect of intensive short-term remediation on academic intrinsic motivation of "at-risk" children. *Journal of Instructional Psychology*, 19, 274–285.

Rawson, H. E., & Cassady, J. C. (1995). Effects of therapeutic intervention on self-concepts of children with learning disabilities. *Child and Adolescent Social Work Journal*, 12, 19–31.

Rawson, H. E., & McIntosh, D. (1991). The effects of therapeutic camping on the self-esteem of children with severe behavior disorders. *Therapeutic Recreation Journal*, 25, 41–49.

Rawson, H. E., & Tabb, L. C. (1993). Effects of therapeutic intervention on childhood depression. *Child and Adolescent Social Work Journal*, 10, 39–52.

Redd, W. H., & Birnbrauer, J. S. (1969). Adults as discriminative stimuli for different reinforcement contingencies with retarded children. *Journal of Experimental Child Psychology*, 7, 440–447.

Rheingold, H. L., Gewirtz, J. L., & Ross, H. W. (1959). Social conditioning of vocalizations in the infant. *Journal of Comparative and Physiological Psychology*, 52, 68–73.

Rosen, B., & D'Andrade, R. (1959). The psychosocial origins of achievement motivation. *Sociometry*, 22, 185–218.

Ryan, R. M., & Deci, E. L. (2000). Self-determination theory and the facilitation of intrinsic motivation, social development, and well-being. *American Psychologist*, 55, 68–78.

Ryan, R. M., Kuhl, J., & Deci, E. L. (1997). Nature and autonomy: An organizational view of social and neurobiological aspects of self-regulation in behavior and development. *Development and Psychopathology*, 9, 701–728.

Sank, L. I., & Biglan, A. (1974). Operant treatment of a case of recurrent abdominal pain in a 10-year-old boy. *Behavior Therapy, 5*, 677–681.

Sapp, A. D., & Vaughn, M. S. (1991). Sex offender rehabilitation programs in state prisons: A nationwide survey. *Journal of Offender Rehabilitation, 17*, 55–75.

Sarafino, E. P. (2001). *Behavior Modification, 2nd ed.* Mountain View, CA: Mayfield.

Sarbin, T. R., & Allen, V. L. (1964). Role enactment, audience feedback, and attitude change. *Sociometry, 27*, 183–193.

Satterfield, J. H., & Schell, A. A. (1997). A prospective study of hyperactive boys with conduct problems and normal boys: Adolescent and adult criminality. *Journal of the American Academy of Child & Adolescent Psychiatry, 36*, 1726–1735.

Schloss, P. J., & Smith, M. A. (1998). *Applied behavior analysis in the classroom, 2nd ed.* Needham Heights, MA: Allyn & Bacon.

Schunk, D. H. (1983). Reward contingencies and the development of children's skills and self-efficacy. *Journal of Educational Psychology, 75*, 511–518.

Schunk, D. H. (1984). Enhancing self-efficacy and achievement through rewards and goals: Motivational and informational effects. *Journal of Educational Research, 78*, 29–34.

Schwartz, B. (1982). Reinforcement-induced behavioral stereotypy: How not to teach people to discover rules. *Journal of Experimental Psychology: General, 111*, 23–59.

Schwartz, B., & Robbins S. J. (1995). *Psychology of learning and behavior, 4th ed.* New York: Norton.

Schwartz, S. (2000). *Abnormal Psychology.* Mountain View, CA: Mayfield.

Schwartz, S. M., Gramling, S. E., & Mancini, T. (1994). The influence of life stress, personality, and learning history on illness behavior. *Journal of Behavior Therapy & Experimental Psychiatry, 25*, 135–142.

Seligman, M. E. P. (1975). *Helplessness: On depression, development, and death.* San Francisco: Freeman.

Seligman, M. E. P. (1990). *Learned optimism.* New York: Simon & Schuster.

Sheeber, L., Hops, H., Andrews, J., Alpert, T., & Davis, B. (1998). Interactional processes in families with depressed and non-depressed adolescents: Reinforcement of depressive behavior. *Behavior Research and Therapy, 36*, 417–427.

Shrout, P. E., Link, B. G., Dohrenwend, B. P., Skodol, A. E., Stueve, A., & Mirotznik, J. (1989). Characterizing life events as risk factors for depression: The role of fateful loss events. *Journal of Abnormal Psychology, 98*, 460–467.

Singer, M. T. & Lalich, J. (1996). *"Crazy" Therapies*. San Francisco: Jossey-Bass.

Sidman, M. (1989). *Coercion and its fallout*. Boston: Authors Cooperative.

Silverman, K., Chutuape, M. A., Bigelow, G. E., & Stitzer, M. L. (1999). Voucher-based reinforcement of cocaine abstinence in treatment-resistant methadone patients: Effects of reinforcement magnitude. *Psychopharmacology, 146*, 128–138.

Skinner, B. F. (1938). *The Behavior of organisms*. New York: Appleton-Century-Crofts.

Skinner, B. F. (1953). *Science and human behavior*. New York: Macmillan.

Skinner, B. F. (1969). *Contingencies of reinforcement: A theoretical analysis*. New York: Appleton-Century-Crofts.

Skinner, B. F. (1971). *Beyond freedom and dignity*. New York: Knopf.

Skinner, B. F. (1974). *About behaviorism*. New York: Knopf.

Skinner, B. F. (1990). Can psychology be a science of mind? *American Psychologist, 45*, 1206–1210.

Skinner, B. F. (1999). Creating the Creative Artist. *Cumulative Record*. Action, MA: Copley (Original work published 1970).

Skinner, B. F. (1999). A lecture on "having" a poem. *Cumulative Record*. Action, MA: Copley (Original work published 1971).

Skinner, B. F., & Vaughan, M. E. (1983). *Enjoy old age*. New York: Norton.

Slaboda, J. A., Davidson, J. W., Howe, M. J. A., & Moore, D. G. (1996). The role of practice in the development of performing musicians. *British Journal of Psychology, 87*, 287–309.

Slaboda, J. A., & Howe, M. J. A. (1991). Biographical precursors of musical excellence: An interview study. *Psychology of Music, 19*, 3–21.

Slot, N. W., Jagers, H. D., & Dangel, R. F. (1992). Cross-cultural replication and evaluation of the teaching family model of community-based residential treatment. *Behavioral Residential Treatment, 7*, 341–354.

Smith, D. (1999). *A coach's life*. New York: Random.

Smith, M. D. (1993). *Behavior modification of exceptional youth and children*. Boston: Andover Medical Publishers.

Snyder, J. J., & Patterson, G. R. (1995). Individual differences in social aggression: A test of a reinforcement model of socialization in the natural environment. *Behavior Therapy, 26*, 371–391.

Snyder, J.J., Schrepferman, L., & St. Peter, C. (1997). Origins of antisocial behavior: Negative reinforcement and affect dysregulation of behavior as socialization mechanisms in family interaction. *Behavior Modification, 21*, 187–215.

Sobel, D. (2000). *Galileo's Daughter*. New York: Penguin Putnam.

Sommers, C. H. (2000). *The war against boys*. New York: Simon & Schuster.

Stawsri, W. (2000). *Kids, parents & money: Teaching personal finanace from piggy bank to prom.* New York: Wiley.

Straus, M. A. (1994). *Beating the devil out of them: Corporal punishment in American families.* New York: Lexington.

Stuart, R. B. (1971). Assessment and change of the communication patterns of juvenile delinquents and their parents. In R. D. Rubin, H. Fernsterheim, A. A. Lazarus, & C. M. Franks (Eds.), *Advances in behavior therapy* (pp. 183–196). New York: Academic.

Sutherland, K. S., Wehby, J. H., & Copeland, S. R. (2000). Effect of varying rates of behavior-specific praise on the on-task behavior of students with EBD [Emotional and Behavioral Disorder]. *Journal of Emotional & Behavioral Disorders, 8,* 2–8.

Tashman, B. (1994, November 15). Our failure to follow through. *New York Newsday* (http://www.uoregon.edu/~adiep/ft/tashman.htm).

Tegano, D. W., Moran, D. J. III, & Sawyers, J. K. (1991). *Creativity in early childhood classrooms.* Washington, DC: National Education Association.

Tellegen, A., Lykken, D. T., Bouchard, T. J. Jr., Wilcox, K. J., Segal, N. L., & Rich, S. (1988). Personality similarity in twins reared apart and together. *Journal of Personality and Social Psychology, 54,* 1031–1039.

The American Heritage Dictionary of the English Language (1992). Soukhanov, Anne H. (Ed.). Boston, MA: Houghton Mifflin.

Thompson, M. L., & Gick, M. L. (2000). Medical care-seeking for menstrual symptoms. *Journal of Psychosomatic Research, 49,* 137–140.

Tkachuk, G. A. (1999, December). Health: Jog your mood. *Psychology Today,* 24.

Tkachuk, G. A., & Martin, G. L. (1999). Exercise therapy for patients with psychiatric disorders: Research and clinical implication. *Professional Psychology: Research & Practice, 30,* 275–282.

Torrance, E. P. (1965). *Rewarding creative behavior: Experiments in classroom creativity.* Englewood Cliffs, NJ: Prentice-Hall.

Toskovic, N. N. (2000). Cardiovascular and metabolic responses and alterations in selected measures of mood with a single bout of dynamic tae kwon do exercise. *Dissertation Abstracts International Section A: Humanities & Social Sciences, 61,* 933.

Turkat, I. D., & Noskin, D. E. (1983). Vicarious and operant experiences in the etiology of illness behavior: A replication with healthy individuals. *Behavior Research & Therapy, 21,* 169–172.

Verplanck, W. S. (1955). The operant, from rat to man: An introduction to some recent experiments on human behavior. *Transactions of the New York Academy of Science, 17,* 594–601.

Vuchinich, R. E. & Tucker, J. (1996). Alcohol relapse, life events, and behavioral theories of choice. A prospective analysis. *Experimental and Clinical Psychopharmacology, 4,* 19–28.

Walco, G. A., Sterliing, C. M., Conte, P. M., & Engel, R. G. (1999). Empirically supported treatments in pediatric psychology: Disease-related pain. *Journal of Pediatric Psychology, 24,* 155–167.

Walker III, S. (1998). *The hyperactivity hoax.* New York: St. Martin's.

Waller, B. (1999). Free will, determinism and self-control. In B. A. Thyer (Ed.), *The philosophical legacy of behaviorism* (pp. 189–208). London: Kluwer.

Waggoner, J. (2001, January 16). Musician says investing in self-practice pays off. *USA Today, 3B.*

Watson, J. B., (1970). *Behaviorism.* (Original work published 1930). New York: Norton.

Watson, J. D., (1968). *The double helix.* New York: Atheneum.

Watters, E., & Ofshe, R. (1999). *Therapy's delusions.* New York: Scribner.

Weisberg, R. W. (1998). Creativity and practice. *Behavioral and Brain Sciences, 21,* 429–430.

Weiten, W. (2000). *Psychology: Themes & variations, briefer version, 4th ed.* Belmont, CA: Wadsworth.

White, M. A. (1975). Natural rates of teacher approval and disapproval in the classroom. *Journal of Applied Behavior Analysis, 8,* 367–372.

Whitehead, W. E., Crowell, M. D., Heller, B. F., Robinson, J. C., Schuster, M. M., & Horn, S. (1994). Modeling and reinforcement of the sick role during childhood predicts adult illness behavior. *Psychosomatic Medicine 56,* 541–550.

Wierson, M., & Forehand, R. (1994). Parent behavioral training for child noncompliance: Rationale, concepts, and effectiveness. *Current Directions, 3,* 146–150.

Williams, C. D. (1959). The elimination of tantrum behavior by extinction procedures. *Journal of Abnormal and Social Psychology, 59,* 269.

Winett, R. A., & Winkler, R. C. (1972). Current behavior modification in the classroom: Be still, be quiet, be docile. *Journal of Applied Behavior Analysis, 5,* 499–504.

Winston, A. S., & Baker, J. E. (1985). Behavior analytic studies of creativity: A critical review. *Behavior Analyst, 8,* 191–205.

Wolf, M. M., Braukmann, C. J., & Ramp, K. A. (1987). Serious delinquent behavior as part of a significantly handicapping condition: Cues and supportive environments. *Journal of Applied Behavior Analysis, 20,* 347–359.

Wolpe, J. (1981). Behavior therapy versus psychoanalysis: Therapeutic and social implications. *American Psychologist, 36,* 159–164.

Wood, P. B., Gove, W. R., Wilson, J. A., & Cochran, J. K. (1997). Nonso-
cial reinforcement and habitual criminal conduct: An extension of
learning theory. *Criminology, 35,* 335–366.

Wyatt, W. J., & Hawkins, R. P. (1987). Rates of teachers' verbal approval
and disapproval: Relationship to grade level, classroom activity, student behavior, and teacher characteristics. *Behavior Modification, 11,*
27–51.

Youngbauer, J. G. (1998). The teaching-family model and treatment dura-
bility: Assessing generalization using survival analysis techniques.
*Dissertation Abstracts International: Section B: The Sciences & Engineer-
ing, 58,* 10–B.

Zajonc, R. B. (1984, July 22). Quoted in D. Goleman, Rethinking IQ tests
and their value. *New York Times,* D22.

Zito, J. M., Safer, D. J., dosReis, S., Gardner, J. F., & Boles, M.L. (2000).
Trends in the prescribing of psychotropic medications to preschoolers.
JAMA: Journal of the American Medical Association, 283, 1025–1030.

APPENDIX 1

The Selection of Behavior

Reinforcement is analogous to natural selection in many ways. Like natural selection, reinforcement is a fundamental process in nature involved in almost all of the situations humans and animals find themselves. Whether or not we are aware of it, the selective process of reinforcement is occurring whenever humans behave. The selective process of reinforcement operates much like the Darwinian process of natural selection. Unfortunately, as is the case with natural selection, reinforcement, and its products, are misunderstood by a large number of educators, social scientists, and the general public.

THE NATURAL SELECTION OF OPERANT BEHAVIOR

Natural selection is a function of variation, selection of particular variations through differential success, retention, and reproduction. Variation of organisms is a fact of nature. Organisms vary through genetic mutation; chromosomal mutation; and for organisms, like humans, who sexually reproduce, through genetic recombination. The environment selects and retains those variations that allow organisms to reach reproductive age and have offspring. As a result the offspring are more likely to survive and retain the adaptive variation that allowed the parent organism to reach reproductive age and to reproduce. Through this differential success and reproduction those variations that are adaptive will be retained and increase in the population.

For example, a lizard that preys on insects, such as grasshoppers, may have offspring. Some of those offspring will run faster than their siblings and, compared to their siblings, will be differentially successful in catching grasshoppers before they can hop away. As a result, an environmental constraint, a food source that can hop away, will differentially select the faster lizards. Therefore, the faster lizards will differentially survive to reproduce (slow lizards will starve), and the genetic material responsible for being fast will be retained and increase in the lizard population.

However, members of the same lizard species may live in an environment where catching prey depends on the ability to stalk, to *slowly* approach the prey, perhaps a fly that will fly off in response to any fast movement in its visual field. Here, organisms that move slowly will be differentially successful. Some lizards will move slower than their siblings and, compared to their siblings, will be differentially successful in catching flies. As a result, an environmental constraint, a food source that flies away in response to fast movement, will differentially select the slow-moving, stalking, lizards. Therefore, the slow lizards will differentially survive to reproduce, and the genetic material responsible for slowness will be retained and increase in that lizard population.

What about the environment that contains some prey that may be caught only with slow movement, and other prey that may be caught only with fast movement? Of course, a medium speed movement will catch neither type of prey. Here the *ability to change* prey tactics based on the particular environmental constraint operating at the moment will be differentially selected. Thus, organisms that can change their behavior in response to differential environmental contingencies, organisms that are behaviorally flexible, organisms that can *learn* will be differentially successful. Lizards that learn to move slowly toward flies and quickly toward grasshoppers will be differentially successful. Lizards that move fast or slow indiscriminately will not be as successful. Therefore, the ability of an organism to change its behavior as a function of changing environmental stimuli and contingencies will be selected. It is this evolved potential of an organism's (lizard or human) behavior to be modified, or selected, that is operant behavior, and the changed behavior is a function of reinforcement. This "operant conditionability represents an adaptive response in evolution because organisms responsive to immediate environmental consequences survived temporally unstable shifts in prevailing environmental features" (Plaud & Holm, 1998, p. 138). A shift could be a change from fly to grasshopper prey for a lizard, or for a human infant the environmental change might be being ignored when crying and attended to when smiling when initially crying produced adult attention and smiling was ignored. That is, human infants who can change their various "attention-getting behaviors" as a function of the prevailing environmental features (different caregivers with different responsiveness to crying and smiling) will be differentially successful compared to infants who persistently cry or smile independent of the consequences of smiling of crying.

Crying by infants may be elicited by painful stimuli such as pinpricks; however the consequences of the crying can acquire reinforcing control of crying behavior, "regardless of the basis for its initial occurrence" (Etzel & Gewirtz, 1967, p. 303). In fact, crying behavior is selected by the consequences of crying. In the classic study "Experimental Modification of Caretaker-Maintained High-Rate Operant Crying in a 6- and a 20-Week-Old Infant (*Infans Tyrannotearus*): Extinction of Crying with Reinforcement of Eye Contact and Smiling" (1967), Barbara C. Etzel and Jacob L. Gewirtz demonstrated that when crying is reinforced with attention and smiles from caregivers crying increases; when crying is ignored or not reinforced, crying decreases. Likewise for smiling. Smiling behavior is selected by the consequences of smiling. When smiling is reinforced with attention and smiles from caregivers smiling increases, when smiling is ignored or not reinforced, smiling decreases. As a consequence of this operant conditioning process, infants increase crying in situations (e.g., the presence of certain caregivers) where crying is reinforced with caregiver attention. Because behaviors, such as crying and smiling, change as a function of their consequences, infants who are highly susceptible to operant conditioning are more likely to have their needs met by their caregiver, which is an adaptive advantage over infants whose behaviors are less suceptable to operant conditioning. Thus, crying and smiling are selected as operant behaviors responsive to immediate environmental consequences.

It is the highly evolved potential of an *individual* human to change her behavior in response to changed environmental contingencies *during the individual's lifetime* that is perhaps the characteristic that most strongly differentiates humans from other species. Only humans can live in the air; on or under the water and land; on the equator or at the poles; and eat vegetables or meat, or both. The ability of humans to live and reproduce in diverse environments is a function of *individual* behavioral flexibility in response to changed environmental contingencies during individuals' lifetimes. Humans may be the most advanced species on earth because their behavior is the most susceptible to complex and multiple reinforcement contingencies.

OPERANT BEHAVIOR AND REINFORCEMENT

Operant behavior is called "operant" because the behavior *operates* on the environment to produce consequences. In turn it is those consequences of behavior that select, strengthen, or maintain the behavior. Consequences that select, strengthen, or maintain behavior are *reinforcers*. The consequence *reinforces* the behavior. *Reinforcement* is the *process* of selecting or strengthening behavior with reinforcers. Reinforcement, or the selection of behavior with reinforcing consequences, operates in an analogous fashion to natural selection. Except for a very limited set of reflexes, almost all human behavior is operant behavior.

Consider human speech, or verbal behavior. Infants (who are "normally formed") from any culture on any continent are capable of making all the sounds for any human language (variation of verbal behavior). Chinese infants living in China learn to speak Chinese, and American infants living in Georgia learn to speak English because verbal behavior that produces sounds approximating Chinese words are differentially reinforced in China, and verbal behavior that produces sounds that approximate English words are differentially reinforced in Georgia (differential success). A Chinese-American infant with Chinese ancestors dating back three thousand years but adopted by English-speaking parents living in Georgia would learn to speak English *with a Southern accent* just as well as any other infant brought up in Georgia (retention and reproduction of behavior).

B. F. Skinner argued that the evolution of the operant control of the vocal musculature is perhaps the most important evolutionary adaptation of humans. This adaptation allows verbal behavior to be selected by its environmental consequences. Verbal behavior is shaped by reinforcement. Verbal behavior operates on the environment to produce consequences. In English-speaking countries, relative to sounds that approximate the Chinese equivalent of "mother," vocal behavior that produces sounds that approximate "mother" are differentially reinforced by the social environment (with hugs, laughter, smiles, tickles, and reciprocal verbal behavior). Through this process of differential success, or reinforcement, in English-speaking countries, saying "mother" will eventually be selected by the environmental consequences that this produces, and in turn the behavior of saying "mother" by the infant operates on the environment to produce reinforcing consequences (e.g., parental attention).

When the current environment supports a genotype responsible for an adaptive physical (e.g., the thick coat of a bear) or behavioral characteristic (e.g., the ability of an organism to change its behavior in response to changed environmental circumstances), that genotype will increase in the population of the species. Similarly when the current environment supports a particular behavior of an organism, that behavioral class or "operant" repertoire will increase in frequency in the individual's population of possible behaviors. When the current environment supports, with caretaker eye contact and smiling, an infant's smiling (or crying), the operant of smiling behaviors (or crying behaviors) will increase in frequency in the infant's population of possible behaviors (Etzel & Gewirtz, 1967).

Likewise, when the environment no longer supports a genetic variation or species, then that variation or species will decrease in frequency and become extinct. For example, the koala bear's only food source is eucalyptus leaves. When the trees were plentiful the bears were plentiful. With increased human population in Australia, eucalyptus trees are decreasing. If the trees decrease to too low levels, the koala will become extinct because the environment no longer supports the evolved inflexible eating behavior and digestive system. (If koalas had evolved more flexible eating behaviors and digestive abilities then their existence would not be threatened by a changed environment, but during their course of evolution the bears *were* highly adapted to their environmental niche.)

Similarly, when the environment no longer supports a behavioral variation of an individual, then that variation will decrease in frequency and become extinct. When the environment, parental comforting, no longer supports the behavioral variation of crying by an infant, then crying will decrease in frequency and become extinct (e.g., Williams, 1959). Likewise, ignoring, not feeding, or looking away—that is, providing no consequences for the behavior of saying "mu-mu"—will decrease the frequency of saying "mu-mu" in an infant's population of verbal behavior. If the infant's mother concurrently differentially reinforces (i.e., attends to, or otherwise provides consequences for) verbal behavior that more closely approximates "mother," then as a function of the environmental consequences provided by the mother, the verbal behavior of saying "mu-mu" will become extinct and eventually saying "mother" will be selected or shaped by the reinforcing consequences of saying "mother."

Whether infants cry or smile in various environments depends in no small part on which behavioral variation has been selected with the reinforcement provided by the caregivers in the relevant environment.

The selective and survival value of operant behavior was clearly demonstrated in the classic study "Enhancement of Neonatal Sucking Through Reinforcement" 1966 by Brown University researchers Lewis P. Lipsitt, Herbert Kaye, and Theodore N. Bosack (1966). When the tube-sucking behavior of newborn infants, aged 35 to 94 hours, was reinforced with a dextrose (sugar) solution tube sucking increased in frequency. Then when tube sucking was not reinforced with dextrose, tube sucking decreased (behavioral extinction). For various reasons, some mothers cannot breastfeed their newborns. If no wet nurses were available and if the sucking behavior of infants was an inflexible "hard-wired instinct" with a flesh nipple as the only eliciting environmental stimulus, that is, if sucking could not be selected as a reinforced operant, if sucking was behaviorally inflexible, then the newborns of mothers who could not breast-feed would starve to death. Fortunately, the sucking behavior of newborns can be selected as an operant behavior through reinforcement. In the presence of a particular environmental stimulus (a tube in the experiment or perhaps an artificial plastic nipple) when sucking is reinforced (with dextrose in the experiment or with formula), sucking is selected and occasioned by the environmental stimuli associated with reinforcement. The reinforcement process, the ability to have behaviors selected by their consequences is a highly adaptive characteristic because, relative to organisms whose behaviors are insensitive to their consequences, the organisms that can have important survival behaviors, such as sucking, shaped by the consequences of those behaviors are more likely to survive to reproductive age.

APPENDIX 2

Basic Terms

Now that the natural selection of behavioral flexibility, and the selective process of reinforcement, or operant conditioning, have been described, it may be advantageous to review and define a few basic terms. It is critical to have an accurate understanding of these basic terms because many myths of reinforcement use terminology haphazardly and whimsically. In order to dispel the myths, accurate knowledge of the terminology is a useful tool.

Reinforcer: a consequence of behavior that increases the frequency of the behavior (or "operant") that preceded the consequence.

Reinforcement: the process of increasing the rate of behaviors (or operants) with reinforcing consequences.

Operant (or operant response class): a class of related behaviors. When a particular behavior is reinforced the entire class of behaviors is reinforced. For example, if the behavior of hitting a spouse produces the reinforcing consequence of compliance by the spouse, then the entire operant class of "abusive behaviors" (hitting, kicking, screaming, etc.) will likely increase. Operant behavior is defined by its function and by the consequences it produces (abuse produces compliance), not by its topography (a right jab). The unwitting reinforcement of operants can, and does, produce problematic situations. But the reinforcement of operants also produces many beneficial outcomes. Reinforcing the behavior of saying "thank-you" may reinforce the operant of "politeness" and thus increase the frequency of saying "please," and "after you, I insist" as well.

251

Extinction: refers to both an environmental procedure, or event, and a behavioral process. The procedure occurs when a previously reinforced behavior is no longer reinforced, as in, "Joe's screaming behavior was being reinforced by my attention, so I put it on extinction by ignoring Joe for two minutes every time he screamed." The behavioral process of extinction refers to the "dying" of a previously reinforced behavior that is no longer reinforced. "Because Joe's screaming no longer produced the reinforcing consequence of my attention, screaming decreased to a rate of zero within a week."

Punishment: a procedure by which consequences *suppress* the preceding behavior. Punishment is different from extinction. A rat's lever pressing is reinforced with food pellets, but if shocks also become contingent on lever pressing, the rate of lever pressing will be suppressed. During extinction a behavior is no longer reinforced. If a rat's lever pressing no longer produces food pellets, eventually lever pressing will extinguish. Conversely, behavior that is being punished may still be being reinforced. For example, a child's "fart noise-" making behavior may be punished with a spanking (assuming spankings are a consequence that would normally suppress the preceding behavior) but the behavior may still be being reinforced with the laughter of friends, or by the adult's attention. The resulting rate of a behavior that is being both punished and reinforced will be determined jointly by the product of the punishing and reinforcing consequences. Punishment is a critical factor in many situations that also involve reinforcement. For example, a reprimand may be intended as a punisher for disruptive classroom behavior, but numerous studies show that the attention provided by reprimands (or even by spankings) usually increase—that is, reinforce—disruptive behavior. Thus, although our examination is focused on reinforcement, on occasion it is necessary to consider punishment.

Positive and Negative Reinforcement: When the word *positive* precedes *reinforcement* or *reinforcer* it refers to a consequence occurring or being presented, or added. When the word *negative* precedes *reinforcement* or *reinforcer* it refers to a consequence not occurring, being removed, or subtracted. Thus, "positive" and "negative" have meaning in the mathematical sense: "One plus positive one equals two. One plus negative one equals zero." Positive and negative do not refer to good or bad, and negative reinforcement *is not* the same as punishment. *Negative reinforcement* is perhaps the most misused term in psychology and education.

Largely because negative reinforcement contingencies are almost never purposefully programmed into educational or behavioral treatment programs, the myths of reinforcement primarily involve a misunderstanding of positive reinforcement. However, negative reinforcement is a fundamental process in nature that greatly affects every human's life.

Positive reinforcement: occurs when an event or stimulus is presented as a consequence of operant behavior and the operant increases. Bar pressing by a rat has been positively reinforced if a bar press produces a pellet of food and the rate of bar pressing increases. If reading a novel reveals a story and excitement and the rate of reading novels increases to reveal more stories and excitement, then reading novels has been positively reinforced by the stories and excitement that reading novels reveals.

Negative reinforcement: occurs when the rate of a behavior *increases* because an aversive event or stimulus is removed (escape behavior) or prevented from occurring (avoidance behavior). Bar pressing by a rat has been negatively reinforced if the rat is being shocked; a bar press turns off the shock and the rate of bar pressing increases. Bar pressing that turns off the shock is escape; bar pressing that prevents the shock from occurring is avoidance. The behavior of saying "not tonight honey; I have a headache" is negatively reinforced if it prevents or terminates unwanted sexual advances. Reading novels may also be negatively reinforced if reading provides escape from the humdrum of everyday life, or allows one to forget, escape from, one's problems.

Both positive and negative reinforcement increase behavior. A behavior, for example, reading novels, may be a function of positive reinforcement at one time and negative reinforcement at another time. "Channel surfing" with the TV remote control is positively reinforced if there are several interesting programs on at the same time and the viewer wants to watch them all. But most of the time channel surfing is likely a function of negative reinforcement because "nothing good is on," so the surfer changes channels to escape bad programs or to avoid commercials. Similarly, drug abuse may occur for positively reinforcing consequences, "to get high," or for negatively reinforcing consequences, "to escape reality." The abuser who engages in drug-taking behavior as a function of negative reinforcement, "to escape," is much more likely to become addicted than the abuser who takes drugs as a function of positive reinforcement, "to get high" (see chapter 11 in this book).

Stimulus control and discriminative behavior: is produced by differential reinforcement. When a behavior is reinforced in the presence of one stimulus and not reinforced (extinguished) in the presence of another stimulus (differential reinforcement), soon it will occur only in the presence of the stimulus that is present when the behavior is reinforced. If a pigeon is reinforced for pecking a key light when it is green but not when it is red, soon the pigeon will only peck the light when it is green. Key pecking is "under stimulus control" of the green color. Key pecking is "discriminated behavior." Similarly, beginning in childhood (often with the children's game "red light, green light"), most humans are reinforced for moving forward in the presence of a green light (or the verbal equivalent), and not moving forward or stopping in the presence of a red light.

Of course, a pigeon *could* peck the red light, and humans *could* go at red and stop at green, but usually we do not. The stimuli in stimulus control *do not make* the behavior occur in a strict mechanical fashion. Instead the "discriminative stimulus" *occasions* the response. Because in the past the behavior has been reinforced in the presence of the discriminative stimulus, and not reinforced, or punished, in the absence of the discriminative stimulus, the behavior comes under the control of the discriminative stimulus. The stimulus discriminates the occasions when the response will be reinforced.

Thus, as environmental stimuli exert selective forces in the survival of a species, discriminative stimuli are a selective force in the probability of behavior. If other environmental stimuli are momentarily exerting strong selective power, the occasioning power of a discriminative stimulus may be overridden. For example, if a man has a wife in labor or a child with a split open head in his car, the discriminative stimulus of a red light may not occasion stopping. But in most other cases the red light does occasion stopping.

The contingency between the discriminative stimulus, response and reinforcer (or Antecedent, Behavior, Consequence, ABC) is known as the three-term contingency. B. F. Skinner and other behavior analysts have argued that the three-term contingency is the *fundamental unit* of behavior (Skinner, 1953, 1969). Indeed, it may be impossible to talk about behavior in any meaningful way without considering, in addition to the behavior itself, the context of the behavior (e.g., the discriminative stimuli) and the consequences (e.g., reinforcement) of the behavior. Is kicking someone in the ribs and punching them in the jaw "appropriate" or "inappropriate" behavior? Is sitting quietly, reading a book "appropriate" or "inappropriate"?

The appropriateness of kicking and punching or reading depend on the context and consequences. In the context of a Muy Tai kick-boxing match, kicking and punching will be positively reinforced by cheers from the crowd and if they produce victory they will be further reinforced with a larger paycheck. However in most other contexts, kicking and punching are not appropriate. A kick-boxing match (discriminative stimulus and antecedent) sets the occasion where kicking and punching (behavior) will be reinforced (consequence; a three-term contingency). Sitting quietly and reading is generally not reinforced, and may be punished with harsh looks or worse from others at football games or at the family dinner table, but sitting quietly and reading is appropriate in many other contexts. Therefore, just like kicking and punching, whether sitting quietly and reading is "appropriate" or "inappropriate," depends on the context and consequences.

The ubiquitousness of reinforcement cannot be understated. Virtually anywhere there is behavior there is reinforcement. A press of a computer key is reinforced with the corresponding letter on the computer screen. If pressing a key did not produce corresponding symbols on the screen, key pressing would cease. Moving pens on paper is reinforced with marks on the paper. Telling a joke is reinforced with laughter. If marks and laughter did not occur, then moving the pen and telling jokes would extinguish. Turning on the air-conditioning avoids or escapes excessive heat and humidity and is thus negatively reinforced.

Shaping: the differential reinforcement of successive approximations to a terminal behavior. How a child may come to say "mother" described earlier, is an example of shaping. Contingencies of reinforcement shape behavior. Understanding the shaping process and its systematic application is one of the greatest achievements of behavior analysts. Dolphins learn to jump over a rope twenty feet above a pool through shaping. Swimming over a rope two feet under the water may be the initially reinforced approximation. Then, successively, new approximations are differentially reinforced and previous approximations are extinguished. Jumping over a rope on the surface of the water may be reinforced while swimming over ropes that are under the water are no longer reinforced. Next jumping over a rope a few inches above the water is reinforced and jumping over the surface of the water is no longer reinforced. This process of differentially reinforcing successive approximations and extinguishing previous approximations continues until the dolphins are regularly jumping over ropes that are much higher than they would otherwise jump. Novelists usually learn to write novels through a lifelong shaping process. Rarely, if ever, is a successful novel a writer's first attempt at writing. Instead, writing an essay for the school newspaper may be the initially reinforced approximation. Writing short stories may be the next reinforced approximation and so on until the writer has built up his writing behavior to the point of writing novels.

Intermittent or partial reinforcement: refers to cases when responding is reinforced only intermittently. Only a partial number of responses are reinforced. A *schedule of reinforcement* specifies the reinforcement contingency. For example, on a fixed ratio five schedule of reinforcement (FR 5) reinforcement is contingent upon five responses. Five lever presses would be required from a rat for a pellet of food, or five completed homework problems would be required for a student to earn a token. On a variable ratio schedule (VR), reinforcement is contingent on a variable number of responses that average to some specific number. For example, lions are successful on an average of only once every five hunts. The environment reinforces the lions' hunting behavior on a VR 5 schedule of reinforcement. Not every response (hunt) is reinforced but *reinforcement maintains responding* (hunting).

There are an infinite number of intermittent reinforcement schedules. Many of the more common schedules have been studied extensively, and many of them produce *predictable characteristic patterns of behavior*. The predictable characteristic patterns of behavior produced by various reinforcement schedules often allow an understanding of behavior in cases where the reinforcement that is maintaining a behavior may not be apparent.

For example, the VR schedule is sometimes called "the addictive schedule," because, even though a majority of responses go unreinforced VR schedules produce a very persistent high rate of responding, much like "addictive behaviors." This is likely because on VR schedules reinforcement *could* occur after any response. Reinforcement is unpredictable, but because each response builds toward whatever the current ratio is, reinforcement becomes more likely with each response. For example, the following specific ratios of responding may satisfy the reinforcement contingency (produce reinforcement) on a VR 5 schedule: 5, 5, 1, 1, 3, 10, 5, 20, 2, 2, 2, 5, 1, 3, and 10. Neither the previous reinforcers or previous responses allow accurate prediction of what the next reinforced response will be, but the more responses, the higher the rate of responding the higher the probability of reinforcement. Thus, ratio schedules reinforce not only responding, but the *rate of responding* as well.

"Addictive behaviors" appear to share two qualities: when they are reinforced the reinforcement occurs immediately after a response, and for the responder, responding is experienced as being reinforced on a VR schedule. Consider a "gambling addiction." When gambling is considered an "addiction," even though the majority of responses may go unreinforced, the behaviors involved occur at a very persistent high rate, often at the expense of important job- or family-related behaviors. Thus the characteristic pattern of behavior is the same or similar to the pattern of behavior generated by VR schedules of reinforcement. Not surprisingly, when "addictive behaviors" are reinforced, they are also reinforced in a manner characteristic of VR schedules. For the gambler, neither the previous wins or previous gambles allow accurate prediction of the next gamble that will win, but the more gambling and the higher the rate of gambling the higher the probability of a win. But unfortunately for the gambler, "in the long run the 'utility' is negative: the gambler loses all" (Skinner; 1971, p. 33; e.g., a gambler may have to place a $2 bet for a .2 chance to win $8; on the average he will win $8 every 5 gambles, and in the long run lose $10 for every $8 won).

Thus even though it may not appear that the "addicted gambler" is being reinforced ("I don't know why he keeps betting his paycheck away; he almost always loses") for his "addictive behavior," his behavior may very well be reinforced, but only intermittently. Even if the behavior is only intermittently reinforced, it may be enough to maintain the behavior to the extent that the behavior is considered "maladaptive." Rather than the result of weak "willpower," "lack of character," or an "inner weakness," "addictions" and other supposed defects, may profitably be understood in terms of the contingencies of reinforcement that maintain and shape the problematic behaviors. One does not become addicted to gambling because of a "weak character," but because one has been exposed to various contingencies of reinforcement that have strong controlling power over behavior. Contingencies of reinforcement produce the behavior and apparent character. The character does not produce the behavior.

Partial reinforcement extinction effect (PRE): intermittent reinforcement makes responding more persistent, or more resistant to extinction compared to a response that has been continuously reinforced (i.e., each response produces reinforcement, an FR 1 schedule). For example, when responding no longer is reinforced, responding that was continuously reinforced on an FR 1 schedule will extinguish, or "die out," relatively quickly compared to a partially reinforced response on a VR schedule. The change from continuous reinforcement to extinction is abrupt and easily discriminated. However, because under partial reinforcement schedules many responses are made without reinforcement but responding is eventually reinforced, the change from partial reinforcement to extinction is much harder to discriminate. Thus it is unclear to the behaving organism when responding is not reinforced because there is an intermittent reinforcement contingency in effect, or because extinction is in effect.

Partial reinforcement also *selects* persistence, or effort, as a dimension of behavior that will then generalize to completely different behavioral domains. For example, students in one group of "learning-disabled" children were reinforced for every five correct spelling words (FR 5, partial reinforcement). Students in another group were reinforced for every correct word (FR 1, continuous reinforcement). Later both groups were systematically observed doing *math*. Even though the reinforcement for math was the same for everyone, the children reinforced for every five spelling words worked twice as long and got twice as many *math problems* correct as the children who were reinforced for every spelling word (Eisenberger, 1992). Here the persistence, the greater effort, required by the intermittent reinforcement in spelling *selected* persistence as a behavioral dimension that generalized to math work. When a dimension of behavior is reinforced, it will be selected. Thus, it may also be profitable to view such socially desirable traits as hard work and persistence as products of selecting environmental reinforcement contingencies rather than products of "willpower," or "moral character." Or if one insists on considering behavior as a result of "character," then it should be admitted that this character, whatever its substance, is a product of dynamic behavior-environment interactions.

NAME INDEX

SUBJECT INDEX

265